GET STARTED WITH PROCREATE

I0823313

A DAVID AND CHARLES BOOK
David and Charles is an imprint of David and Charles, Ltd, Suite A, Tourism House, Pynes Hill, Exeter, EX2 5WS

First published in the UK and USA in 2025

A catalogue record for this book is available from the British Library.

ISBN-13: 9781446314678 paperback
ISBN-13: 9781446314685 EPUB

This book has been printed on paper from approved suppliers and made from pulp from sustainable sources.

Printed and bound in China.

10 9 8 7 6 5 4 3 2 1

Conceived, edited, and designed by
The Bright Press, an imprint of The Quarto Group,
1 Triptych Place, London, SE1 9SH,
United Kingdom.
T (0)20 7700 6700
www.Quarto.com

Publisher: James Evans
Editorial Director: Isheeta Mustafi
Art Director: Emily Nazer
Managing Editor: Jacqui Sayers
Commissioning Editors: Anna Southgate, Sorrel Wood
Senior Editor: Dee Costello
Project Editor: Lindsay Kaubi
Design: Lindsey Johns

David and Charles publishes high-quality books on a wide range of subjects.

For more information visit www.davidandcharles.com.

Follow us on Instagram by searching for @dandcbooks.

Layout of the digital edition of this book may vary depending on reader hardware and display settings.

Picture Credits
L = left, R = right, T = top, B = bottom
The Bright Press would like to thank the following:

Shutterstock: 18 Marina Rich, 77TL Ground Picture, 77TR Followtheflow, 77BL myboys.me, 77BR Ground Picture, 95TL Gergely Zsolnai, 95TR Creative Travel Projects, 95BL Galyna Andrushko, 95BR Creative Travel Projects, 101 Adisa.

While every effort has been made to credit copyright holders of the images used in this book, The Bright Press would like to apologize should there have been any omissions or errors, and would be pleased to make the appropriate correction for future editions of the book.

GET STARTED WITH PROCREATE

The 10-Step Guide to Drawing on Your iPad

Liz Kohler Brown

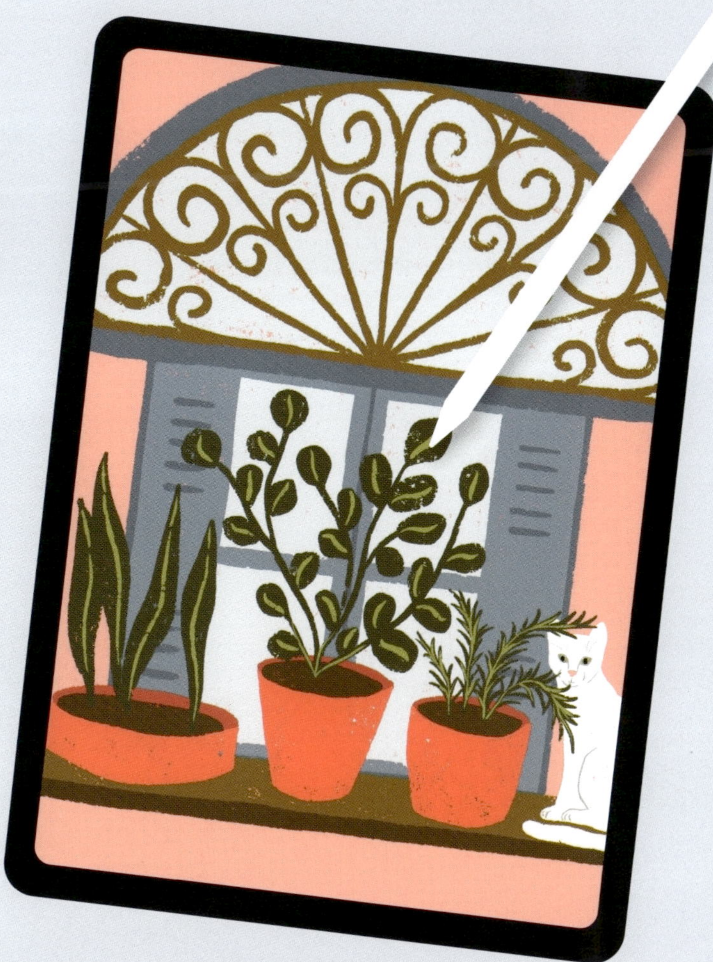

DAVID & CHARLES
—PUBLISHING—

www.davidandcharles.com

Contents

The Projects

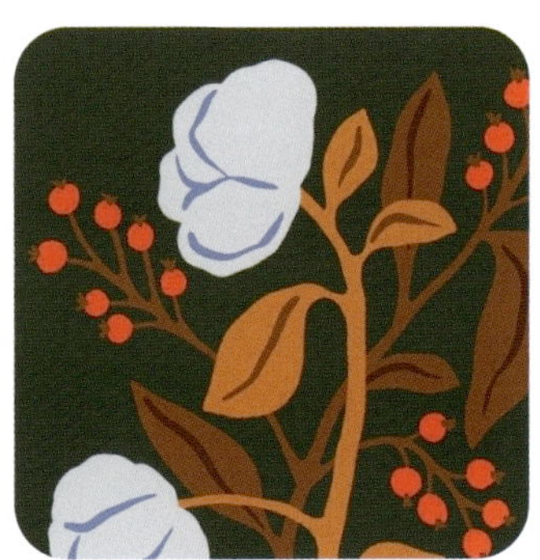

Beginner ★★★

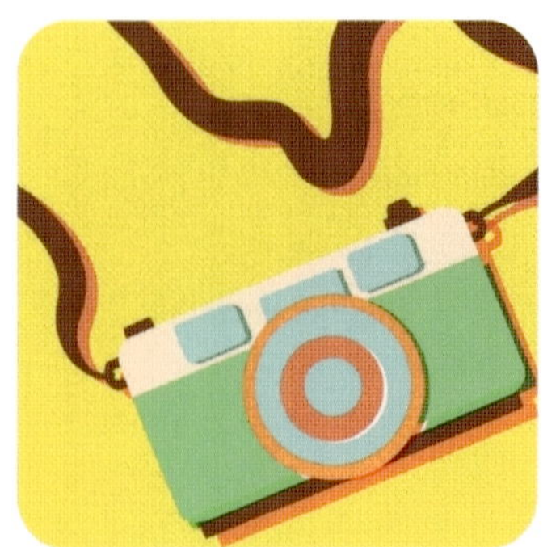

Intermediate ★★★

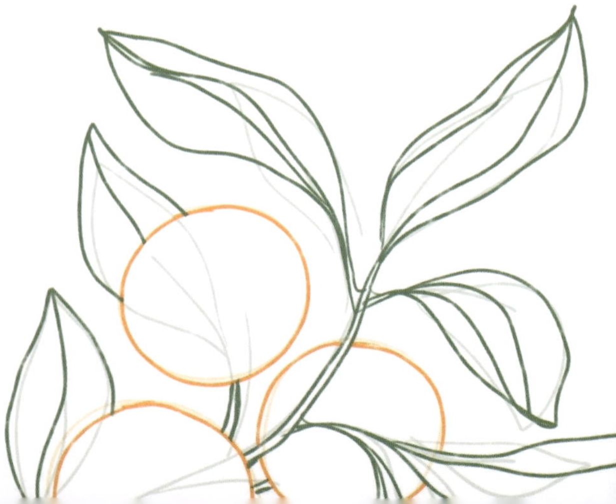

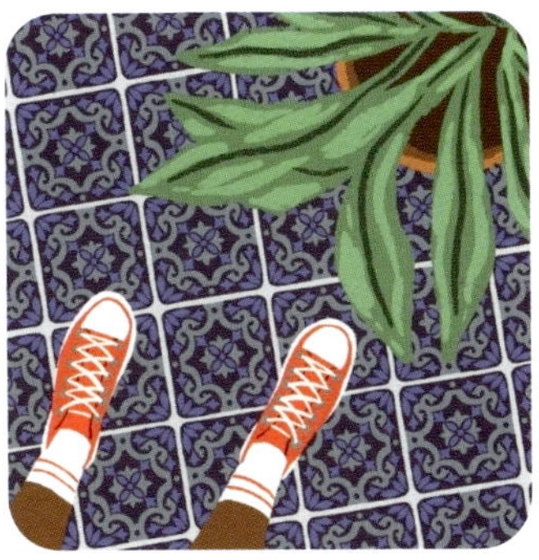

Advanced ★★★

Letter from the Author

With this book, I hope all of you artists, designers, and creatively curious people will discover how working with digital brushes and colors can open up a whole new world of artistic possibilities. Gone are the days of worrying about "wasting" paints and paper or "messing up" an expensive canvas. When you work digitally, you can experiment with colors, shapes, and realistic brushes without even getting your art supplies off the shelf.

Learning Procreate will inevitably transform and speed up your creative process.

P.S. This is my signature, drawn in Procreate with the Sketching Pencil at 9%. Yes, that nerdy digital art talk will make sense to you soon, and you'll be ready to sign your own artwork in just a few pages!

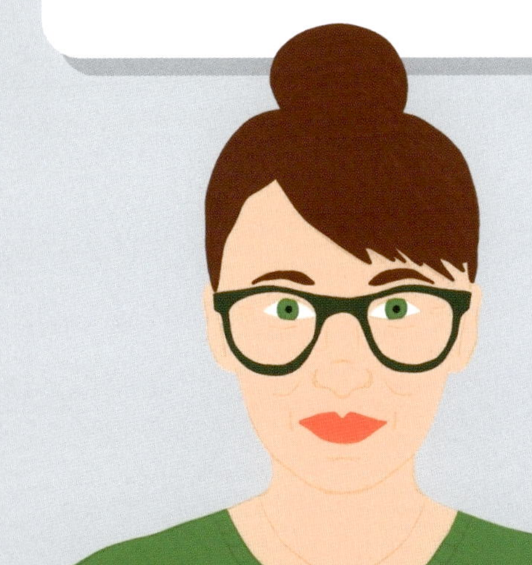

AN INTRODUCTION TO *Procreate*

When I discovered Procreate, I was in a creative dry spell. I wanted to travel and be mobile, but art supplies are heavy and take up a lot of space. I invested in a refurbished iPad and immediately went down the rabbit hole of color, texture, and limitless possibilities that were at my fingertips.

WHY PROCREATE?

Procreate has the most realistic feel of all of the iPad-based drawing apps and has become a favorite tool for iPad-based artists. As we dive into the projects in this book, you'll see that Procreate has a unique brush interface that allows you to use (or create) any brush effect you can imagine. Whether you are trying to create a realistic watercolor composition or a bold black-and-white ink-pen look, you can achieve the exact texture and feel that you could create on paper or canvas. Let's look at some of the advantages of working digitally.

Work Anywhere

When you work digitally, you can pull out your "digital studio" wherever you go, whether you are sitting in your favorite cafe, waiting to pick up your children after school, or stuck in an airport terminal when your flight is delayed. Just a warning here—after you go through the projects in this book, you may start hoping your flights are delayed so that there is nothing to do but draw on your iPad!

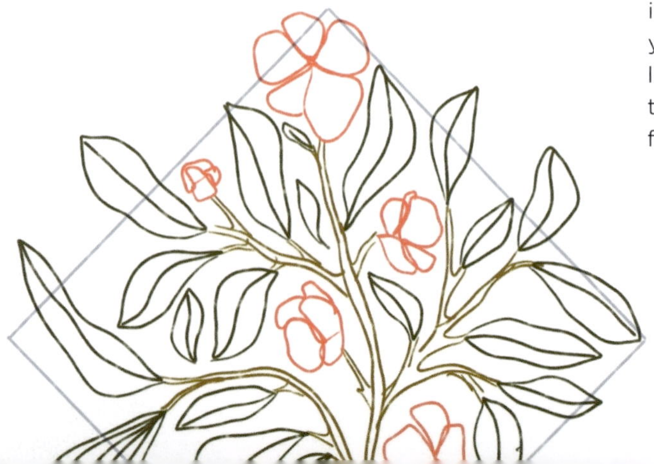

Drop the Guilt

Many creatives find working digitally to be more freeing than traditional materials. Financial pressures (and concerns about wasting materials) can put a strain on your creative brain and even cause creative block. You may have asked yourself in the past, "is my creative skill even good enough to be worthy of this expensive canvas?" When you work with digital brushes, you can hone your skills and find your style without ever facing the guilt of wasting expensive materials. You can even abandon artwork halfway through and start a fresh canvas without considering that you're being wasteful.

Ease and Speed

It's no secret that traditional art takes time. The prepping of materials alone can eat away at the precious moments we have to draw, especially for those of us juggling jobs, family, and other responsibilities. Digital art can be more efficient. The more you practice your digital art skills using the steps in this book, the faster your art-making process will be. Before you know it, you'll be facing the problem of organizing your folders because you can't find what you're looking for amid the hundreds of canvases on the page (more later on how to organize your folders of artwork).

Art Prints: You can create art prints featuring illustrations, lettering, or even simple geometric shapes, just as I did for this American-quilt-inspired composition.

Stationery: You can create repeat patterns and motifs for things like notebooks, scrapbooking paper, and gift wrap. See Project 19 for more on repeat patterns.

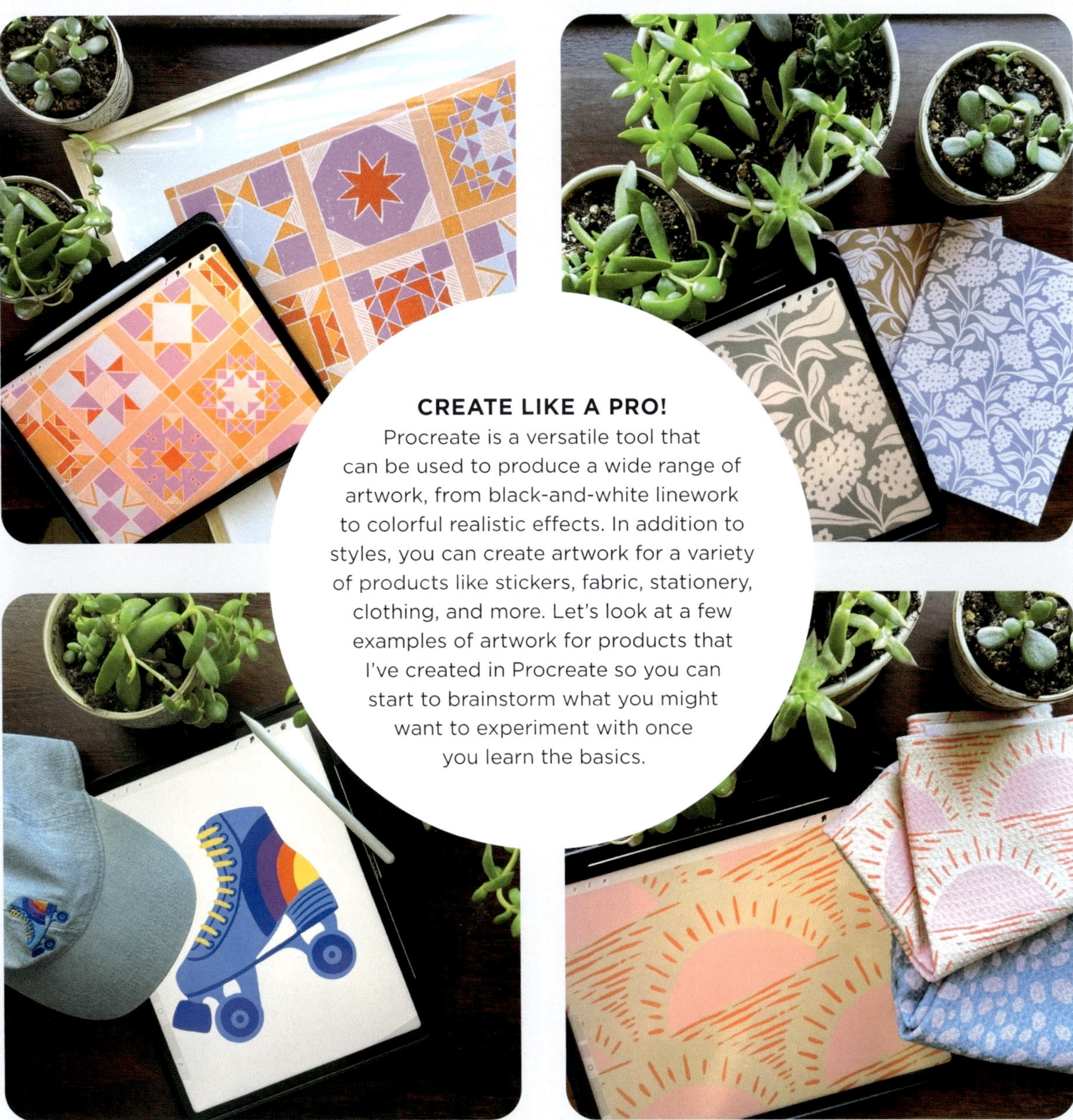

CREATE LIKE A PRO!

Procreate is a versatile tool that can be used to produce a wide range of artwork, from black-and-white linework to colorful realistic effects. In addition to styles, you can create artwork for a variety of products like stickers, fabric, stationery, clothing, and more. Let's look at a few examples of artwork for products that I've created in Procreate so you can start to brainstorm what you might want to experiment with once you learn the basics.

Clothing: You can use illustration, lettering, or a combination of the two to design clothing like shirts, hats, or other wearable items.

Fabrics: You can create illustrations or repeat patterns for printing onto fabric using an on-demand print website.

About This Book

This book is structured around 20 Procreate art projects, which are designed to work from the ground up, sequentially building skills and knowledge of tools. Each project is categorized as Beginner, Intermediate, or Advanced skill level. The skill level of the projects is indicated on the contents page—and at the foot of each project page—with a star rating; one star for beginner, two stars for intermediate, and three for advanced.

While you could start with any project in the book, you may feel frustrated if you jump to a more advanced project without having learned the skills from the previous sections.

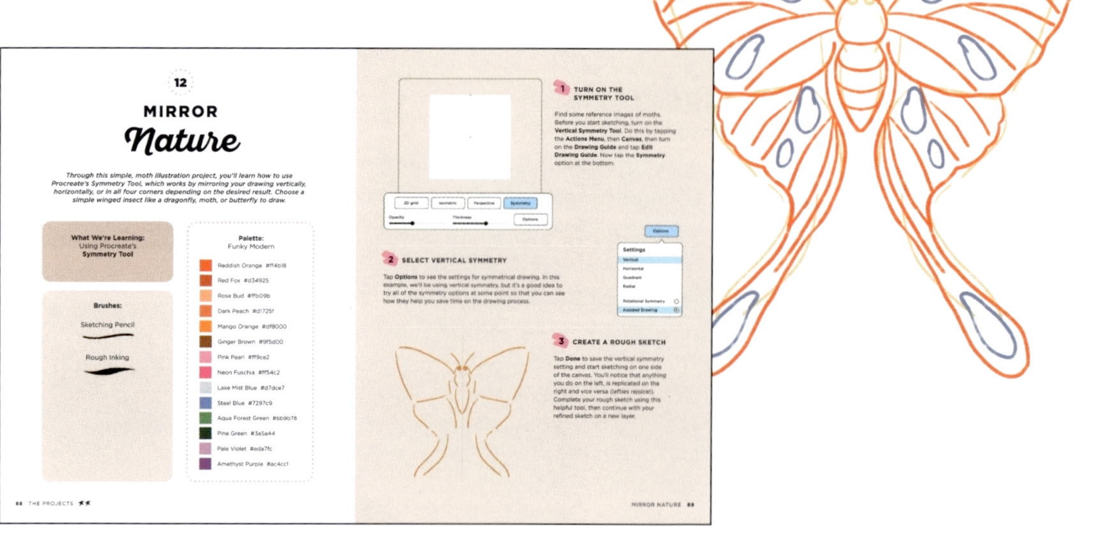

12

MIRROR
Nature

Through this simple, moth illustration project, you'll learn how to use Procreate's Symmetry Tool, which works by mirroring your drawing vertically, horizontally, or in all four corners depending on the desired result. Choose a simple winged insect like a dragonfly, moth, or butterfly to draw.

What We're Learning:
Using Procreate's **Symmetry Tool**

Brushes:
Sketching Pencil
Rough Inking

Palette:
Funky Modern

Reddish Orange #ff4b18
Red Fox #d34925
Rose Bud #ffb09b
Dark Peach #d1725f
Mango Orange #df8000
Ginger Brown #9f5d00
Pink Pearl #ff9ce2
Neon Fuschia #ff54c2
Lake Mist Blue #d7dce7
Steel Blue #7297c9
Aqua Forest Green #6b9b78
Pine Green #3a5a44
Pale Violet #eda7fc
Amethyst Purple #ac4cc1

88 THE PROJECTS ★★

1 TURN ON THE SYMMETRY TOOL

Find some reference images of moths. Before you start sketching, turn on the **Vertical Symmetry Tool**. Do this by tapping the **Actions Menu**, then **Canvas**, then turn on the **Drawing Guide** and tap **Edit Drawing Guide**. Now tap the **Symmetry** option at the bottom.

2 SELECT VERTICAL SYMMETRY

Tap **Options** to see the settings for symmetrical drawing. In this example, we'll be using vertical symmetry, but it's a good idea to try all of the symmetry options at some point so that you can see how they help you save time on the drawing process.

3 CREATE A ROUGH SKETCH

Tap **Done** to save the vertical symmetry setting and start sketching on one side of the canvas. You'll notice that anything you do on the left, is replicated on the right and vice versa (lefties rejoice!). Complete your rough sketch using this helpful tool, then continue with your refined sketch on a new layer.

MIRROR NATURE 89

Each project is created by following 10 steps that will help you gain the skills you need to make the next one. All projects are produced at the same canvas size and each is presented with details of the palette and brushes used, so that, if you wish to, you can recreate it almost exactly.

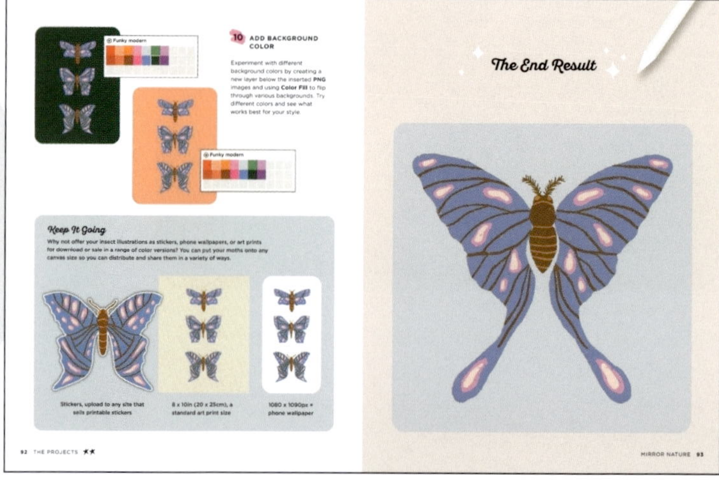

10 ADD BACKGROUND COLOR

Experiment with different background colors by creating a new layer below the inserted **PNG** images and using **Color Fill** to flip through various backgrounds. Try different colors and see what works best for your style.

Keep It Going

Why not offer your insect illustrations as stickers, phone wallpapers, or art prints for download or sale in a range of color versions? You can put your moths onto any canvas size so you can distribute and share them in a variety of ways.

Stickers, upload to any site that sells printable stickers

8 x 10in (20 x 25cm), a standard art print size

1080 x 1090px = phone wallpaper

92 THE PROJECTS ★★

The End Result

MIRROR NATURE 93

WHAT TYPE OF CREATIVE ARE YOU?

I have been working with creatives long enough to know that there are several different types of inspired brains, each with their own unique learning style. Let's talk about three different ways you could use this book, so that you can choose the style that works best for you.

1. The Star Student

The Star Student will enjoy following the steps in this book exactly as they are shown, perhaps even copying the project exactly. This is a great way to work when you want to focus on learning the app and tools, without having to worry about creating a composition at the same time. Feel free to use this method if you want to learn the tools first, then produce your own artwork later.

2. The Rule Breaker

The Rule Breaker applies creativity to everything they do, including following rules, so following the projects exactly will not work for this kind of artist. If this is you, you should feel free to go "outside the box" with any of the projects, and skip around to find the process or technique you want to learn.

3. The Rebel

The Rebels have probably already skipped reading this intro because they don't like to be confined to the predetermined order of a book's contents. Just in case there is a rebel reading this though, I want you to know that you should feel free to go "off the rails" with all of the projects in this book, not that a rebel would need my permission to do so.

Of course, you may find that you don't fit perfectly into any of these categories, or that your approach to the projects changes as you progress. Limiting creativity is the worst thing we can do for our creative process, so go with your gut and use this book in any way that makes you feel excited to draw.

FINDING YOUR STYLE

Finding your style as a creative is an ongoing process, and at this early stage, it's best to try everything you can imagine so that you get an idea of what is available to you. The more artwork you create, the more you will start leaning toward certain colors, brushes, and themes that you enjoy, which in turn will start to help you uncover your own creative style.

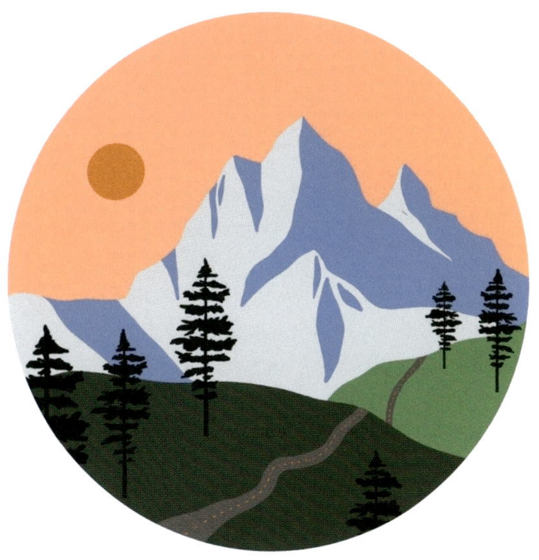

GETTING *Started*

To get started in Procreate you'll need the right equipment, along with some basic skills and knowledge so that you can open the app and start exploring its features.

EQUIPMENT

Since Procreate currently only functions on iPads and iPhones, those are the recommended devices you should use. The iPhone version of Procreate, known as Procreate Pocket, can be used with this book but the features on that app are somewhat limited so you may find that not everything discussed in the book is available in Procreate Pocket. For that reason, an iPad is recommended. The Apple Pencil is a great choice for a drawing stylus as it has the most lifelike feel of any of the available styluses, but you can certainly use a different stylus if you find one that is pressure sensitive. Without the pressure-sensitive feature, you cannot make use of the Procreate brush interface that makes brush strokes thicker or thinner depending on how hard you press down on the stylus. Having said that, use whatever stylus you currently have, keeping in mind that you can always upgrade later.

YOUR "CANVAS"

The first step to creating artwork in Procreate is creating a new document. This is where a lot of artists get stuck. They wonder what size to use and what all the seemingly complicated options on the document creation page mean. We are going to keep things simple and use the same canvas size for all of the projects, but in the future you may want to use a different size depending on what you are creating. For example, if you want to create a 8½ x 11in (21.6 x 28cm) art print, you would make your canvas 8½ x 11in (21.6 x 28cm) at 300 DPI.

What is DPI?

DPI (dots per inch) refers to the number of pixels inside an inch. The standard for most modern printers is 300 DPI, so that is typically what you'll use for all your artwork. However, there are some printers who use a different DPI, so check with each company you use to print your artwork first

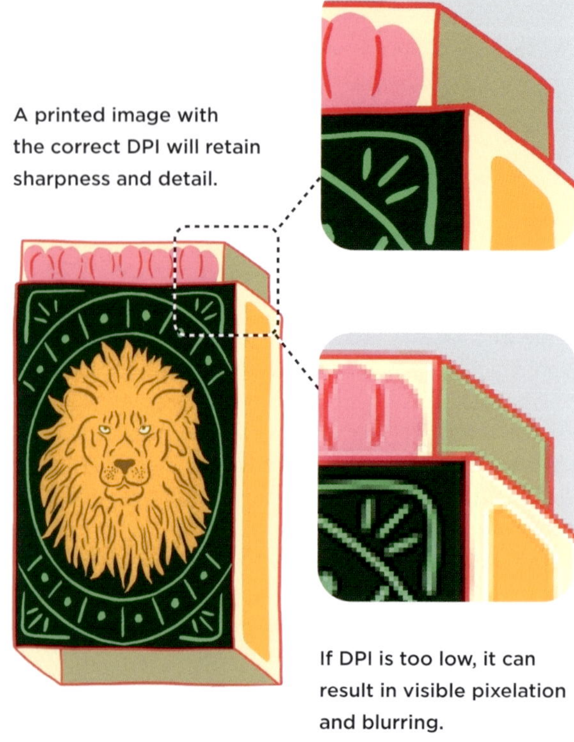

A printed image with the correct DPI will retain sharpness and detail.

If DPI is too low, it can result in visible pixelation and blurring.

HOW TO UNDO, REDO, AND ZOOM

Procreate has built-in finger gesture tools that can save a lot of time in your drawing process, so it's important to understand and practice them before you get started. Below is a guide to some of the most helpful finger gestures.

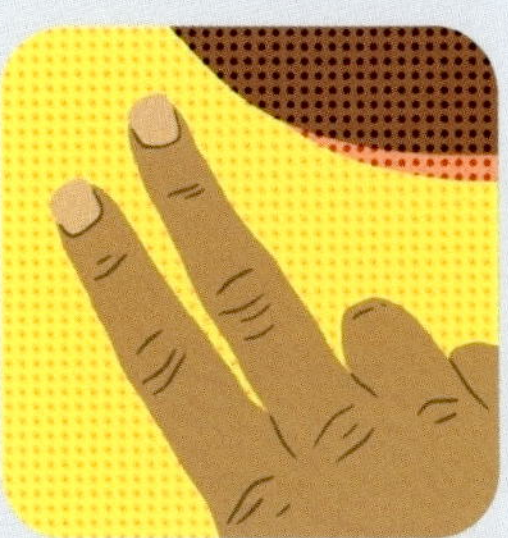

Undo Gesture

A **two-fingers** tap on the canvas will undo one step, and continued two-fingers tapping will keep undoing past steps. If you close your canvas by tapping **Gallery**, the "undo memory" is reset. So you cannot open a document and start two-fingers tapping once it is reset.

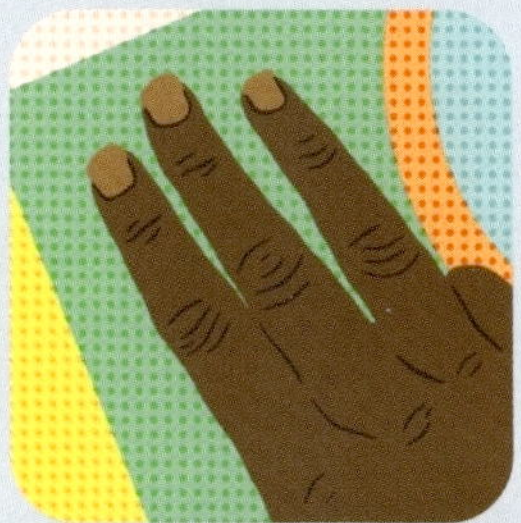

Redo Gesture

Three fingers tap to redo the step you just undid! Sometimes we accidentally tap undo, or just want to redo/undo a line several times to see how the composition looks with/without it, and this helpful gesture allows us do that.

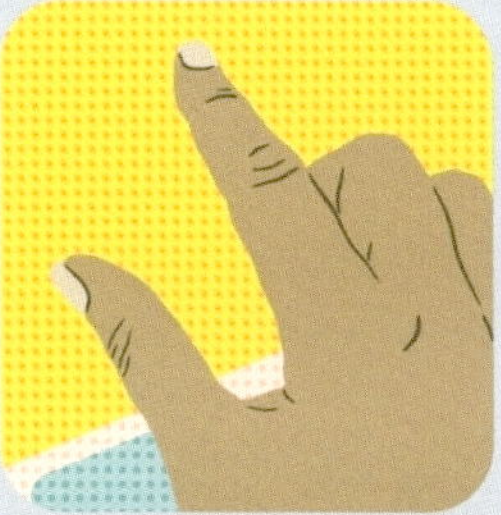

Zoom Gesture

You can **pinch your fingers** on the canvas to zoom in and out of your artwork. This makes it easy to do fine detail work without craning your neck and hurting your eyes by keeping your face close to the bright canvas.

Take some time to play with zooming in and out and undoing, and redoing, the brushstrokes you have created to see how these functions work.

Scale and Blur

Have you ever seen a menu at a restaurant or a sign in a shop that was blurry? The reason this happens is that the artwork is smaller than the object it was printed on, so it was upsized to fit the product. This process creates blurriness because there aren't enough pixels to print a crisp line. For this reason, you should not scale artwork up, only down, so keep that in mind when creating new artwork. It's always better to work at a size larger than you need and size down later than to upsize and get blurry results!

What size are the projects?

For each of the projects in this book, the document, or canvas, size is:

10 x 10in (25.4 x 25.4cm) at 300 DPI (also known as 3000 x 3000 pixels).

That means you'll be able to print out artwork at 10 x 10in (25.4 x 25.4cm) or smaller, but not larger!

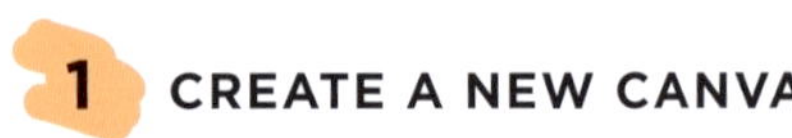

Make a Practice Page

1 CREATE A NEW CANVAS

Make a practice page by tapping the **+** symbol, then tapping the **New Canvas** symbol to create a new canvas.

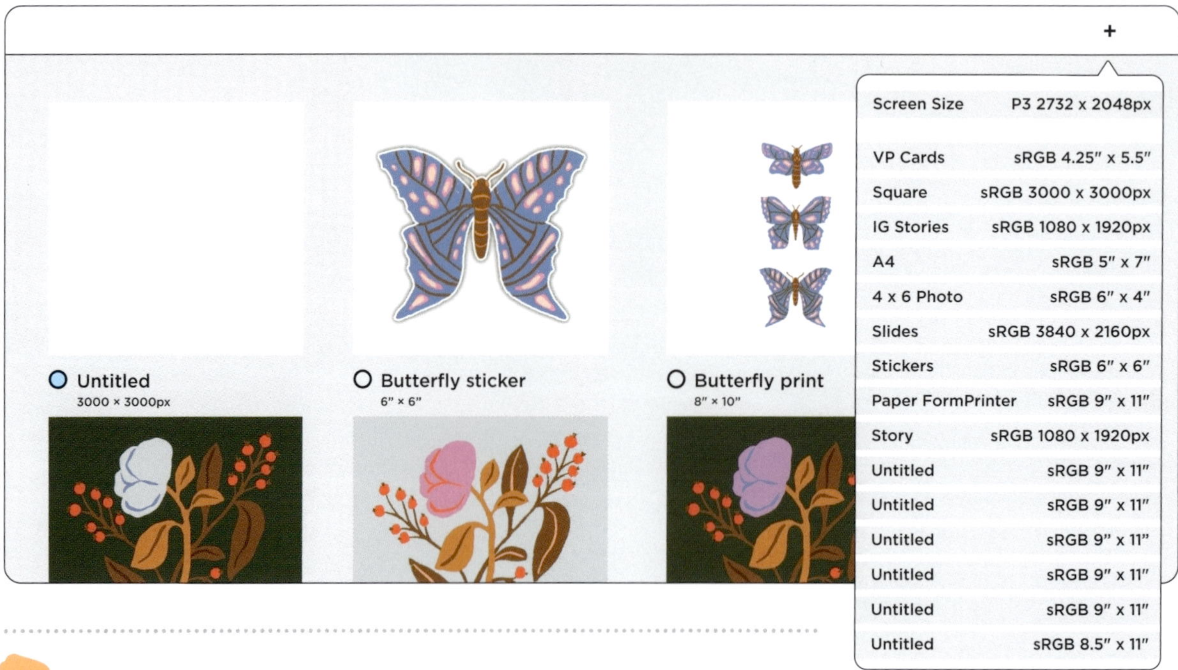

2 SET THE DOCUMENT SIZE

Enter 3000 x 3000 as the pixel dimensions. You'll notice that you could change the measurement unit to millimeters, centimeters, or inches if you choose. You may need to do this in the future if you work with a client or company that requests a specific type of measurement.

Custom canvas	Untitled canvas	
Dimensions	Width	3000px
Color profile	Height	3000px
Time-lapse settings	DPI	300
Canvas properties	Maximum layers	204

Tip When you change the size of your document, the **Maximum Layers** number changes. This number tells you how many layers you can use in your artwork based on the device you have and the size of your document (we'll talk more about layers soon, but for now, just know that more layers is a good thing!). So if you create a document at 30 x 30in (76 x 76cm), and this page says you have three layers, you may want to consider working smaller as limited layers translates to limited flexibility in changing color and style.

3 CHOOSE A COLOR PROFILE

Now tap on the **Color Profile** section. This is where you'll find a list of color profiles (i.e. ways of displaying color that printers use). The default is typically one of the variations of RGB, and you'll find that most home printers, print-on-demand companies, and digital printing companies use this profile. There are some cases where other color profiles are preferred and in those cases the company or client should communicate exactly what color profile their printers use. For now, you can just leave it as the default. Tap on **Create** to open your blank canvas.

Custom canvas
Dimensions
Color profile
Time-lapse settings
Canvas properties

Untitled canvas
RGB
CMYK
Import
Cancel
Create
Display P3
sRGB IEC61966-2.1
sRGB v4 ICC Appearance
sRGB v4 ICC Preference
sRGB v4 ICC Preference Display Class

4 THE BRUSH LIBRARY

The first thing you'll notice when you open your canvas is that the interface is straightforward, with only a few tools lined up at the top of the screen. The tool you'll be using most is the **Brush Library**, so tap on that, then tap on it again to select one of the **Brush Sets**. You'll then see all the brushes available in that set. Choose one and draw with it on the canvas. Repeat the same process with other brushes, opening several different **Brush Sets** to experiment with a wide range until you have a feel for how each brush differs in thickness, texture, and behavior.

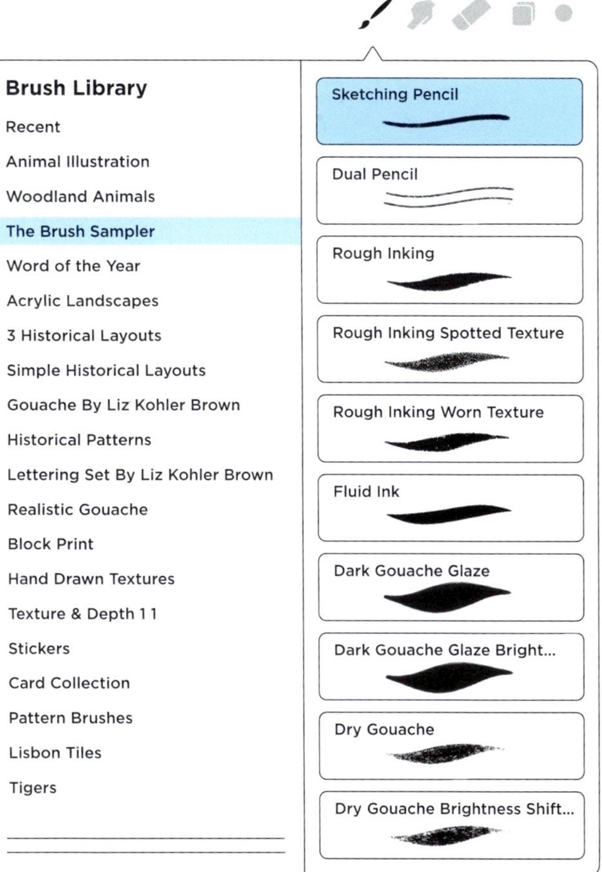

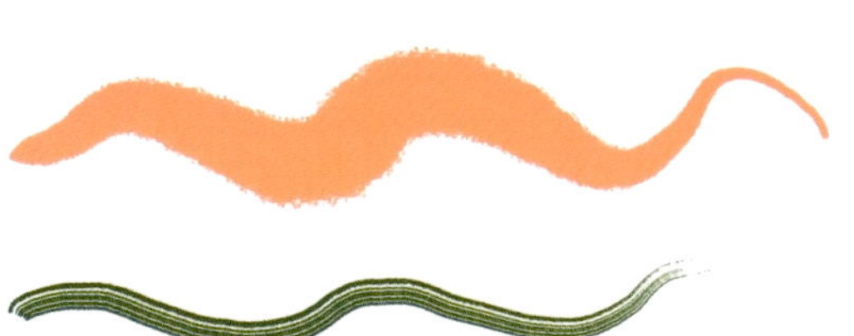

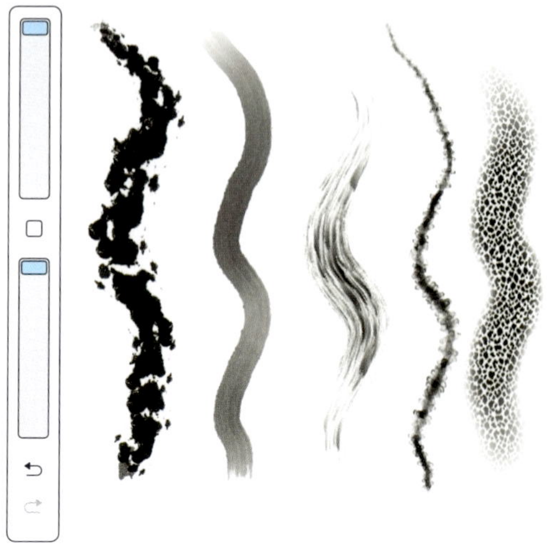

5 BRUSH SIZE AND OPACITY

The sliders on the left side of the screen allow you to adjust the **Size** (top slider) and **Opacity** (bottom slider) of each brush. So if a brush is too large, too small, or too dark, you can adjust it there.

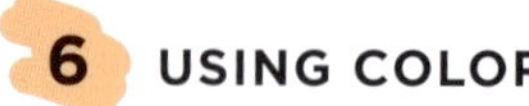

6 USING COLOR

Add some color to your page by tapping on the **Color Disc** and selecting a color. You can drag your finger around the outer disc to choose the color, then use the inner circle to choose the brightness/saturation of that color. Once you have chosen a color that you like, select a brush and draw with it on the canvas. Repeat that same step with a variety of colors until you have a colorful, messy page.

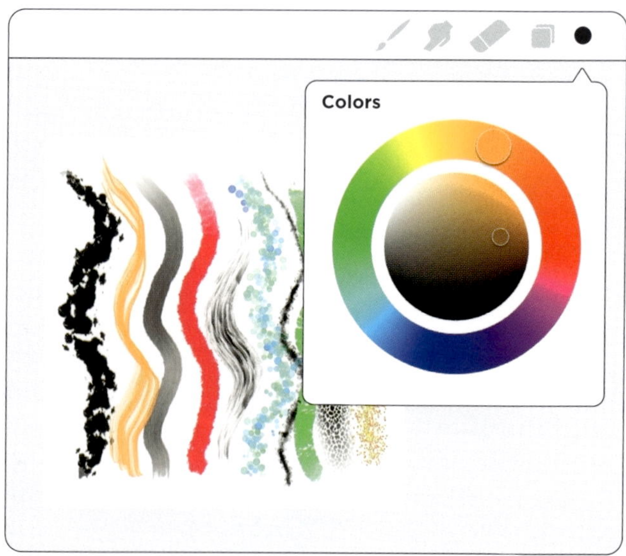

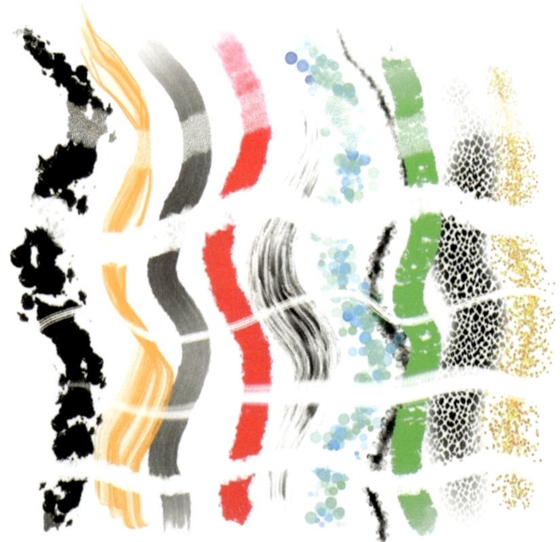

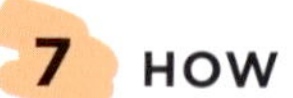

7 HOW TO ERASE

There are multiple ways to erase in Procreate, including the **Undo Gesture** described on page 11. You can also use the **Eraser Tool** in the toolbar to choose erasers made of all the brush shapes. To try this, tap on the **Eraser Tool**, then tap it again to choose a brush. Erase lines horizontally and choose different brushes to see how each eraser brush creates a different effect. Some eraser brushes remove marks with a sharp edge, whereas others have a soft, airbrushed edge.

8 MAKE A NEW LAYER

Layers are the essential building blocks of digital art. You can use them to save time, remain organized, and adjust your artwork as you work. Think of layers as pieces of transparent paper stacked one on top of the other.

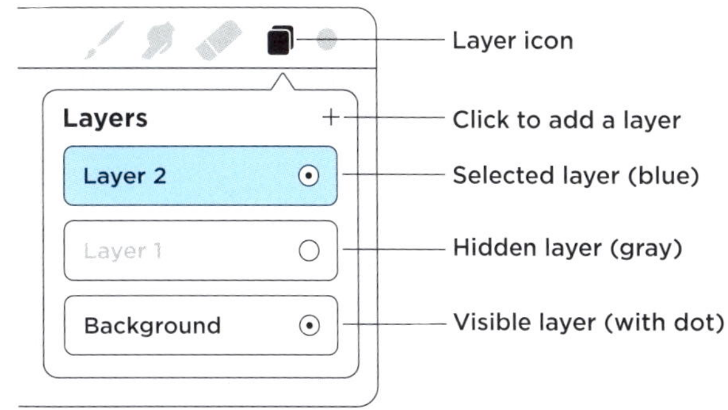

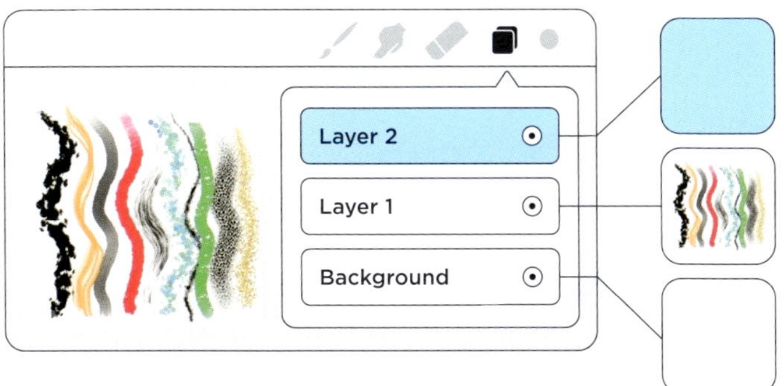

To get some practice with layers, tap on the **Layers Panel** icon, then tap the **+** symbol to create a new layer.

Tip You can swipe left on a layer to see the option to **Lock**, **Duplicate**, or **Delete** the layer. Locking prevents you from editing or deleting a layer.

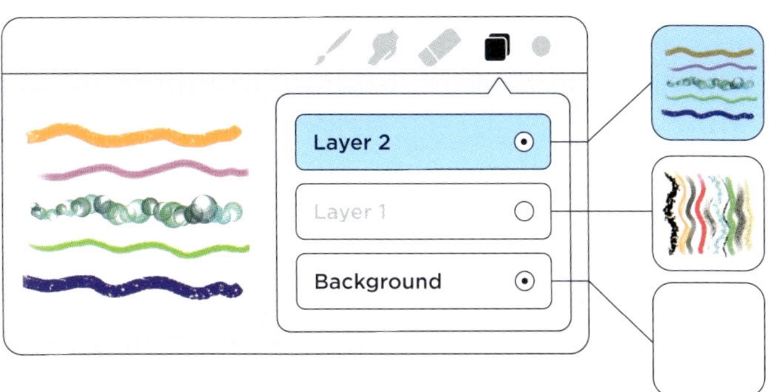

Make a new practice page on the new layer by selecting a brush and drawing with it on the canvas. Try a variety of colors until you have another colorful, messy page.

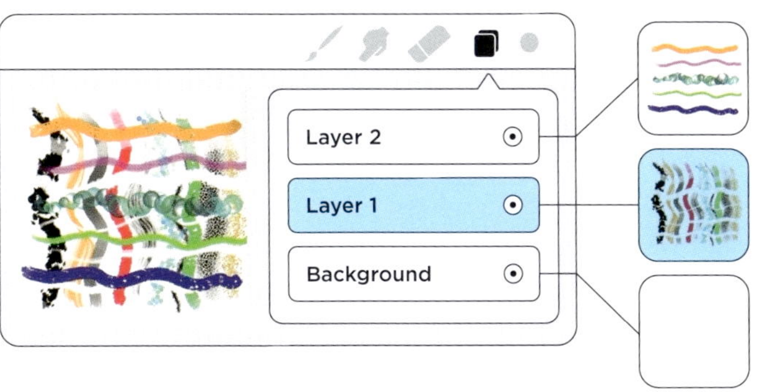

Then see what happens when you erase on that new layer. It only erases the layer you currently have selected in blue in the **Layers Panel**. Now you can tap the **Layers Panel**, select your first layer, then draw and erase on that without affecting Layer 2. Each layer is its own little "world" that you can work on without affecting the other layers.

9 CLEAR YOUR CANVAS

Now, clean up your canvas so you can play with some other tools. To do that, tap on a layer, then on the flyout menu that appears, and tap **Clear**. This erases everything on that layer, and you can repeat that step with both layers. This is the third method for erasing material in Procreate—this one is great for removing a large amount of material at once.

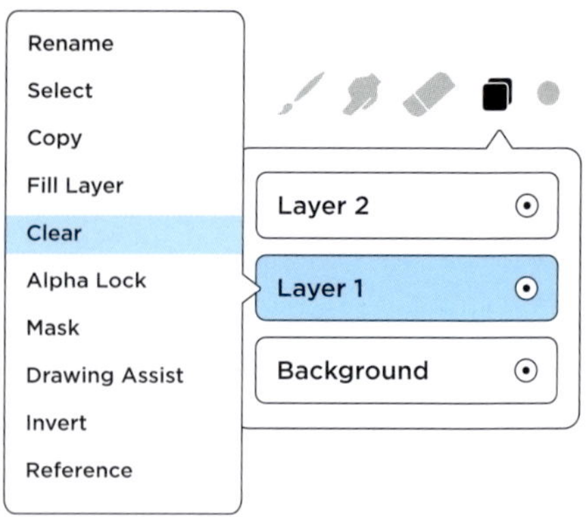

10 THE ADJUSTMENTS TOOLS

To see how the **Adjustments Tools** work, create a new layer and put some color down on the canvas. Use a solid brush to create two big blocks of color that are touching one another.

Swipe left on that layer, then tap **Duplicate**. Repeat that same process nine times so that you have 10 duplicates in total. We're going to experiment with each layer using the **Adjustments Tools**, so having the duplicates will make that easy to do.

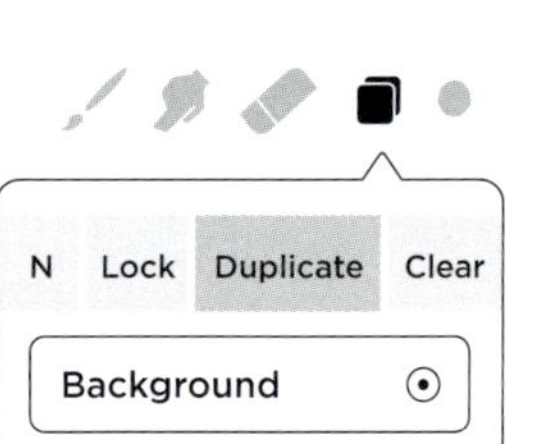

Tap on the top layer in the **Layers Panel** and make sure it is highlighted in blue, tap on the **Adjustments Menu**, then tap **Hue**, **Saturation**, **Brightness**. Adjust the sliders on the bottom of the screen to see how your page changes.

Repeat this process with all the **Adjustments Tools**, each time using a different layer from your series of duplicated color blocks. Follow the steps below for the tools that don't have obvious toolbars at the bottom. You can tap the check mark on the layers you've already adjusted to make them invisible, which reveals the next layer on the list.

11 FINGER-SLIDE ADJUSTMENTS TOOLS

Most of the **Adjustments** options are relatively self-explanatory, but a feature of some of these tools that may not be intuitive for beginners is the finger slide. You can practice this feature with the **Gaussian Blur Tool**. Tap on the layer you want to blur, then tap on **Gaussian Blur** in the **Adjustments Menu**. Drag your finger across the canvas from left to right to see the percentage on the top change. The higher the percentage the blurrier your artwork will be. One hundred percent will create an even gradient look that you could apply to the background of any artwork.

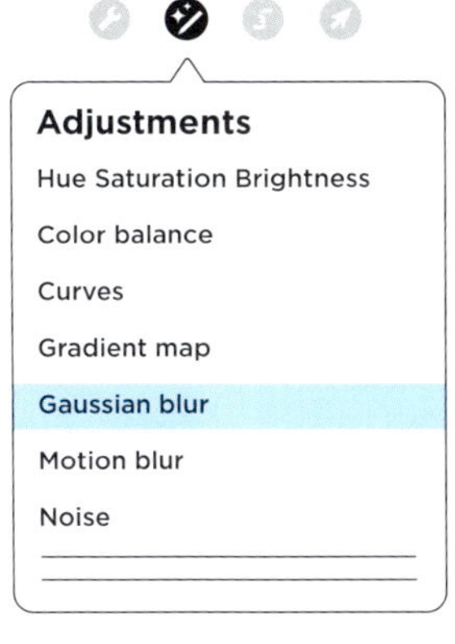

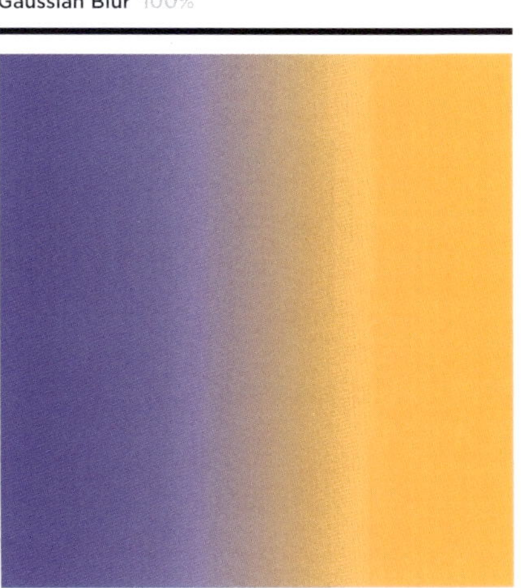

Try this out with all the other **Adjustments Tools** that require a finger slide to see how they change your layers. You will know that they require a finger slide if a menu doesn't pop up at the bottom. Here is an example showing the **Glitch** feature, which gives your artwork a digital glitch effect.

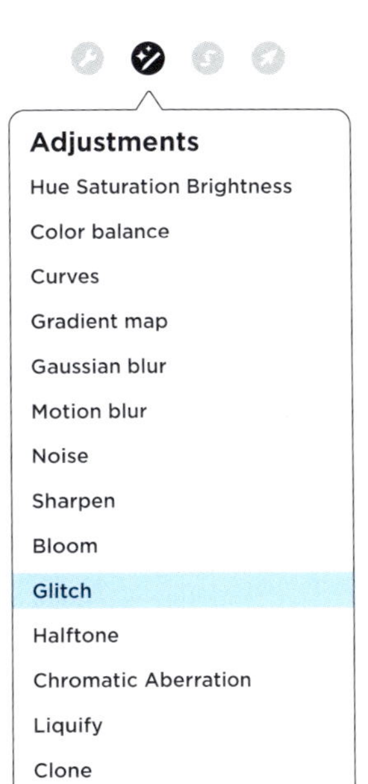

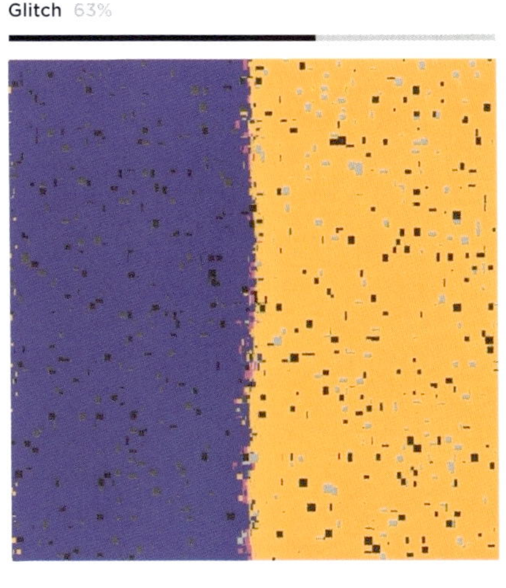

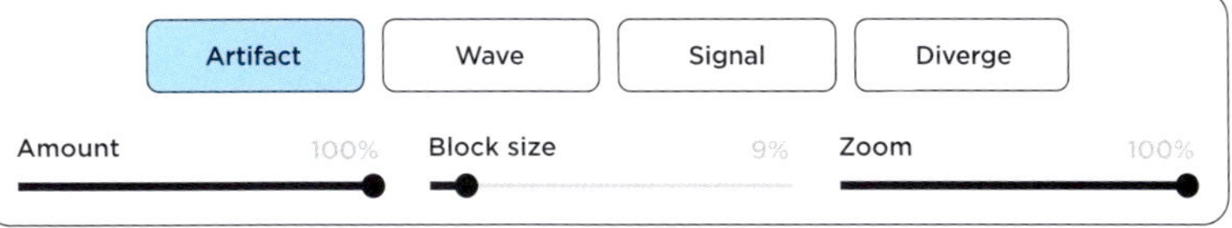

Using Reference Images

WHERE TO GET THEM

There are online resources for reference images, but use these with caution. Most images will be held under copyright, so it's best to avoid using pictures you find online as direct references—even redrawing a product or image can be considered copyright infringement. An exception to this is artwork that is in the creative commons. One of my favorite resources for reference images is the Flickr Commons, where you can find images that are no longer protected by copyright and can be used as reference images worry-free. However, most of us prefer to make work that is 100 percent unique and doesn't resemble any previous works, so I would recommend keeping that as your goal. One option is to take your own photos to build a personal image library (see below).

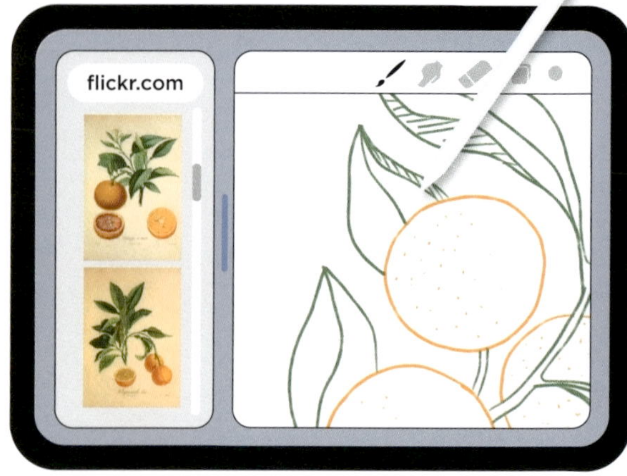

Using a Split Screen

Procreate can be used with the built-in split screen feature that all iPads allow, which lets you see two apps at once. You can use split screen by opening an app that you want to see alongside Procreate (in this case, Google Chrome), then swipe up from the bottom of the screen to see the app icons appear, and, finally, drag the app icon over to the left side of the screen to see it beside your Procreate canvas. The picture below shows a vintage orange illustration from 1861 that was uploaded to Flickr Commons by the Boston Public Library.

Start Your Own Image Library

There is only one thing better than finding great, copyright-free reference images and that is taking your own pictures. This is a great time to start your own library of reference images, so that whenever you start a new drawing project, you have some images to inspire you. If you're about to eat a delicious donut from your local bakery, STOP! Take a picture of it before you take a bite, and then go ahead and snap a picture of your friend's donuts too, because you really can't have too many good donut reference images.

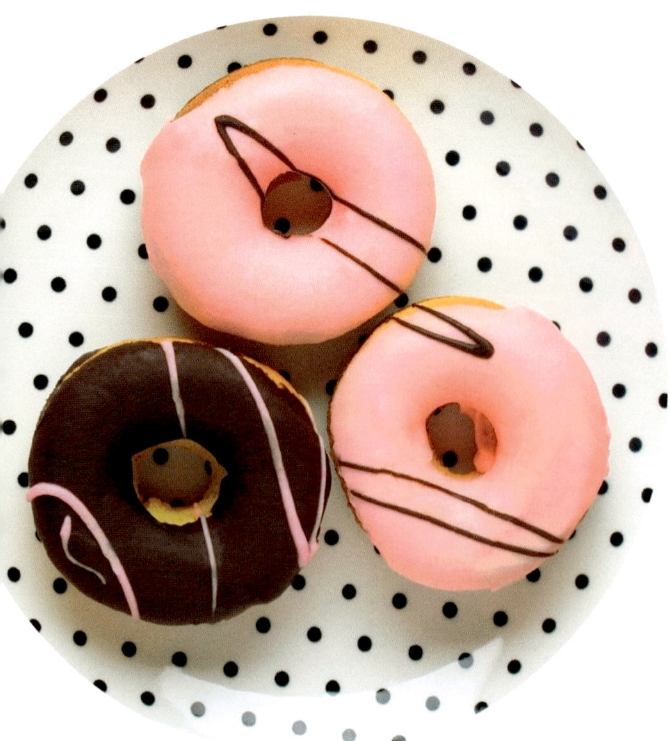

SAVING AND EXPORTING FILES

The last thing you need to think about after creating some artwork is saving it and sharing it with the world. To do this, tap the **Actions Menu**, tap **Share**, then choose a file type. For social media and home printers, **JPEG** is a great option. Now tap **Save Image** since that allows you to save the file to the Photos app on your iPad. Once there, you can share it to any other locations you'd like.

Saving is Automatic

Procreate has an automatic saving feature, which means that whenever you create some artwork and then press **Gallery** to go back to your home gallery space, the document is saved as it is. This means you never have to worry about tapping a save button; however, the downside of this feature is that if you press **Gallery** accidentally and then try to open the document to **two-fingers tap** and undo a step, you'll find that nothing happens because your progress was saved when you pressed **Gallery**.

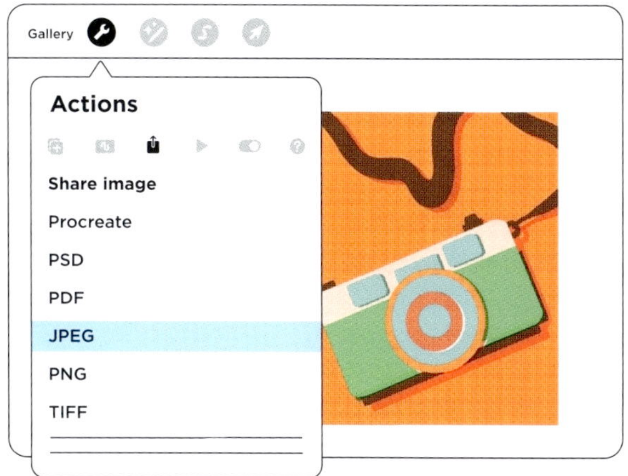

CREATING FOLDERS

To stay organized in Procreate, it's helpful to group your artwork into folders, which are known as **Stacks**.

1. To do this, head back to the **Gallery** by tapping **Gallery** on the top left of the screen. Tap **Select** and then tap on your artwork. Tap **Duplicate** a few times to make some duplicates of your art.

2. Tap the **X** to undo that selection, then tap **Select** again, tap on all the artworks you have just duplicated, and tap **Stack**.

3. Now you can tap on your **Stack** and see all your artworks there, separated from the rest of your art. This is helpful for staying organized and focused as you build your artwork library. You can name both your **Stack** and individual artworks by tapping on the **Stack/Artwork** name in the **Gallery** and typing a new name.

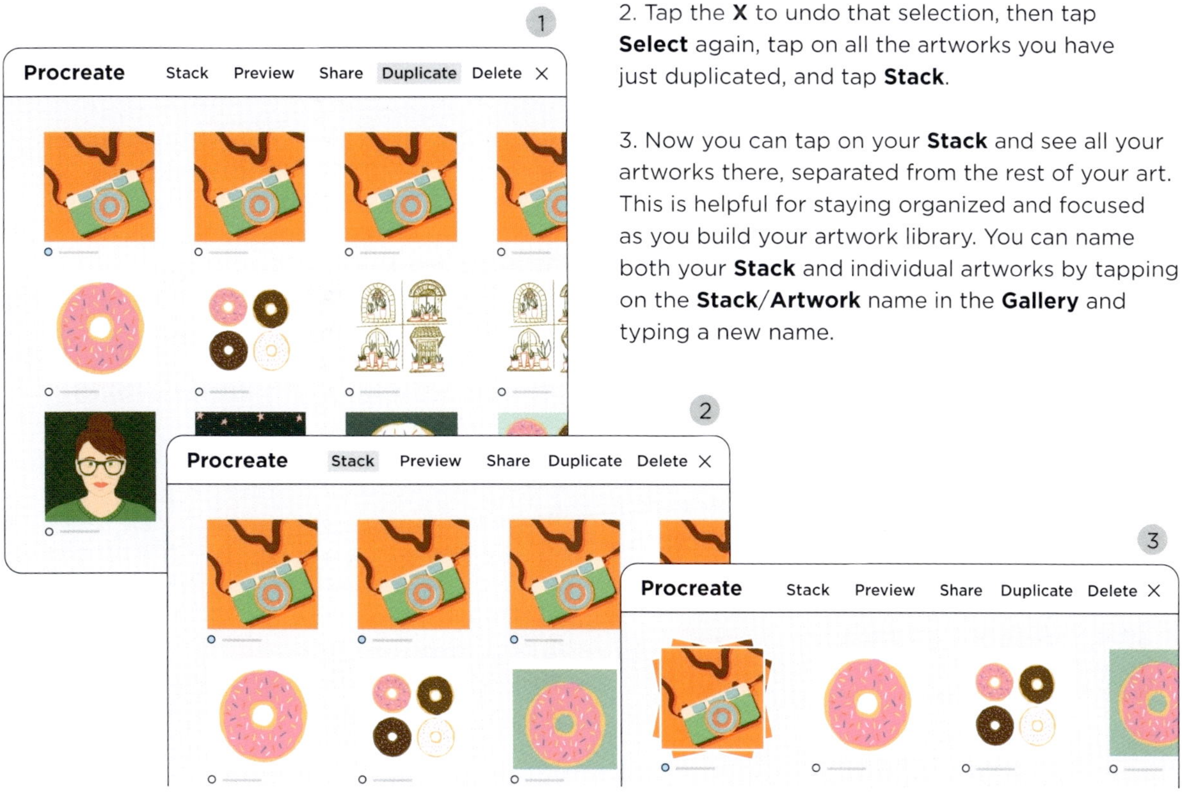

ADDITIONAL RESOURCES

Throughout the book, I'll reference the **Brush Sampler**, **Color Palettes**, and reference images found at: LizKohlerBrown.com/10steps. You'll find instructions for loading those into your Procreate app there as well. These are optional resources that are a supplement to what is already included with Procreate. If you'd like to get the resources, go to the page listed above and you'll find:

The Brush Sampler

This is a custom Procreate **Brush Set** designed to help you experience the full potential of Procreate. Each of these brushes will be discussed later on in the book, but for now you may want to download the **Brush Set** to load it into your Procreate **Brush Library**.

The Color Palettes

There are five specially designed **Color Palettes** used these in the projects in this book. If you'd like to use them, please load the palettes into your **Saved Palettes** using the same process described above.

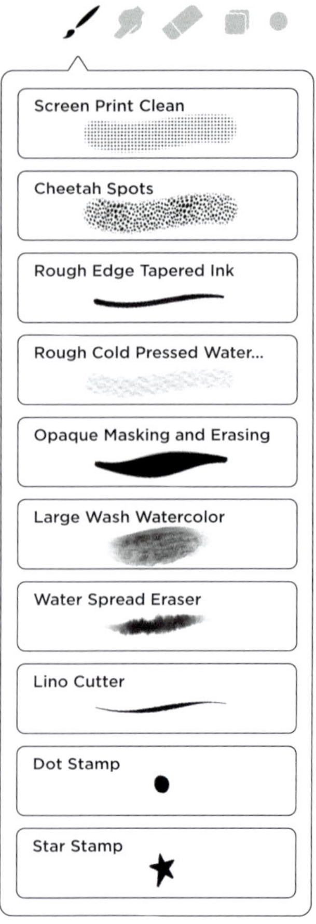

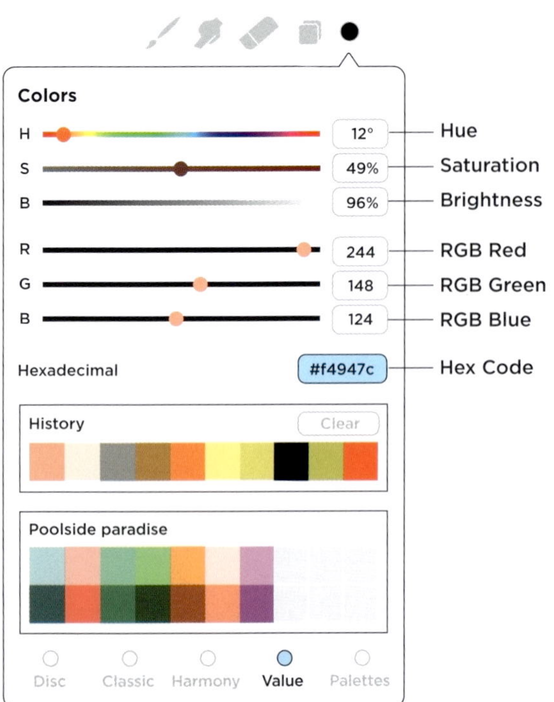

Hex Codes

Each project palette also includes hex codes. Hex codes (short for hexadecimal codes) are a way of representing colors in digital form that translates to nearly any app. In a hex code, colors are represented by a combination of six alphanumeric characters, which include numbers 0–9 and letters A–F.

Hex codes allow you to create palettes in your Procreate library based on color combinations you find online. For example, if you search "trending desert palette" online, you'll likely find a selection of interesting color combinations, some of which have six-digit numbers to indicate the hex code. You can put this number into your Procreate palette.

To input a hex code into your color library, tap on the **Value Menu** at the bottom of the **Colors Menu**, then enter the six-digit code in the Hexadecimal section.

THE
Projects

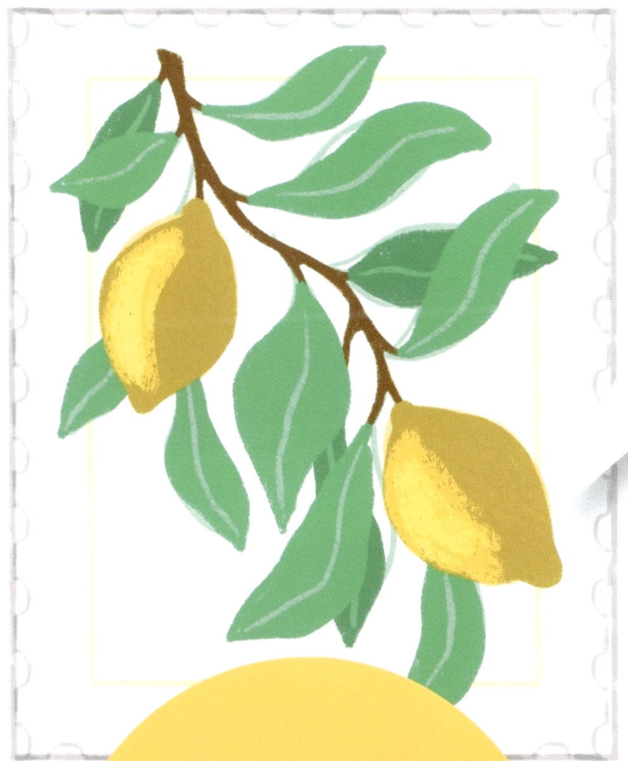

Let's Get Started!

You now have everything you'll need to start creating artwork in Procreate. Let's jump right into the first project, where we'll dive into sketching, organizing layers, and using reference images.

1

SKETCH SOME *Fruit*

Create a simple sketch of fruit on a branch, and during the process you will become familiar with the basic tools and processes that will be used throughout this book. You can choose any fruit tree as your subject or simply draw the orange branch shown here.

What We're Learning:
How to sketch in layers and use transform tools to resize and move

Brushes:

Sketching Pencil

Palette:
Poolside Paradise

Robin Egg Blue #98f2f4

Faded Jade #347373

Cherry Blossom #ffb9bd

Watermelon Pink #ff6472

Seafoam Green #77f0b5

Eucalyptus #3d845f

Pale Green #9cf08c

Astroturf Green #395f36

Butterscotch Orange #ffad56

Pumpkin Skin #ad5a00

Dawn Pink #ffebe2

Coral Pink #f4947c

Lavender Ice Cream #eea8f2

Dark Lilac #a465aa

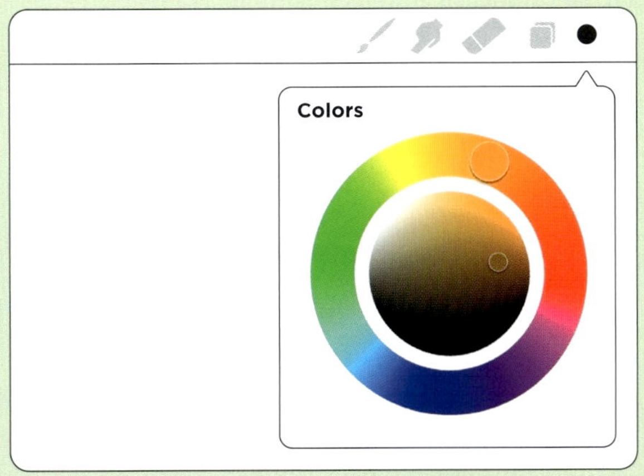

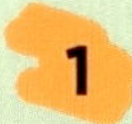

1 CHOOSE YOUR PALETTE

Tap the circle in the top-right corner of your screen to open the **Color Disc** and choose some colors for your sketch. In this example, the leaves are dark green, and the oranges are bright orange, using shades from the Poolside Paradise Palette. Sketching in different colors will help you stay organized and make the inking process easier. It also makes your sketches look beautiful and eye-catching.

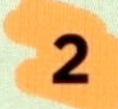

2 CHOOSE A BRUSH

Select a brush by tapping on the **Brush Library** icon and select either the Sketching Pencil from the **Brush Sampler** (see page 20) or any Procreate sketching brush that you prefer. Test your brush size by drawing some marks on the canvas, then **two-fingers tap** to undo the test marks. Here, the Sketching Pencil is used at 24%, but you can use any size that you would like.

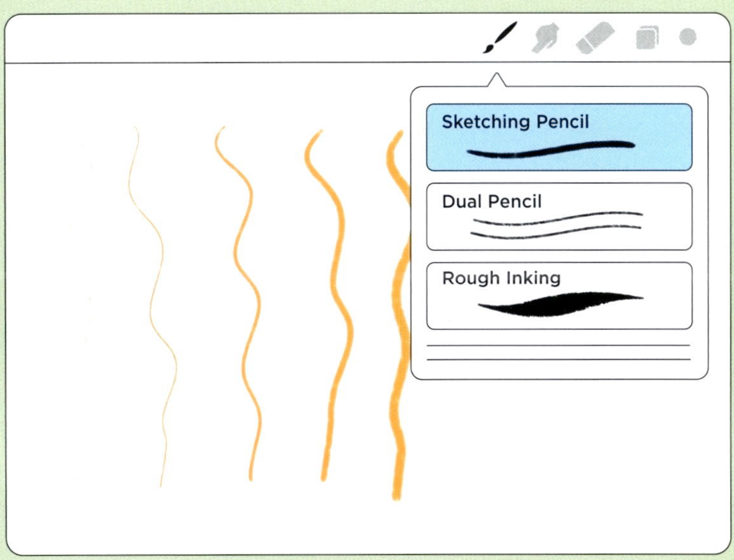

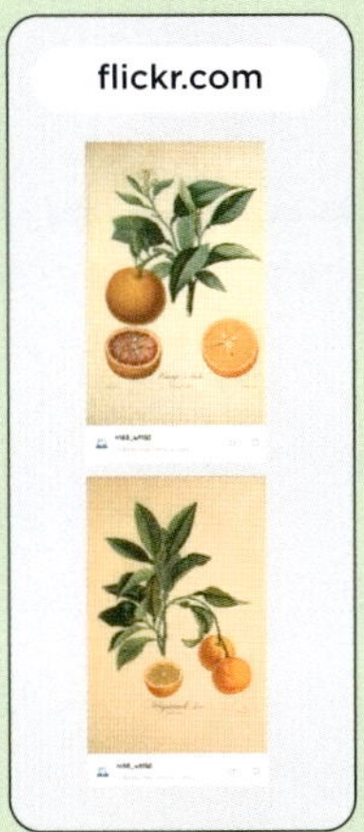

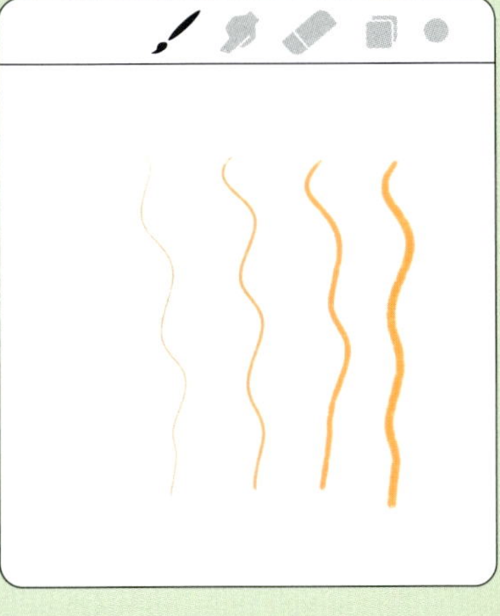

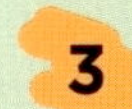

3 FIND REFERENCE IMAGES

Search online to find some images of oranges. Remember not to copy any single image, but rather sample shapes from various sources. If you would like to use the same images as I did, there is a gallery of orange pictures in the Creative Commons on Flickr that you can access through the resources mentioned on page 18. Pull your reference images up beside your canvas so that you can see both them and the canvas at the same time.

4 SKETCH LOOSE SHAPES

Create some loose circle shapes to identify where your oranges will be on the page. Repeat the same process with the leaves, remembering to put each color on its own layer. Name your layers as you create them by tapping on the layer and tapping **Rename**, then type a name for the layer.

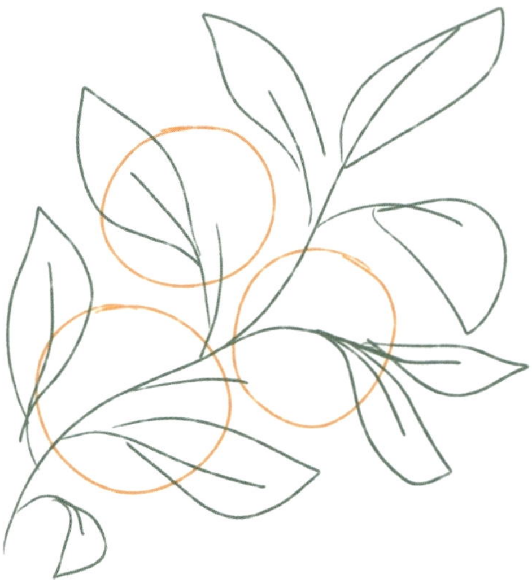

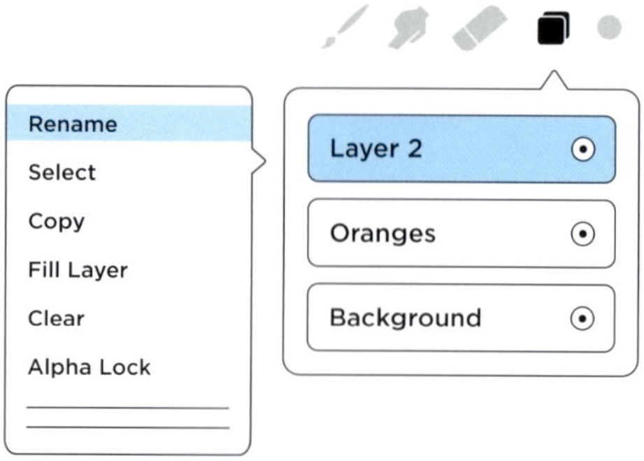

Rename
Select
Copy
Fill Layer
Clear
Alpha Lock

Layer 2
Oranges
Background

Freeform
Uniform
Distort
Warp

5 RESIZE YOUR SKETCH

At this point, you may have realized that your drawing is too big, too small, or skewed to one side of the page. If that is the case, tap on one layer in the **Layers Panel**, swipe right on the other layer (which allows you to select multiple layers at once), then tap the **Move Tool**. Now use your finger to pull the blue dots in the corner of your artwork to resize.

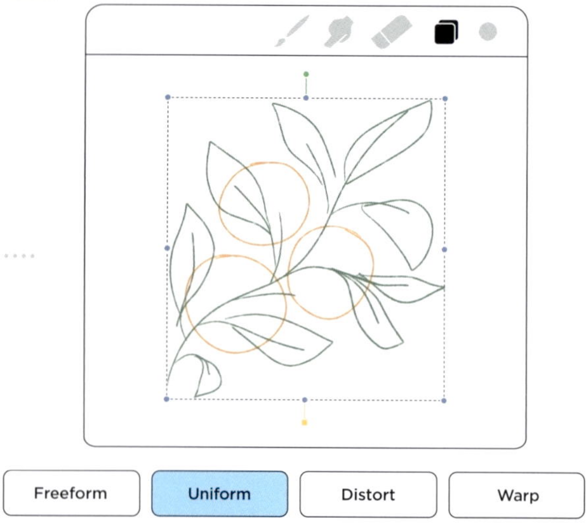

Tip If you want to move objects on the page, you can slide your finger on the side of the canvas rather than putting your finger on the artwork itself. This makes it easier to see what you're doing.

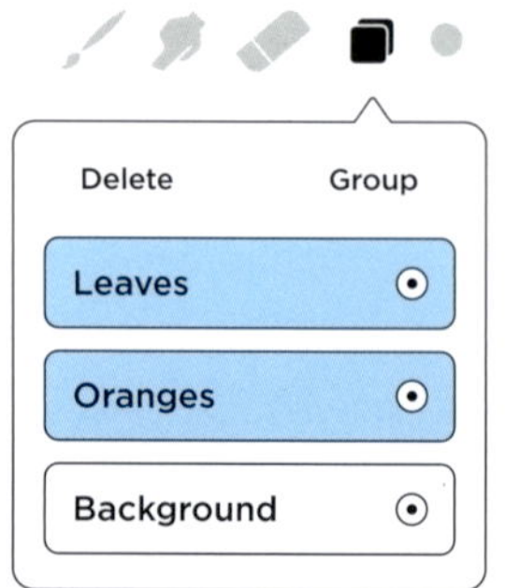

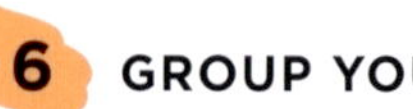

6 GROUP YOUR LAYERS

While you still have the Layers open, tap on the **Layers Panel** and then tap **Group** on the top right of the **Layers Panel**. You can choose to rename the group just as you did for the layers if you'd like to stay organized.

7 REFINE YOUR SKETCH

To make it easier to see the next layer of sketches, change the rough sketch to semi-transparent. To do this, open the **Group** by tapping the arrow beside the group name, tap on one of the layers, tap the **N** symbol beside the layer name, and then reduce the opacity. If you reduce it to 30%, you should still be able to see the rough sketch, but it won't be distracting.

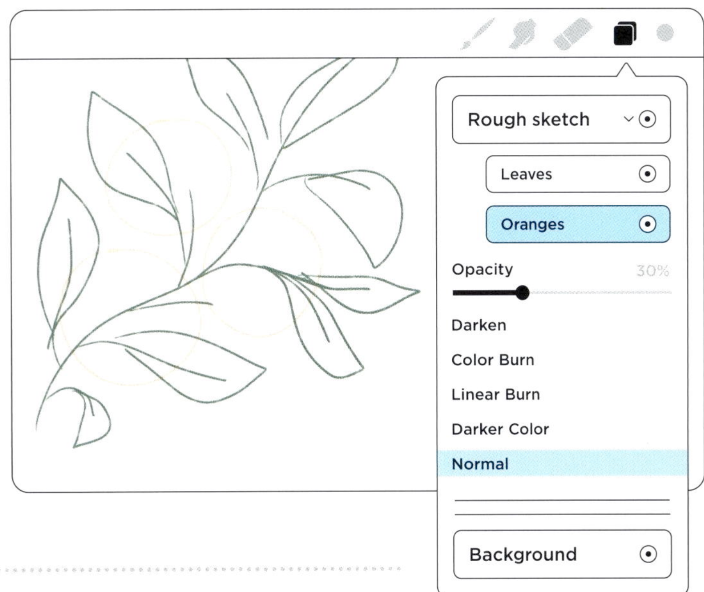

8 PLACE DIFFERENT ELEMENTS ON DIFFERENT LAYERS

Create new layers for the oranges and leaves. At this point, you can sketch in details like the thickness of the vine and variation in the shapes of the oranges. You may need to erase parts of the drawing to show where the objects overlap. This is when you'll be glad you placed elements on separate layers, because you can erase on one layer without erasing other parts of your drawing.

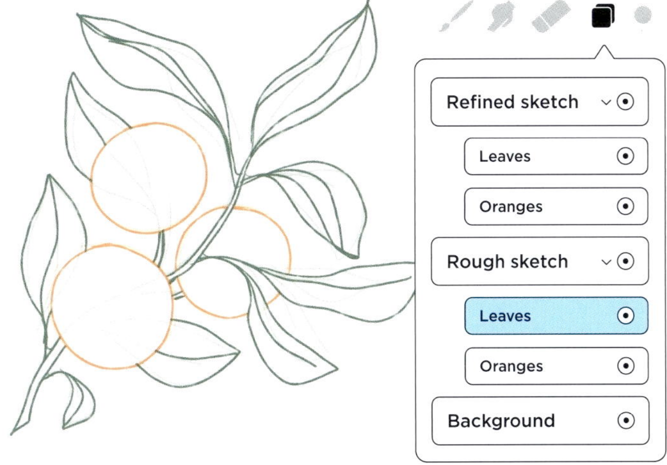

9 REVIEW YOUR SKETCH

At this stage, you could choose to do additional sketch layers or just call this drawing finished. I typically do at least three or four sketch layers, so don't worry about redoing the drawing. This is a great time to add shading, more variation to your leaves, or even some texture on the orange if you decide you want to.

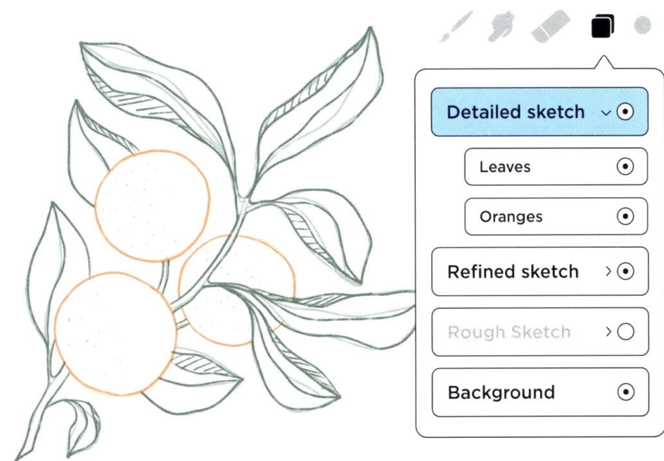

10 SHOW YOUR WORK

Finally, make the rough sketches invisible by tapping the check mark beside the layers you want to hide. Or leave all the layers on to show the progression of your drawing. Remember that while people love seeing your final project, they also love seeing the messy and rough parts of your creative process, so don't be afraid to share your messes!

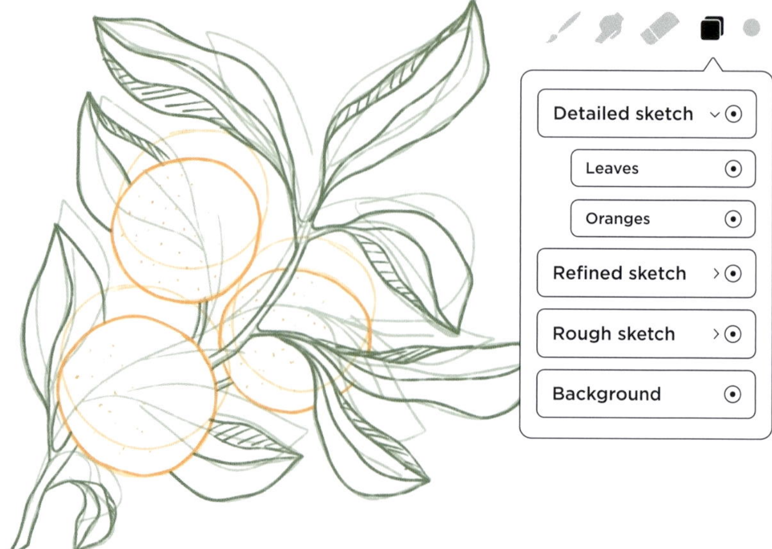

Keep It Going

Play around with sketching in various colors and brush thickness levels, and try using different brushes to see how they transform the look of your sketches. In these examples, the Sharp Pastel brush from the **Brush Sampler** was used at 44% size and in both a pure black and a multicolored version.

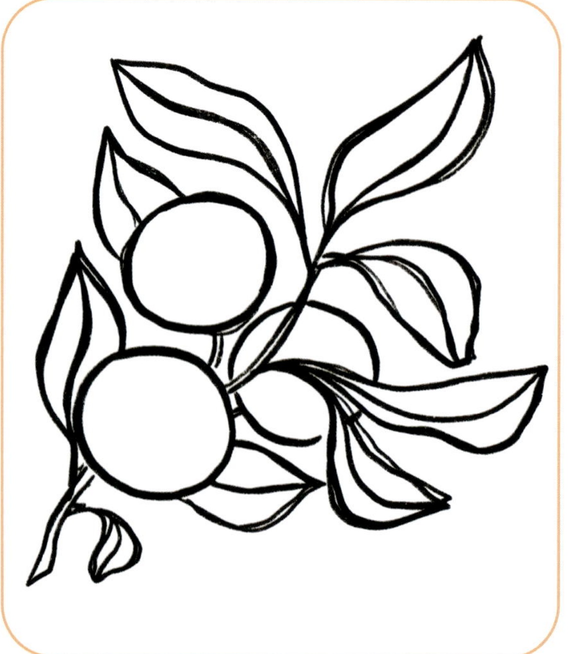

The End Result

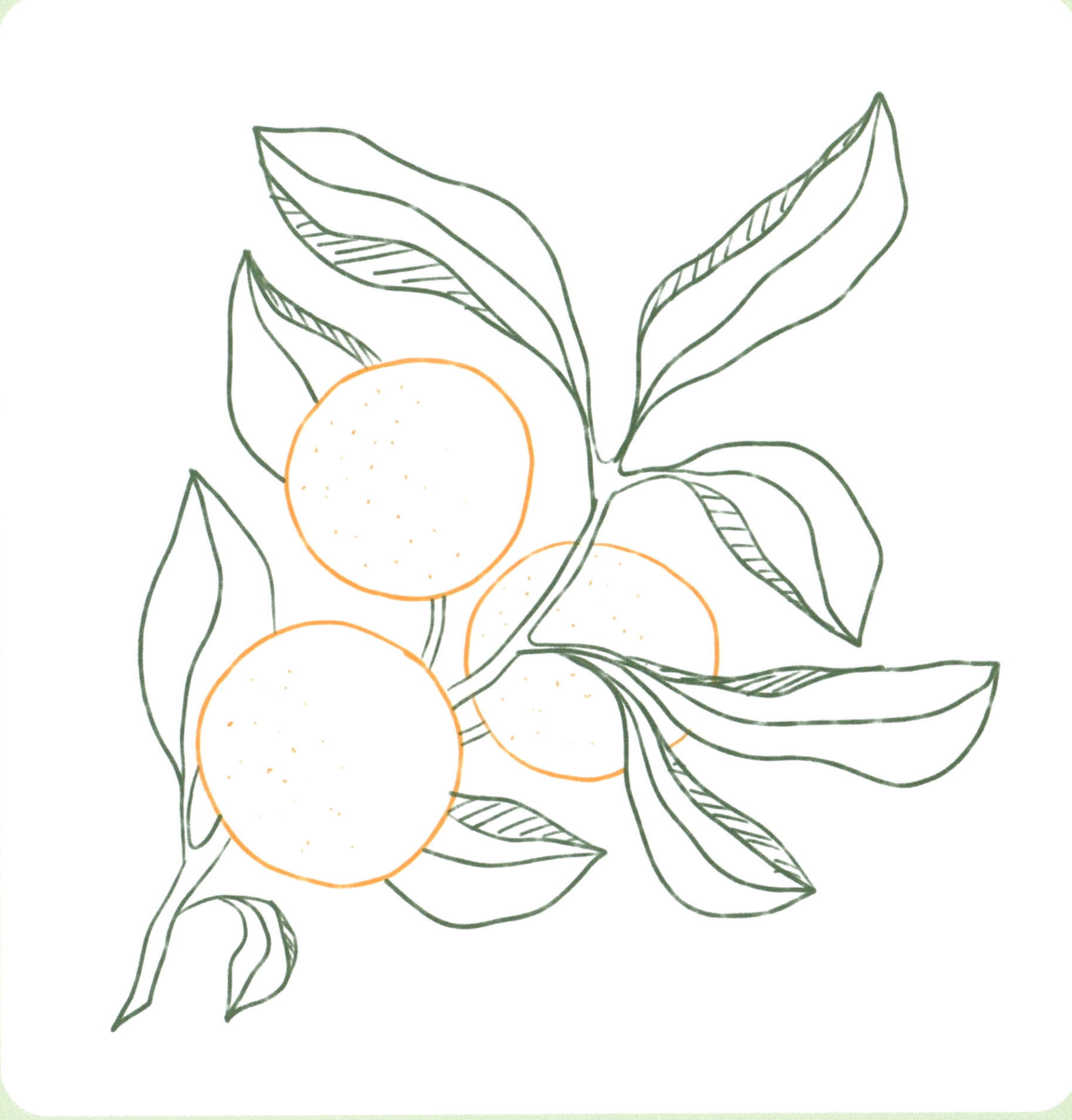

2

DRAW AND INK *Your Drink*

Draw your favorite hot drink to practice building a composition from sketch to finished artwork. You'll notice that the first few projects all use the same brush. Using the same brush simplifies things, so you don't have the additional worry of choosing the "right brush."

What We're Learning:
How to ink artwork in layers and change colors

Brushes:

Sketching Pencil

Rough Inking Worn Texture

Palette:
Funky Modern

Reddish Orange #ff4b18

Red Fox #d34925

Rose Bud #ffb09b

Dark Peach #d1725f

Mango Orange #df8000

Ginger Brown #9f5d00

Pink Pearl #ff9ce2

Neon Fuschia #ff54c2

Lake Mist Blue #d7dce7

Steel Blue #7297c9

Aqua Forest Green #6b9b78

Pine Green #3a5a44

Pale Violet #eda7fc

Amethyst Purple #ac4cc1

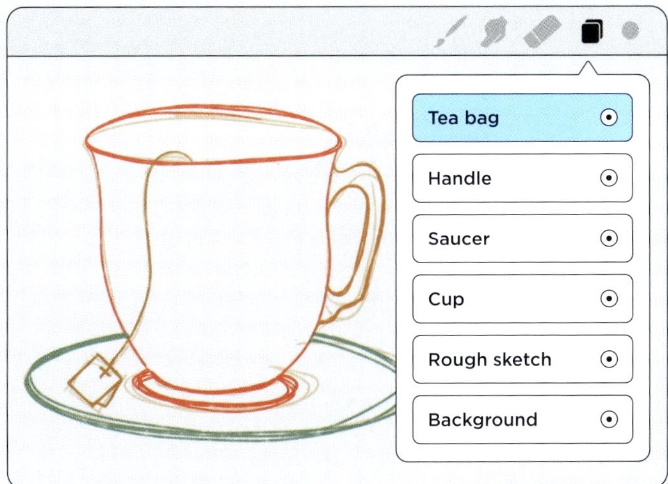

1 FIND INSPIRATION

Find some images of cups that you like. A simple teacup and saucer are shown here, but you could sketch a cappuccino cup, espresso cup, or even a paper to-go cup. You might find one cup with a shape you like and another with some interesting decoration. Combining various features from your reference images, create a sketch of your cup following the steps from the Fruit Sketch project. Name each layer as you create it to stay organized.

Quickshape is a "smart tool" that senses what you want to draw and helps you draw it more accurately. To draw the oval shapes on the cup, draw the oval then, rather than releasing your stylus, hold it in place for a moment. Procreate will invoke "Quickshape," which will help smooth out your oval.

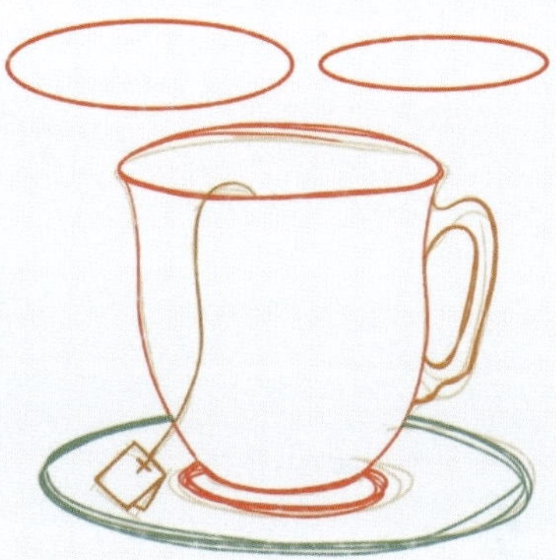

2 CHOOSE YOUR BRUSH

Select a brush from the **Brush Sampler** set or a Procreate brush and test the thickness on your canvas to make sure you have the right size. The Rough Inking Worn Texture brush is used here at 42%. Start the inking process by drawing around your shapes' edges, then turn up your brush size to fill in the inner parts of your drawing.

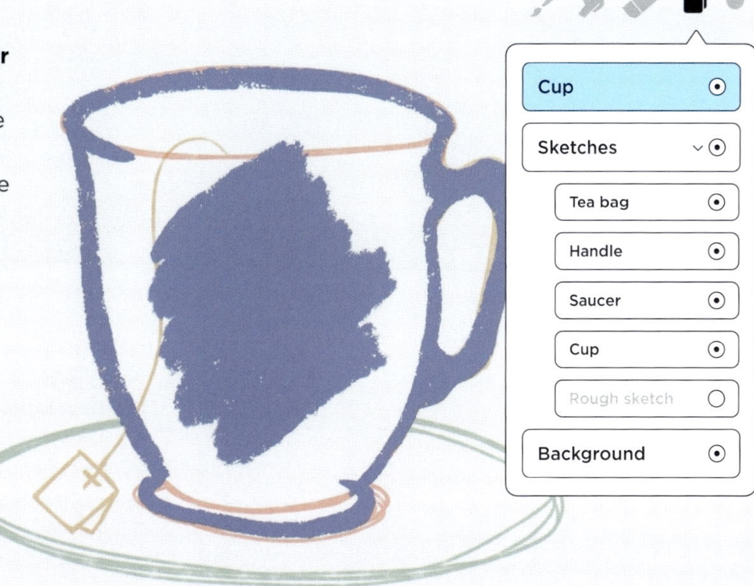

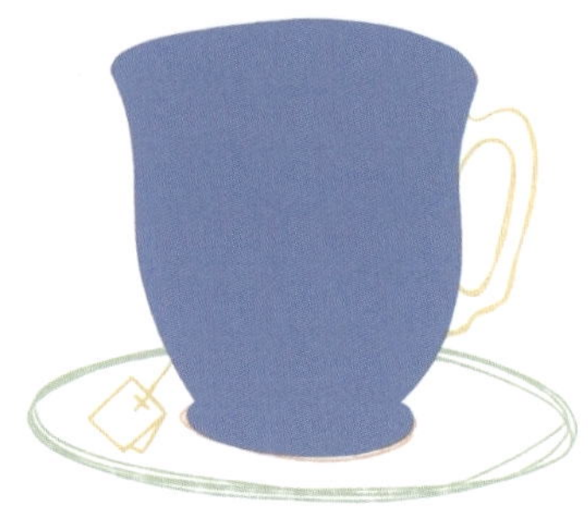

3 INKING INSIDE YOUR OUTLINE

It is only necessary to manually ink the inner parts of your shape if you want to retain the texture of the brush. If you are using an untextured brush like the Fluid Ink brush from the **Brush Sampler**, you can drag and drop color into any closed shape. Test this technique by drawing a circle with the **Color Drop Tool**, then dragging the color from the **Color Disc** into the center of your shape.

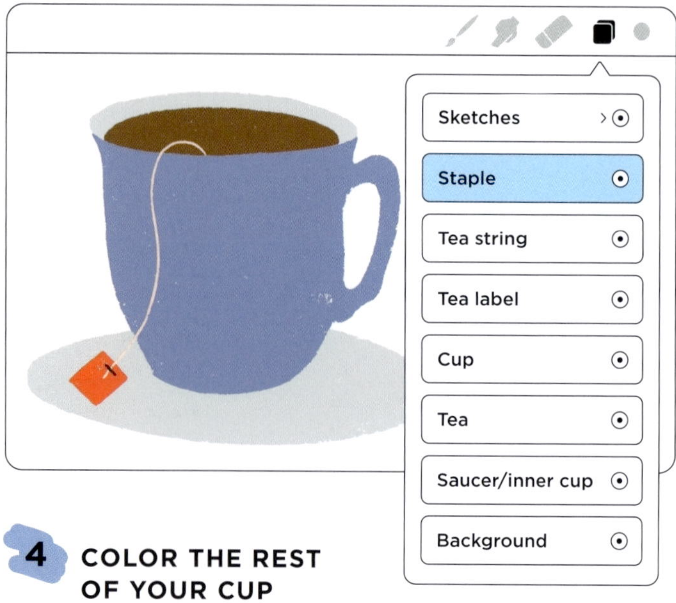

4 COLOR THE REST OF YOUR CUP

Repeat the coloring process on all the parts of your cup. If needed, use the eraser when you go outside the lines; however, keep in mind that going over the lines can help to give your drawing a handmade, unique feel, so don't be afraid to work loosely.

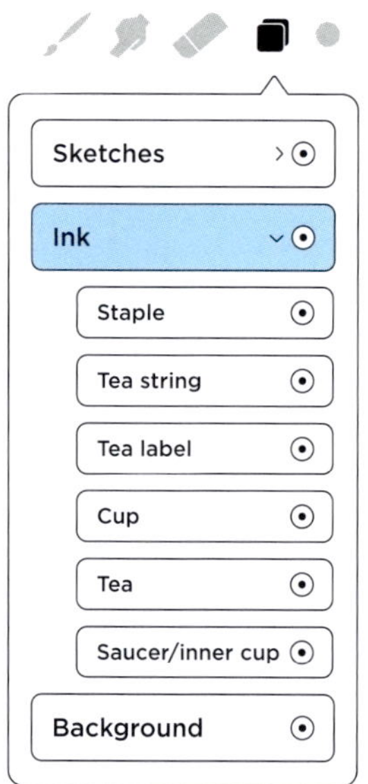

5 ORGANIZE YOUR LAYERS

Make sure that each new object goes onto a new layer so that you can easily change colors at the end of the process, then group all your inking layers. You will never regret taking time to create an organized **Layers Panel**!

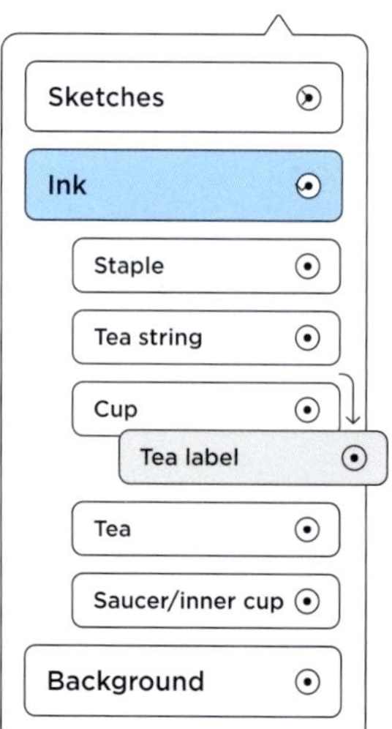

6 ADJUSTING THE SEQUENCE OF THE LAYERS

If you realize a layer needs to be above or below another element, you can easily use your finger to drag it to the right spot in the **Layers Panel**. First hold your finger on the layer for a moment, then you'll see it "pop out" of the **Layers Panel** so you can drag it to where you want it to be.

7 ADD A BACKGROUND COLOR

To add a background color, first choose a color. Then create a new layer, drag it below all the other layers, tap on the layer, and then tap **Fill Layer**.

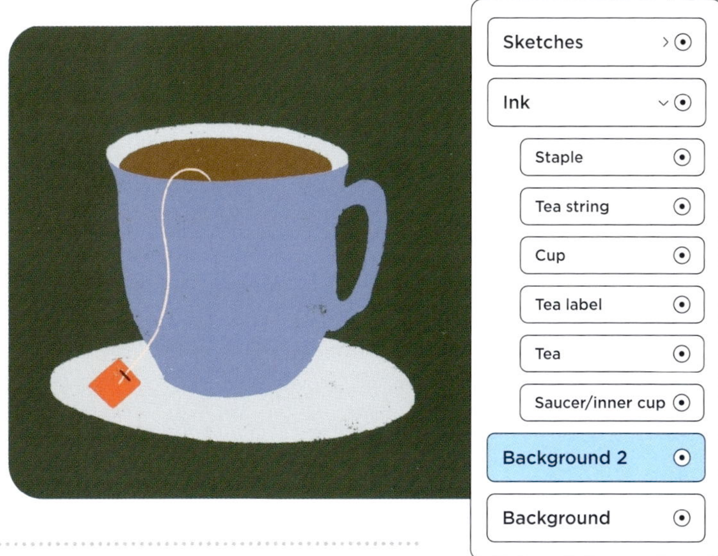

8 ADD DECORATION TO THE CUP

Tap on the layer you want to add decoration to, in this case, the cup body, then tap **Select** on the flyout menu. You should see everything except your cup shape covered in diagonal lines. This indicates what is not selected (the area in which you cannot draw). Tap the **+** symbol at the top of the **Layers Panel** and start drawing lines, dots, or any other design you want to use.

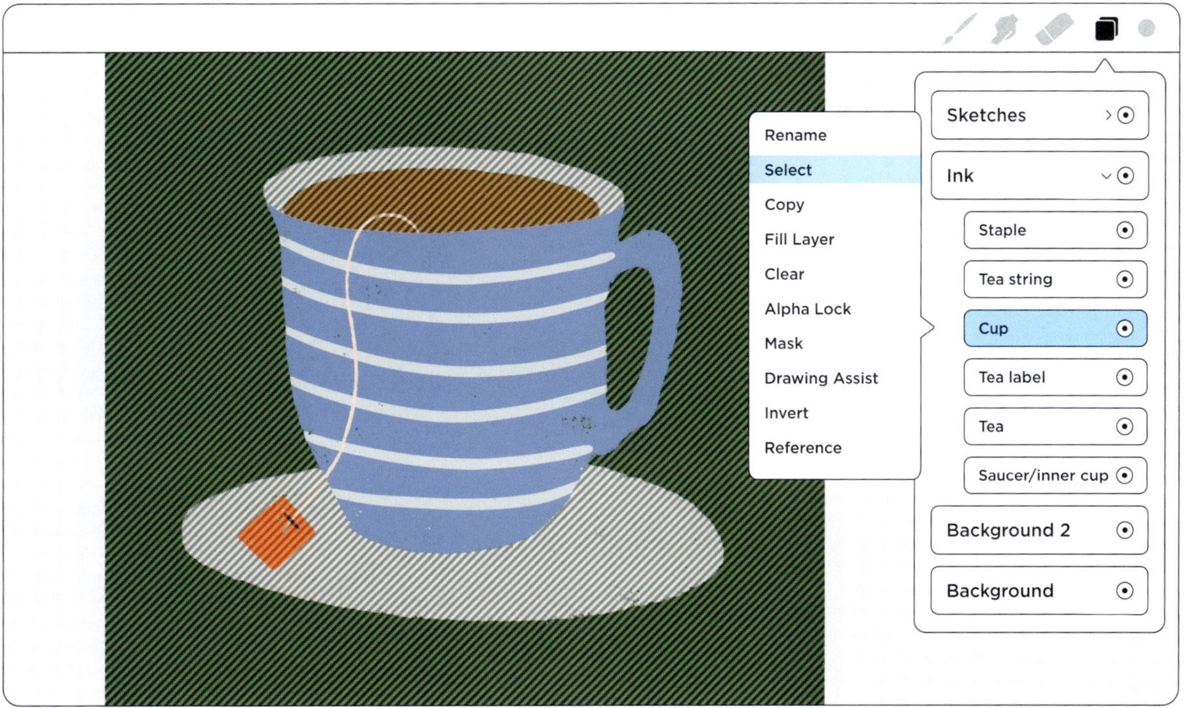

9 CHANGE THE COLORS

There are several ways to change colors in Procreate, and we'll cover them all in this book, but for now let's keep it simple by tapping on the layer you want to change, selecting **Alpha Lock**, choosing a color, tapping on the layer again and tapping **Fill Layer**.

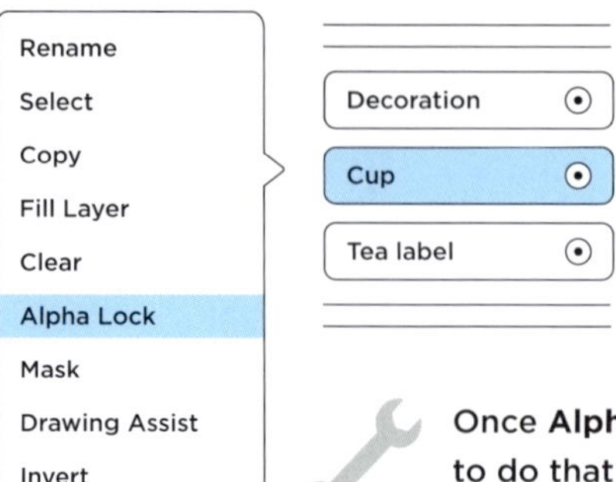

Once Alpha Lock is on, you don't have to do that step again for that layer, so you might as well go ahead and put all your inked layers on Alpha Lock so that you can easily just tap each layer, then tap Fill Layer to change its color.

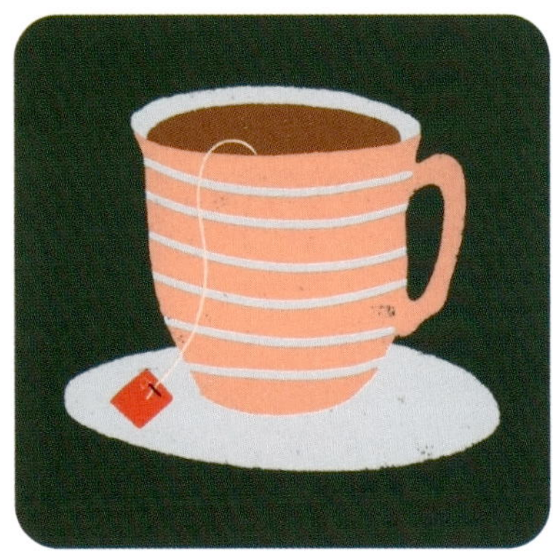

10 FIND THE PERFECT COLOR COMBINATION

Repeat the **Fill Layer** process described in step 9, trying various different colors on each layer (including the background layer) until you find a combination that you are happy with.

Keep It Going

Why not try a few different types of decoration and a variety of color combinations? Changing just one or two features of your artwork can give it a totally different look and feel.

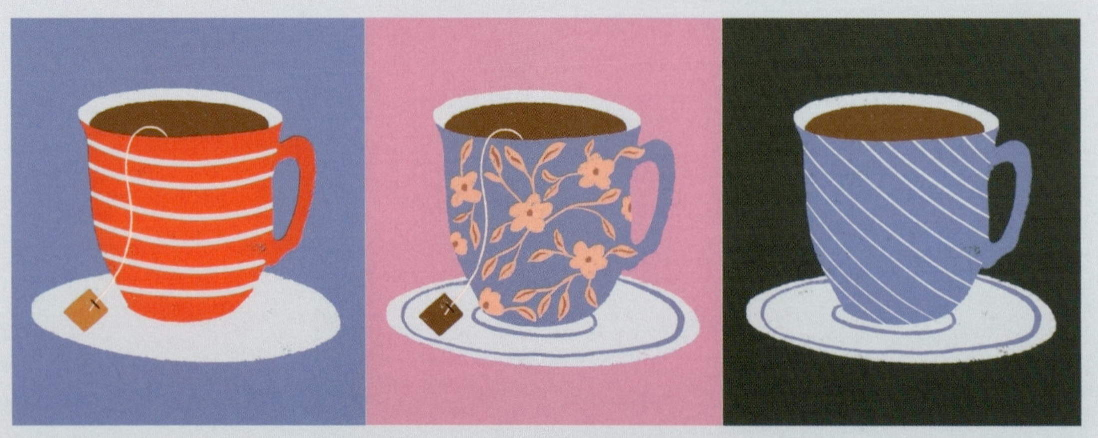

The End Result

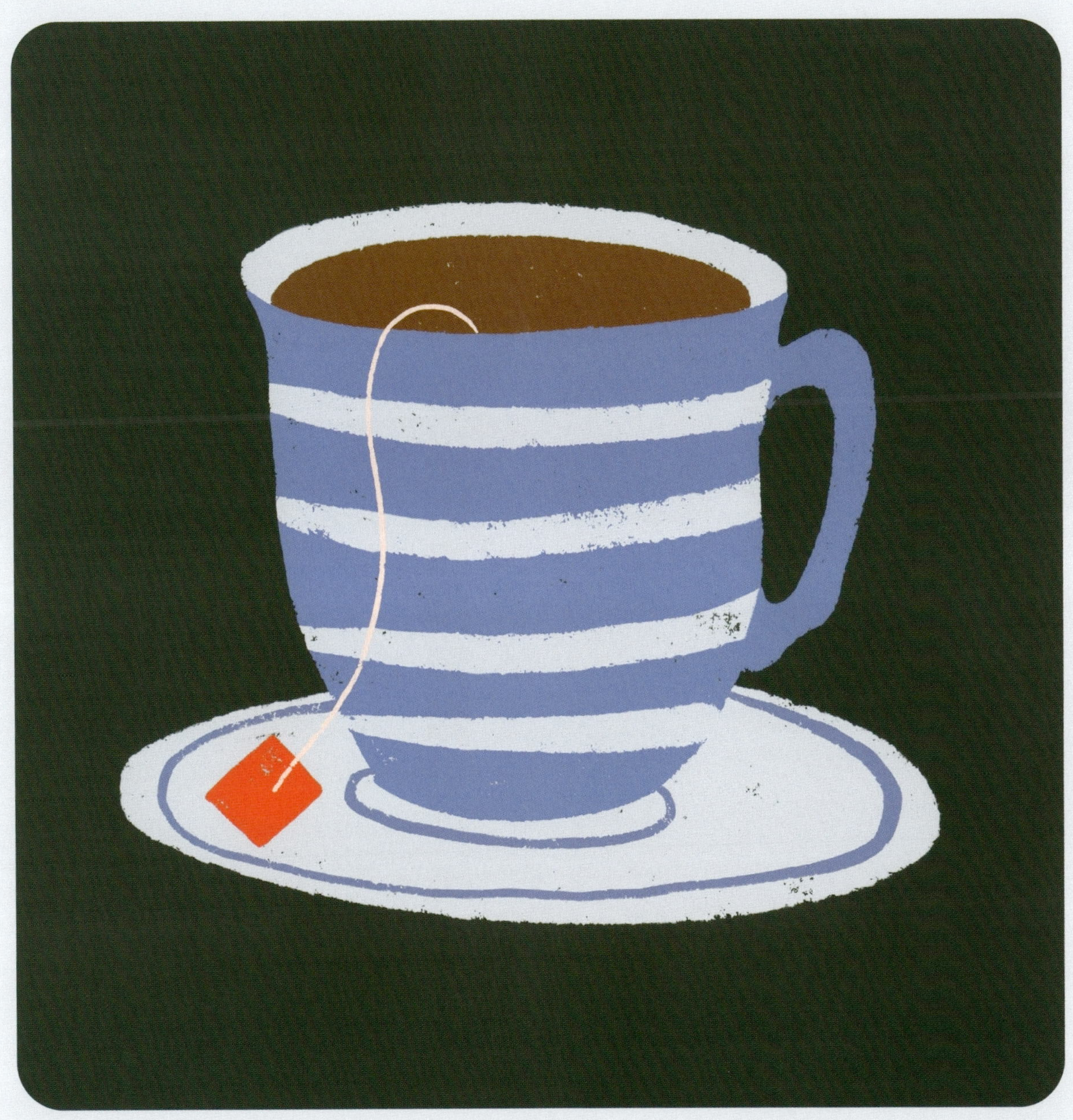

3

DESIGN

Donut Palettes

In this project, you'll be drawing your favorite bakery treat. Try choosing something colorful like donuts, macaroons, or cookies since the main goal of this project is to practice creating palettes by sampling colors from photographs.

What We're Learning:
How to create **Palettes** and sample color from photographs

Brushes:

Sketching Pencil

Rough Inking Worn Texture

Palette:
Photo Sampled

Muted Sunset Orange #f2c27d

Blood Orange Red #b54c2f

Barbie Pink #ff94c9

Light Cornlower Blue #7895c3

Hot Pepper Red #f85c35

Chocolate Brown #7d5113

Dark Chocolate Brown #7d5113

Cherry Lips Red #992935

Jacaranda Lilac #9f91f0

Sea Glass Turquoise #9acebf

Apple Green #87a34e

Zesty Lime Green #bac53a

Banana Yellow #ffda68

Burnt Orange #c68836

1 MAKE A SKETCH

Just as you have done for the previous projects, start by finding some pictures of your bakery treat and sketching it on your canvas. Donuts are a good choice because they give you the chance to play with color on the sprinkles and icing, making for a colorful composition.

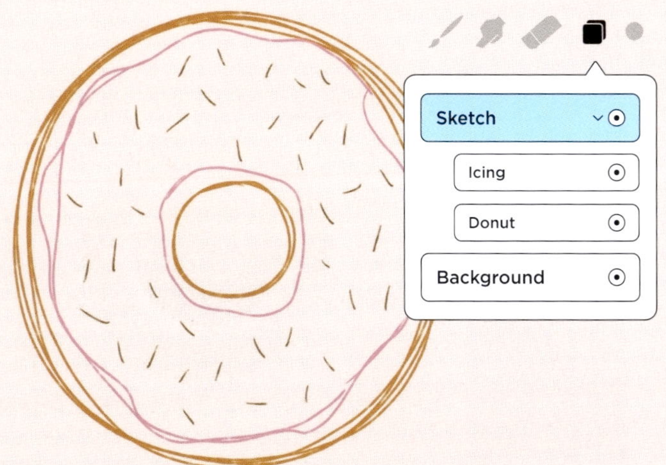

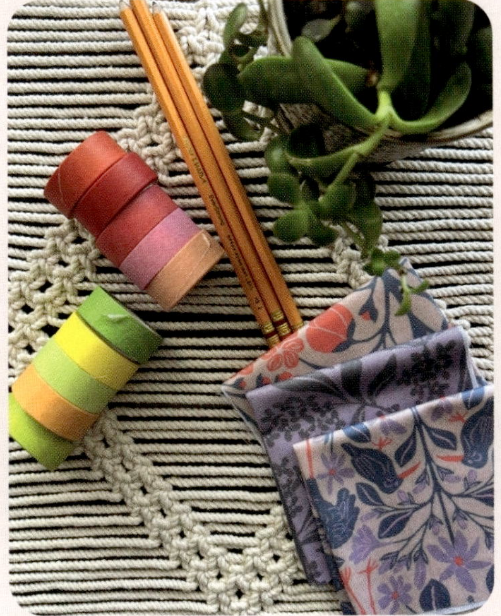

2 PHOTOGRAPH YOUR PALETTE

To get started with making a palette, you will need a photograph that contains the colors you want to sample. If you don't have a colorful donut at your disposal, gather some items from around your home that contain colors that you like and take some pictures of them. You can do this with your iPad camera to avoid the step of transferring photos from your camera or phone to your iPad.

3 ADD THE PHOTO TO YOUR CANVAS

Once you have the photos on your iPad, tap the **Actions Menu**, tap **Add**, then **Insert a Photo**. Choose your photo from the **Photo Gallery** and it will drop down onto your canvas. You can resize it using the little blue dots on the corners if you want to make it smaller before creating your palette.

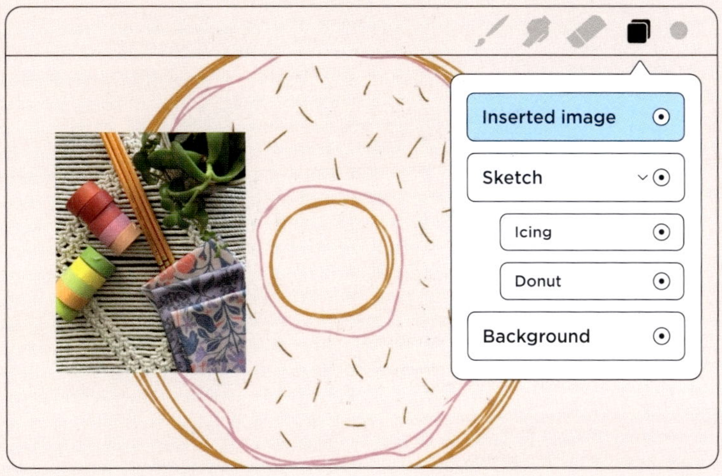

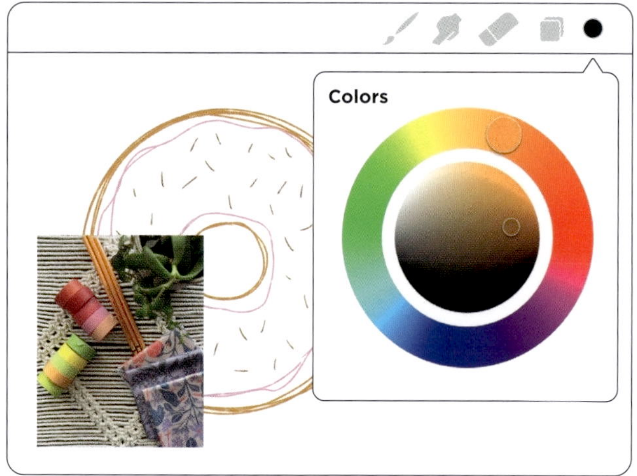

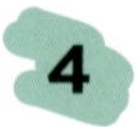

4 OPEN THE COLOR MENU

Next, tap on the **Move Tool** to position your photo, then tap the **Colors Menu** so that you can start creating a new palette that will be saved in your Procreate app.

5 CREATE A NEW PALETTE

Go to **Palettes** on the **Color Disc** and tap the **+** symbol to create a new palette. Rename it by tapping on the word Untitled, then go back to the **Color Disc** to see your empty palette.

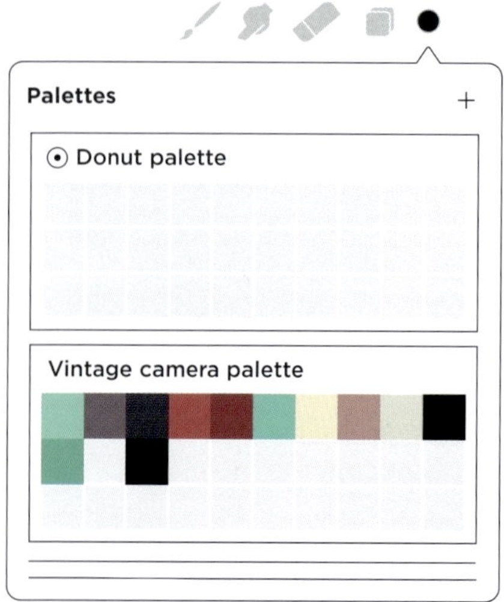

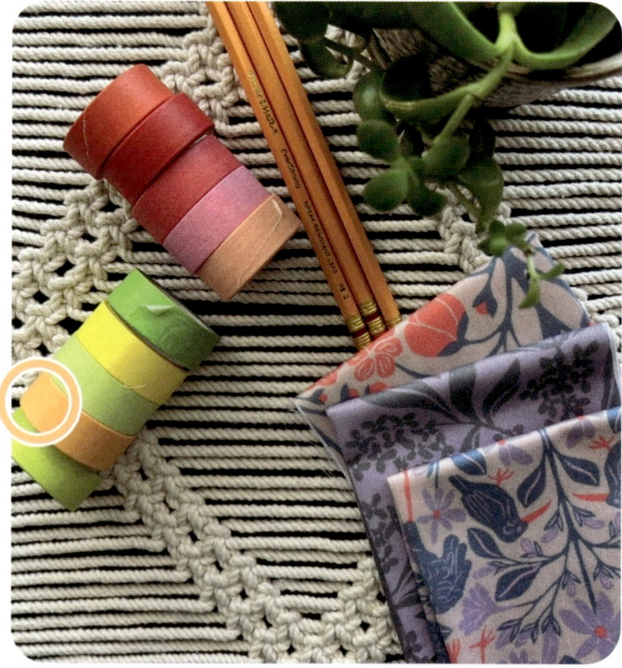

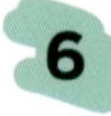

6 SAMPLE A COLOR FROM YOUR PHOTOGRAPH

To sample a color, press and hold your finger down on a color in your photo. If you move your finger around without picking it up, you will find different colors to sample from your photograph. Once you find a color you like, lift up your finger and you should see that color selected in the **Color Disc.**

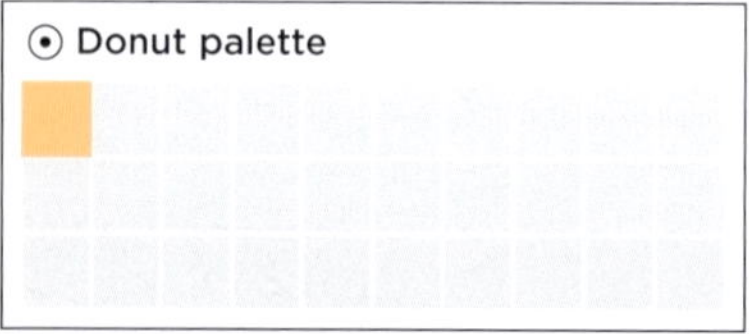

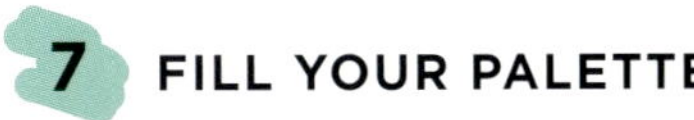

7 FILL YOUR PALETTE

Tap on the first square on your palette to add the first sampled color, then repeat the steps for sampling color and tapping your palette until you have sampled all the colors you want to save.

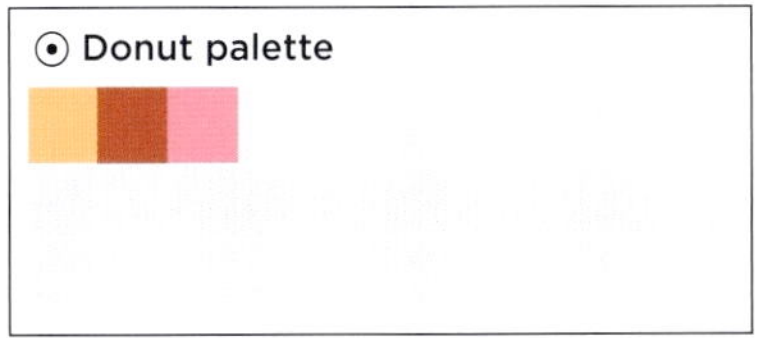

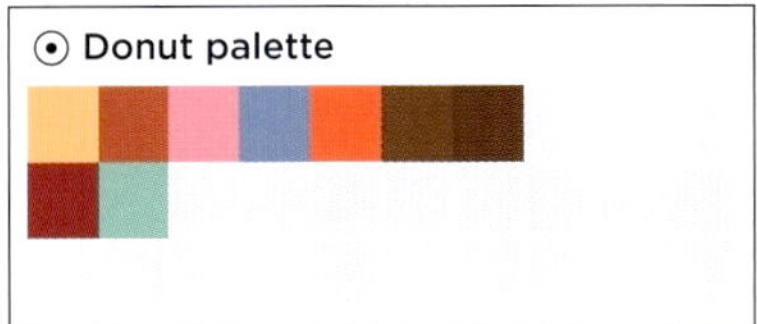

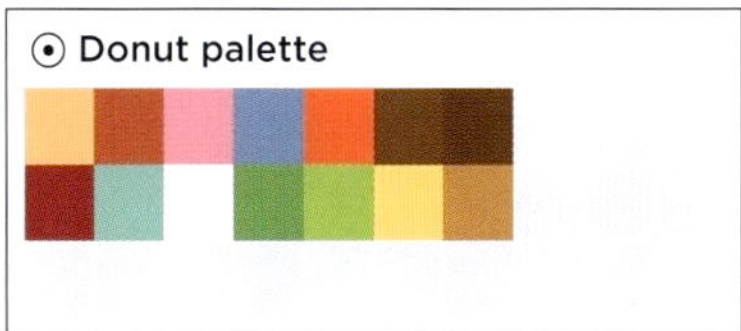

8 COLOR YOUR DRAWING

Now it's time to add some color! Using colors from the palette you have created, color your drawing, following the steps described in Draw and Ink Your Drink, trying out various brushes to get the level of smoothness or texture that you prefer.

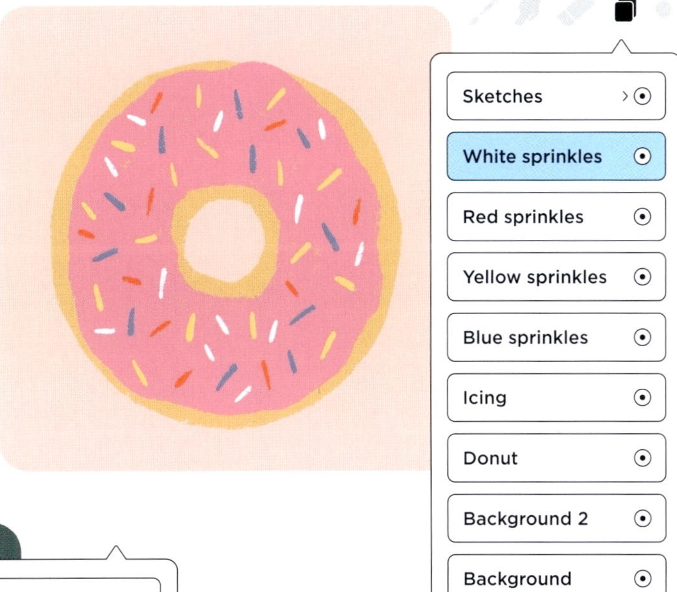

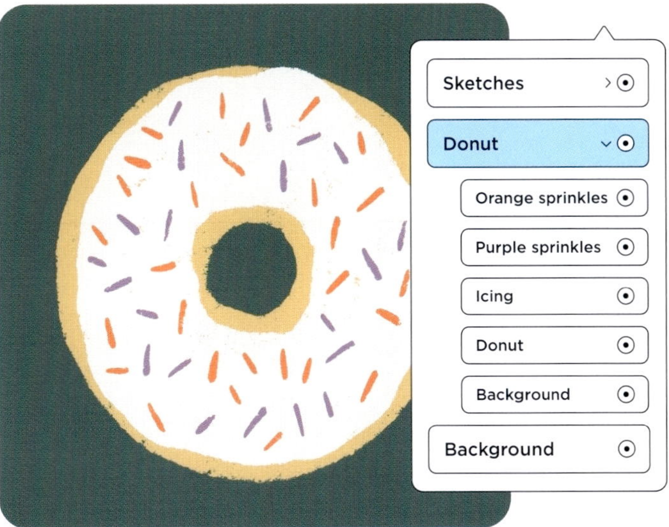

9 USE ALPHA LOCK TO INK YOUR DRAWING

Remember, you can use the **Alpha Lock** and **Fill Layer** method that was introduced in the last project to change the colors of your donuts, using either a color in your palette or a different palette altogether. It's a good idea to group your inked layers at this point to stay organized.

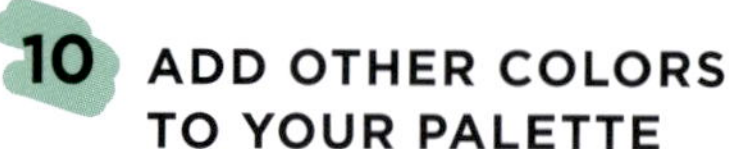

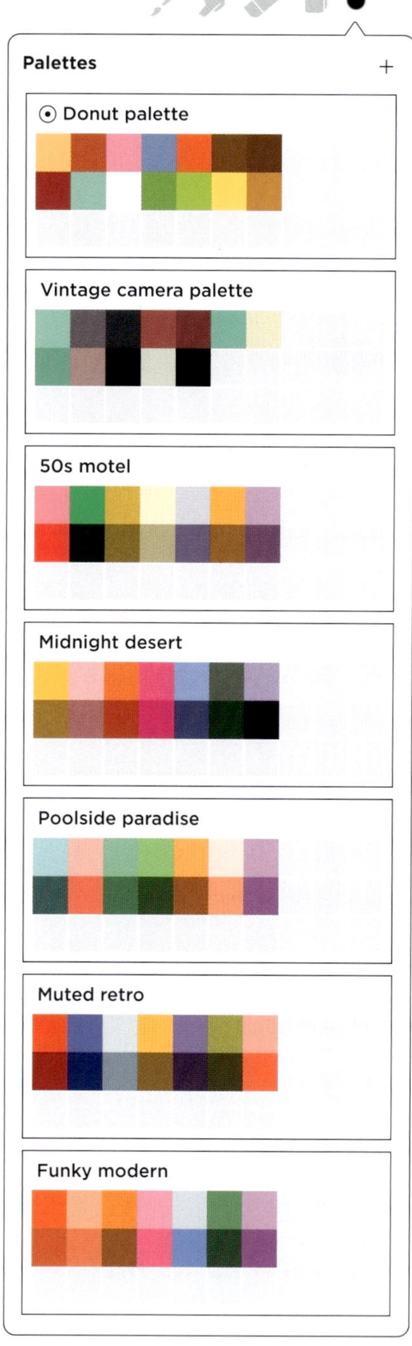

10 ADD OTHER COLORS TO YOUR PALETTE

If you discover other colors that would work well in your palette, add them now by tapping on one of the blank squares. It's always helpful to have a variety of your favorite colors to choose from when you create artwork, so this is a great time to create a few palettes featuring your favorite shades that you can use throughout the projects in this book.

Keep It Going

Create a more interesting composition by combining multiple donuts on the same canvas. Duplicate the donuts by swiping left on the Inked donut group, then resize the duplicated group to a quarter of its original size by tapping the **Move Tool** and adjusting the blue **Transform Dots**. Note that the original donut group can be made invisible by tapping the check symbol in the **Layers Panel**. Then resize the Donut group, duplicate, and arrange into a composition of four. The frosting and sprinkle colors can be changed using **Fill Layer**.

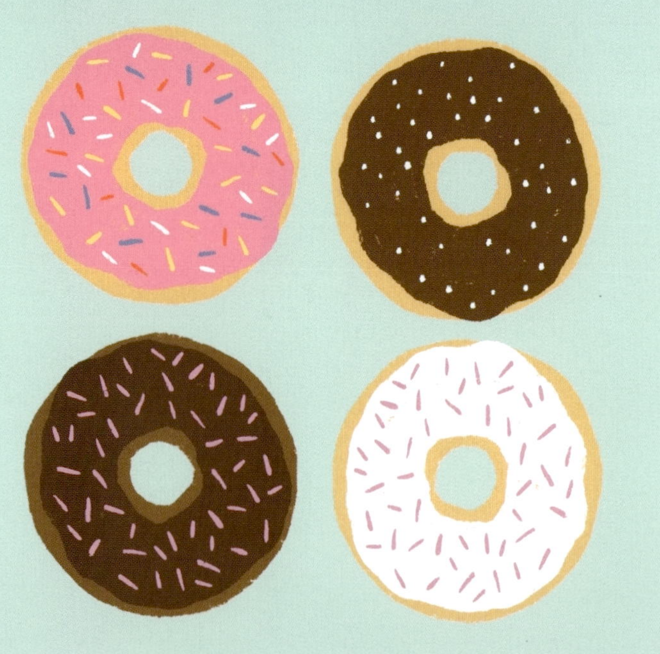

The End Result

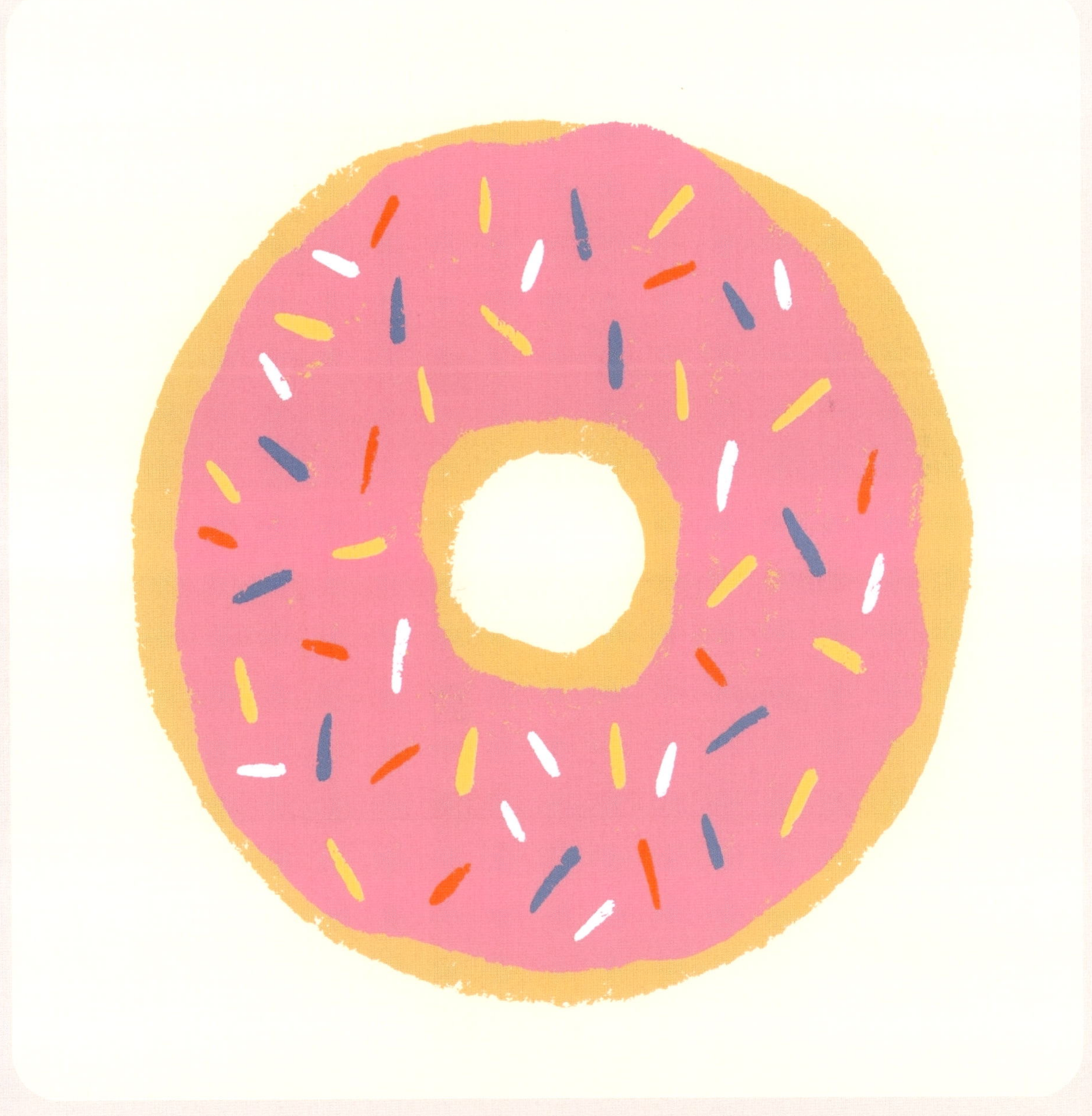

4

MAKE Fast Calls

Quickline is a tool that most illustrators use daily; it allows you to quickly create shapes to speed up your drawing process. In this project, we'll use Quickline to create an image of a cell phone displaying a simple music player.

What We're Learning:
How to use **Quickline** to create straight lines and interesting shapes

Brushes:

Sketching Pencil

Rough Inking Worn Texture

Palette:
Poolside Paradise

Robin Egg Blue #98f2f4

Faded Jade #347373

Cherry Blossom #ffb9bd

Watermelon Pink #ff6472

Seafoam Green #77f0b5

Eucalyptus #3d845f

Pale Green #9cf08c

Astroturf Green #395f36

Butterscotch Orange #ffad56

Pumpkin Skin #ad5a00

Dawn Pink #ffebe2

Coral Pink #f4947c

Lavender Ice Cream #eea8f2

Dark Lilac #a465aa

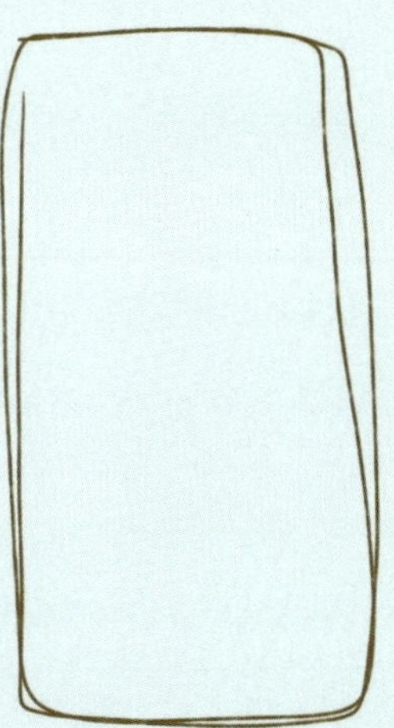

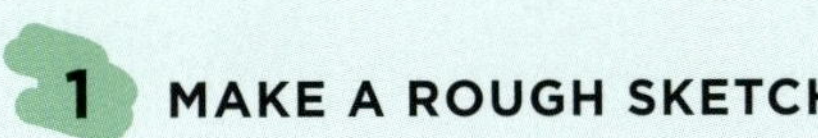

1 MAKE A ROUGH SKETCH

Using the sketching process you've already learned in Project 1, draw a cell phone using loose lines, capturing the basic proportions of your phone

2 REFINE THE LINES

Make your rough sketch semi-transparent using the **Opacity Slider** on the layer, then on a new layer, draw a line. Before picking up your stylus, hold still for a moment. You'll notice that your line snaps to your stylus and you can drag it around in a circle. If you continue to hold your stylus down and put one finger on the screen using the other hand, the line will snap to a 45-degree angle. This is especially helpful in a project like this, where you want to create a rectangular shape. Take some time to get used to how **Quickline** works.

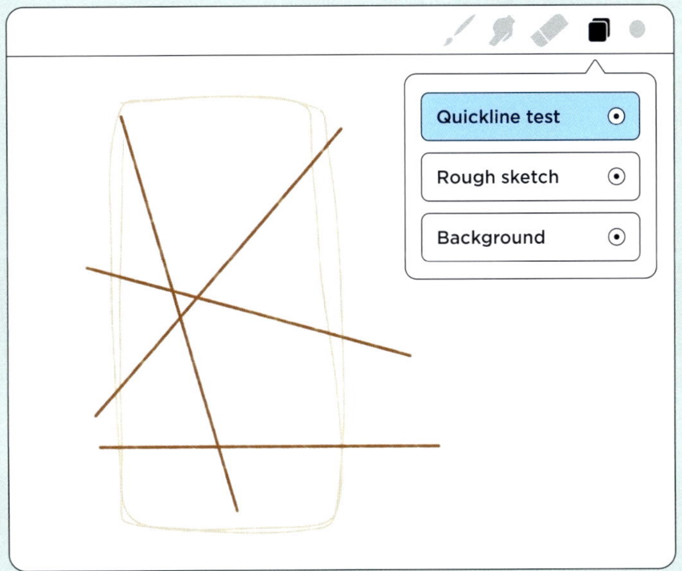

3 START DRAWING THE LINES OF YOUR PHONE

Next, go ahead and make the vertical line for the side of your phone, and another for the top.

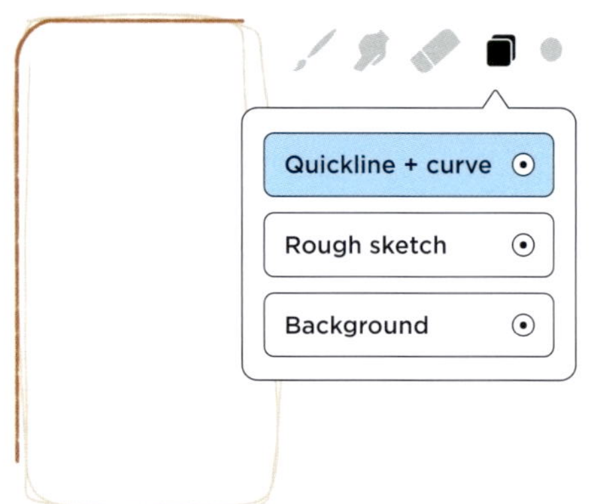

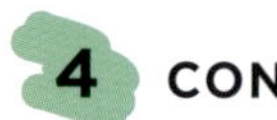

4 CONNECT THE LINES

Draw a smooth curve to connect the two lines you have drawn, then go to the **Layers Panel**, swipe left on that layer and tap **Duplicate**.

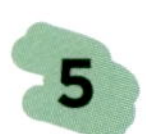

5 REPEAT AND FLIP THE IMAGE

Tap the **Move Tool**, then tap **Flip Horizontal** to get a mirror image of the top and left sides of your phone. You may need to drag the second layer a bit to get your phone drawing to the right width. Then repeat the same process to create the bottom of your phone.

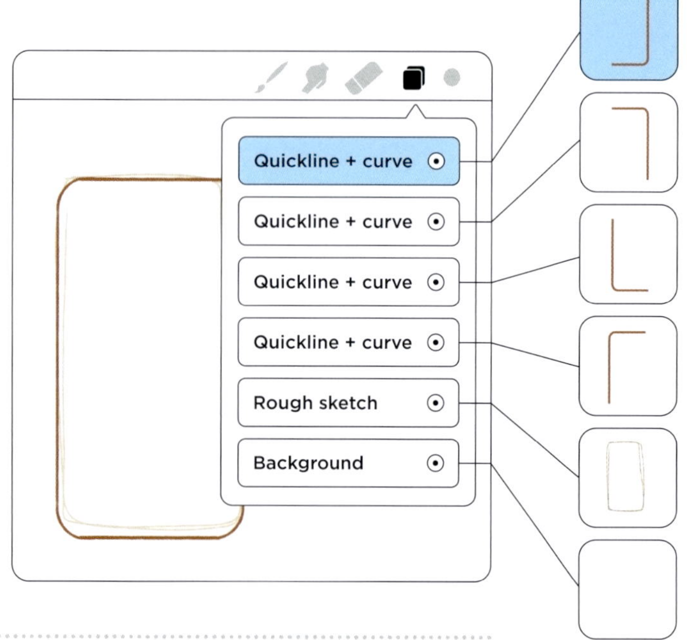

6 MERGE THE LAYERS

Next, you can merge these four layers into one shape by pinching them with your fingers in the **Layers Panel**, then create another rough sketch to map out the remaining parts of your phone screen. In this example, that's an app icon and music player, but feel free to put anything on your phone that you want to share with the world!

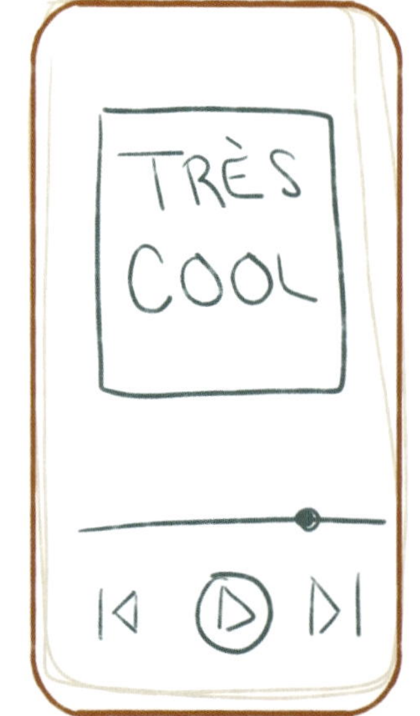

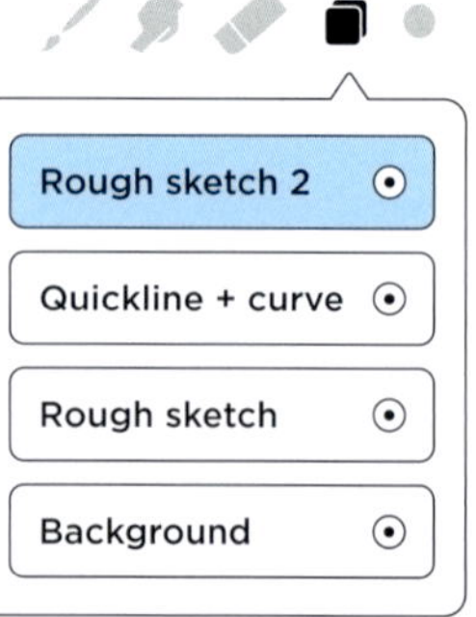

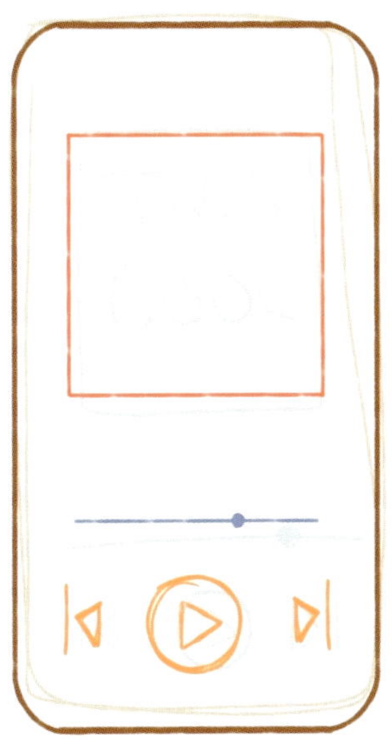

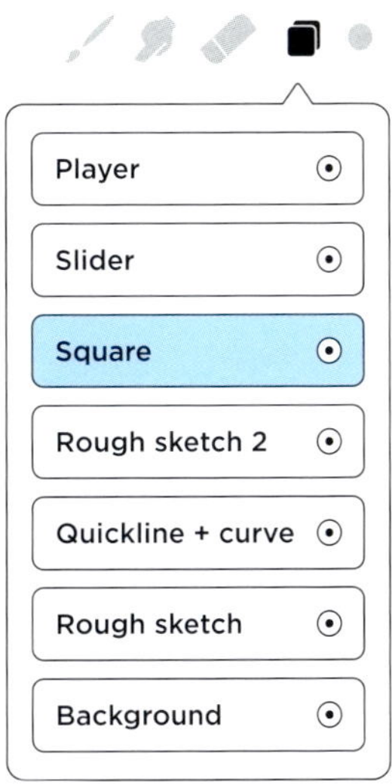

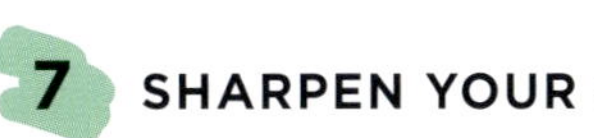

7 SHARPEN YOUR SKETCH

Using **Quickline** in the same way you did in the previous steps, you can sharpen up your sketch. For example, for the square on the phone screen, you can draw just one line, then duplicate that four times to get a perfect square.

8 ADD LETTERING

If you want to add some words to your phone screen, you can use **Quickline** to make some simple lettering guides to keep your hand lettering in line.

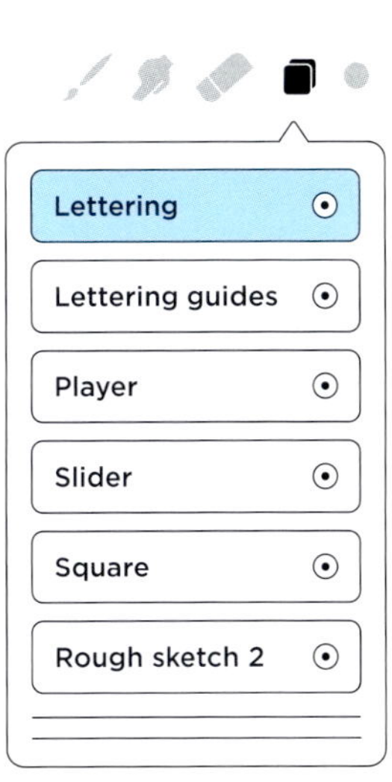

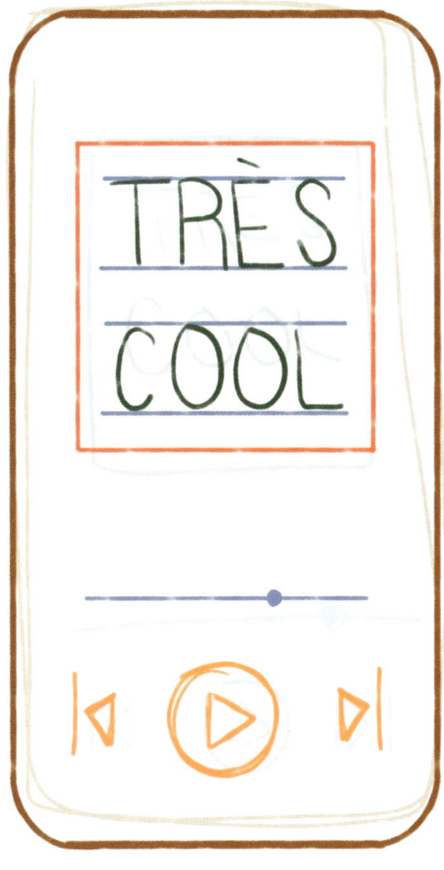

Tip When you first get started in digital art you may wonder, "when do I create a new layer?" Here is an easy-to-remember mantra that you can use as a beginner: "new color, new layer." Every time you lay a new color down on the canvas, switch to a new layer. That means you can always go back and adjust that color without affecting any other part of the artwork.

9 CHANGE THE COMPOSITION

Ink all the layers just as you did in the previous projects, remembering to keep each new color on its own layer. To make a more dynamic composition, tap on the group that contains all of your inked layers, tap the **Move Tool**, then move the **Rotate Bar** to rotate your phone. You can also add a background color.

Freeform | Uniform | Distort | Warp

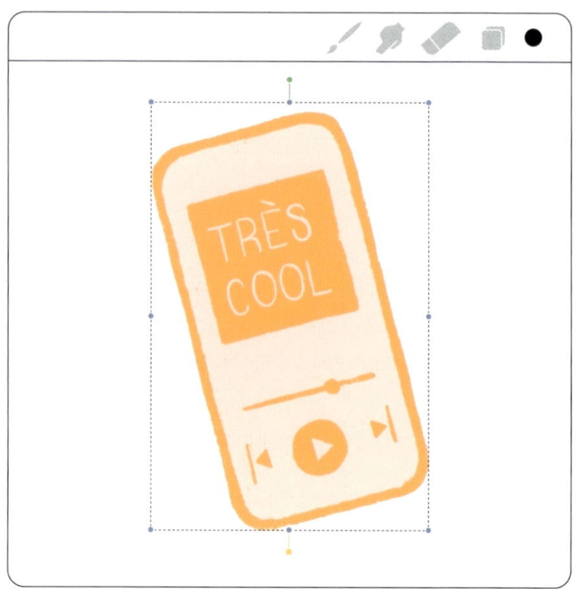

10 THE FINAL TOUCHES

You can add more elements to your page using **Quickline** or just draw them by hand. Here, an earphone cord gives the composition some movement and a notebook with lined paper and a pencil have been added to imply the phone's owner has been writing. A wood-grain effect has been added to the background by hand-drawing some fluid lines. Each element you add to your illustration helps tell the story of the scene.

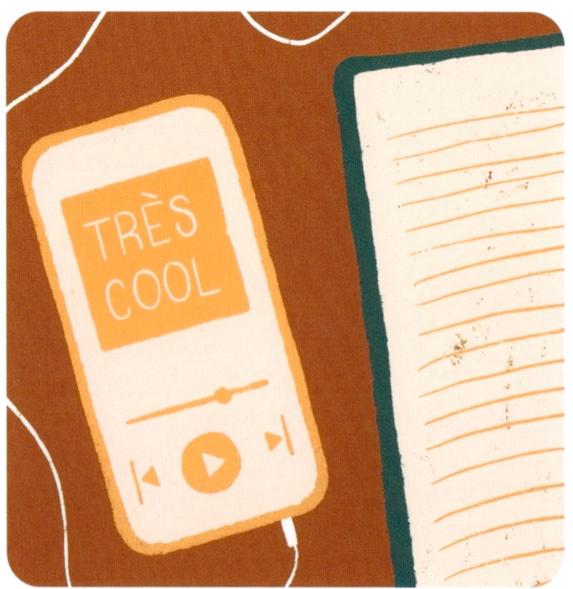

The End Result

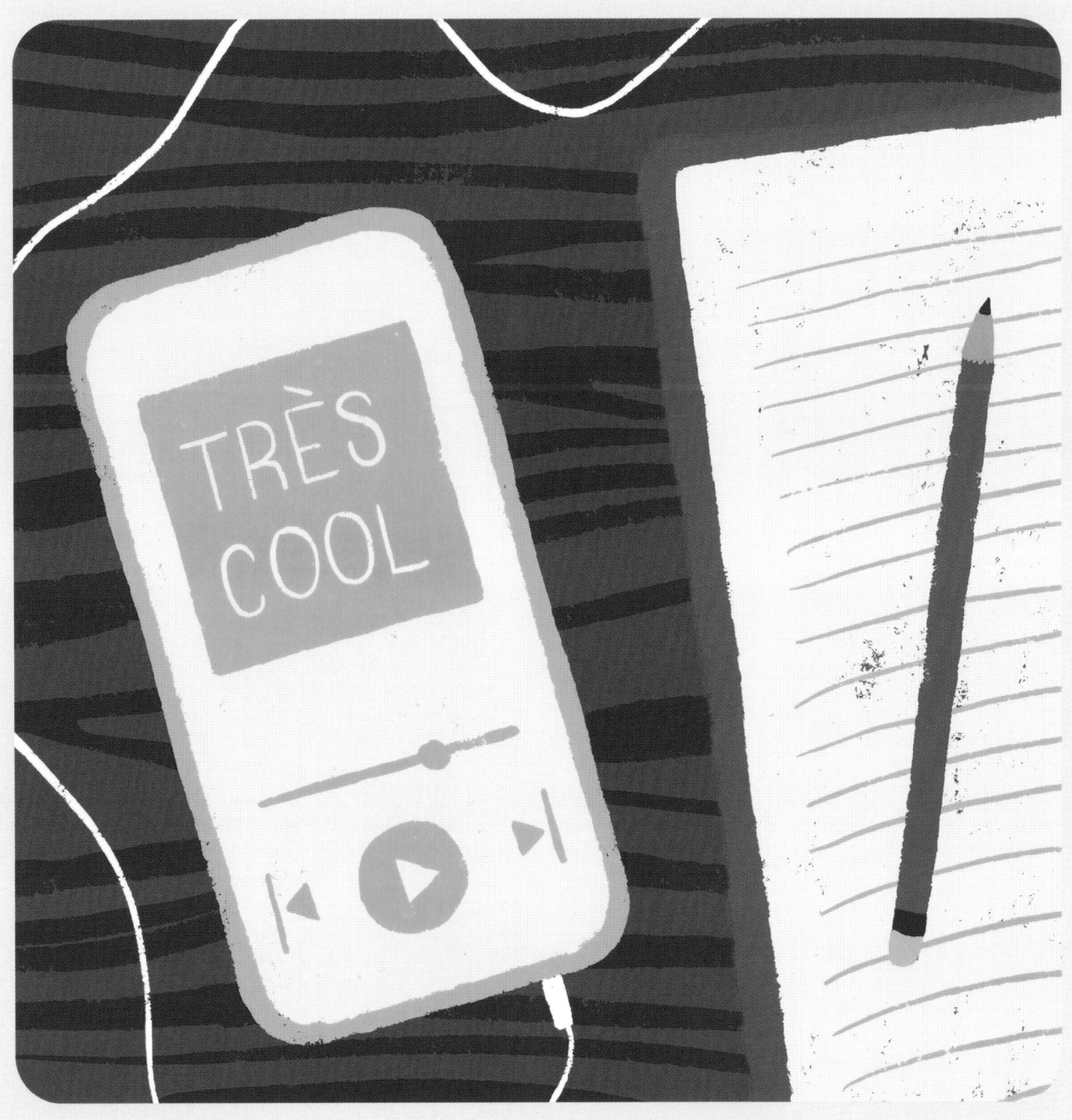

5

TEST
Floral Colorways

By creating this simple, vintage, botanical-inspired illustration you'll learn how to quickly change the color of any element in your compositions using a tool that makes creating color versions fast and easy.

What We're Learning:
How to quickly change colors using **Color Fill**

Brushes:

Sketching Pencil

Fluid Ink

Palette:
Funky Modern

- Reddish Orange #ff4b18
- Red Fox #d34925
- Rose Bud #ffb09b
- Dark Peach #d1725f
- Mango Orange #df8000
- Ginger Brown #9f5d00
- Pink Pearl #ff9ce2
- Neon Fuschia #ff54c2
- Lake Mist Blue #d7dce7
- Steel Blue #7297c9
- Aqua Forest Green #6b9b78
- Pine Green #3a5a44
- Pale Violet #eda7fc
- Amethyst Purple #ac4cc1

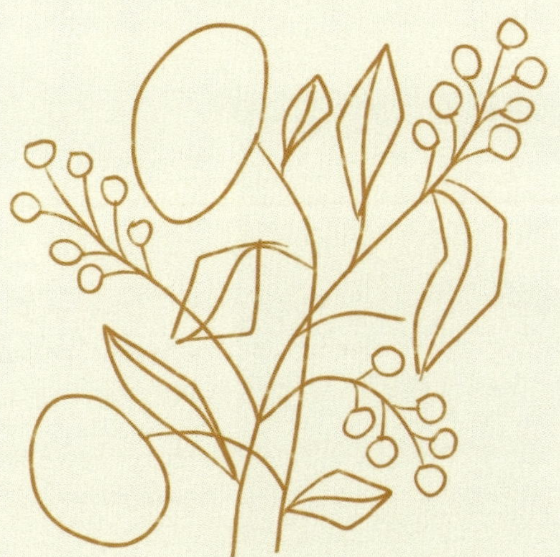

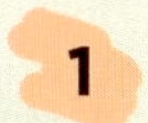

1 FIND YOUR INSPIRATION

First, look for some vintage, botanical reference images and choose two different plants to inspire a rough sketch. Two different plants with contrasting shapes work well here—one large flower with fluid petals and one with small, round berries. Choosing two very different shapes is a great way to add visual interest to your work.

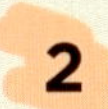

2 REFINE YOUR SKETCH

Create a more detailed sketch, working in a new color and on a new layer. Mark some of the areas where you'd like to add details like the veins on a leaf and the petals of a flower.

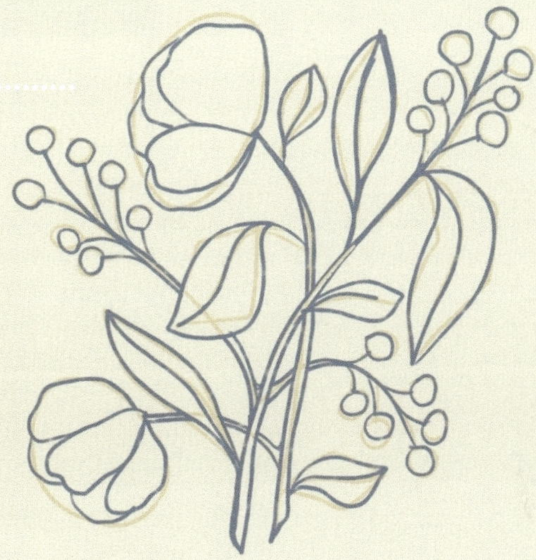

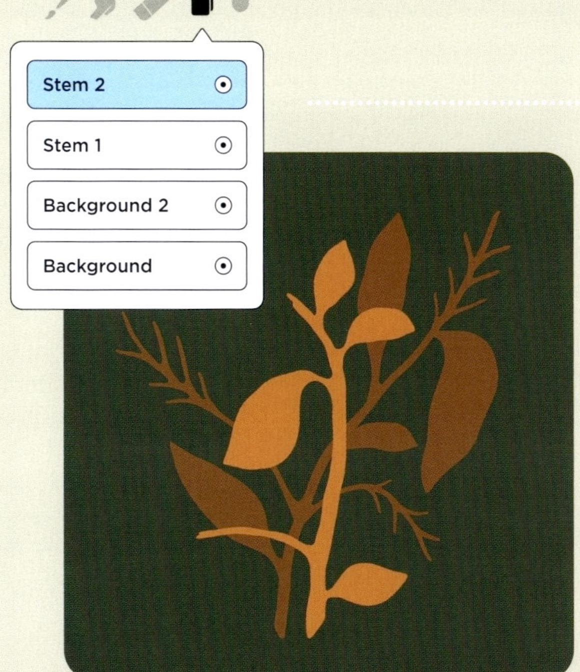

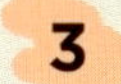

3 START ADDING COLOR

Add a background color, then ink each of the plant stems on separate layers. If you're working with overlapping shapes like the plant stems, it's a good idea to use two very different colors to ink them so that you can easily see the difference between the two. The Fluid Ink brush from the **Brush Sampler** was used here to get a soft, fluid effect, but you can use any brush you like for this step.

4 COLOR THE FLOWERS AND BERRIES

Repeat the process used in step 3 but this time for the flowers and berries. Choose bold colors that contrast with the stems so that the stems and berries or flowers don't blend. Also, since the flowers and berries are the most important aspects of this composition, make sure the color you choose helps them stand out.

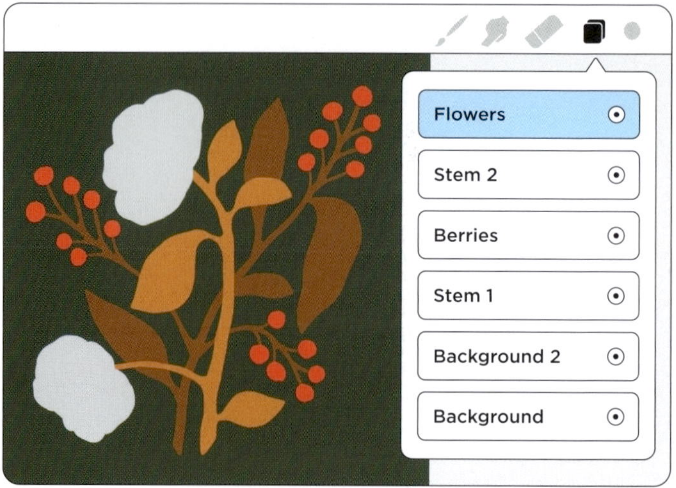

5 DRAW IN SOME DETAILS

Add detail marks like veins and separations between the flower petals on separate layers. In this step you can add as much or as little detail as you'd like. Artwork with a lot of detail can be powerful online and in print, but simple artwork is also captivating and sellable, so take some time to find the level of detail that speaks to your style and preferences.

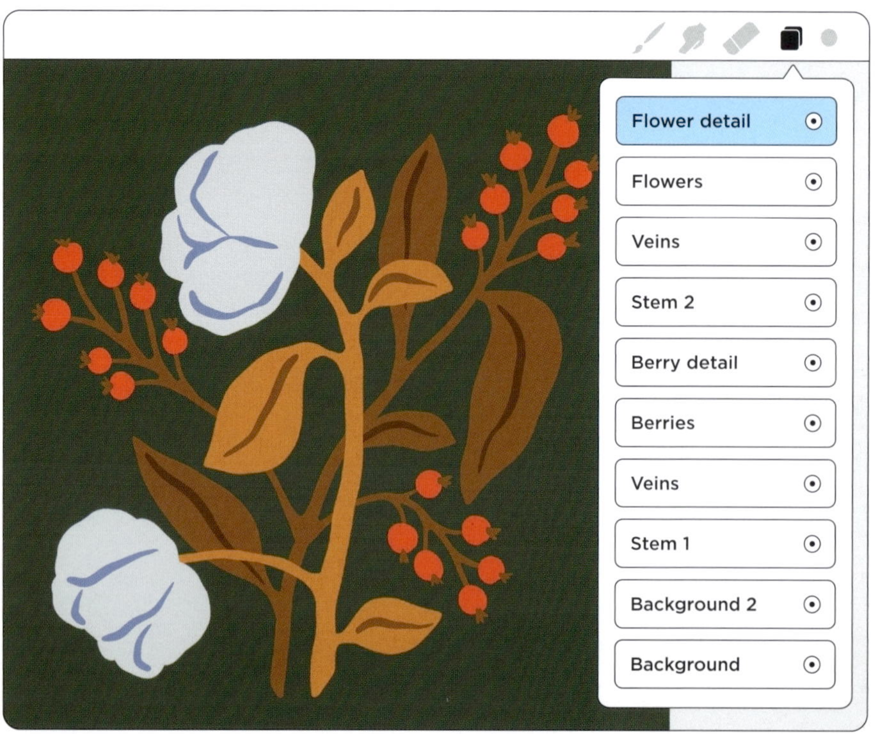

6 TURN ON COLOR FILL

To invoke **Color Fill**, tap on any layer, then tap the **Selection** menu. Tap **Color Fill** on the lower menu to make sure the tool is on. Now the **Color Fill** option is on, so any selection you make will automatically fill the shape completely with color (keep this in mind if you have some problems with selecting in the future as you will need to turn **Color Fill** off when you don't want to use it).

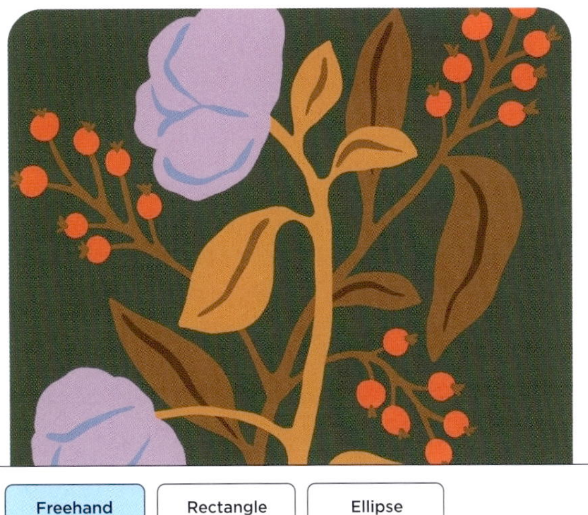

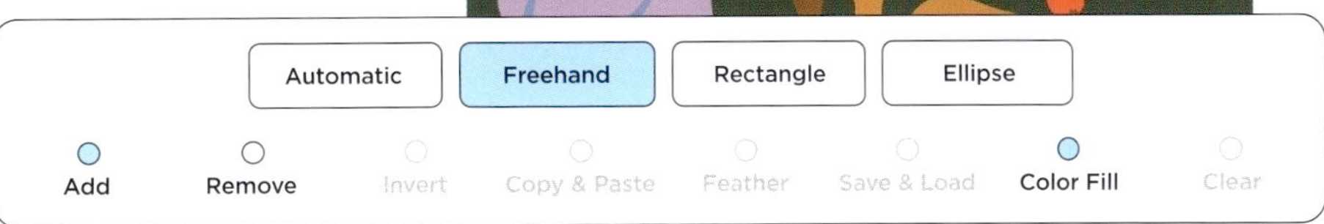

7 USE COLOR FILL TO CHANGE COLORS

Next, open up your **Layers Panel** and tap on one of the flower layers, then tap **Select**. The flower should change to whatever color is selected on your **Color Disc**.

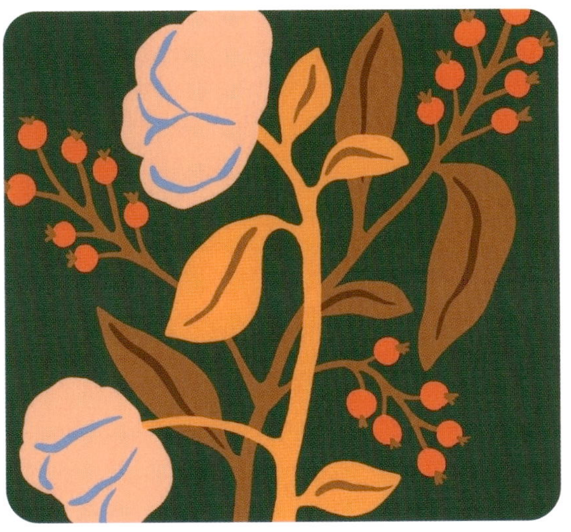

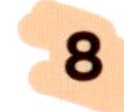

8 EXPERIMENT WITH DIFFERENT COLORWAYS

Now select different colors from your palette or **Color Disc** to see the flowers change color. You might try creating a high-contrast combination (like light pink and dark green) or a low-contrast combination (like light blue and light pink). There is no "right answer" to color combinations; it is really just a matter of personal taste and style.

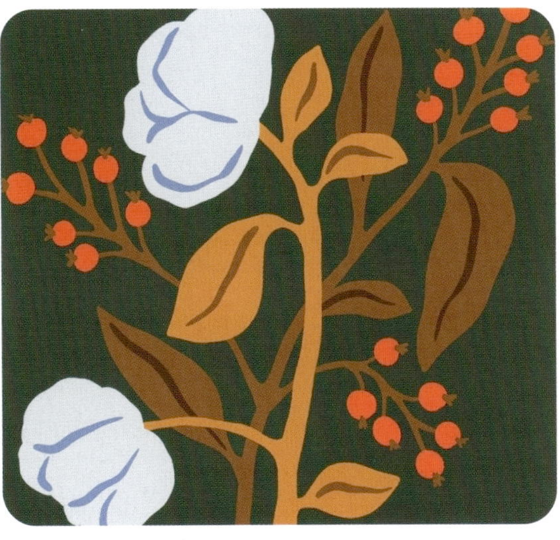

9 CREATE MULTIPLE COLOR SCHEMES

Now you can quickly flip through a variety of colors for each layer in your document. This saves time compared to the **Fill Layer** method, which involves more taps for each color change. That may not seem like a big deal now, but when you're creating large batches of artwork regularly, saving a few minutes here and there will make a big difference to your overall productivity, and reduce the number of steps you must take to get to your final goal.

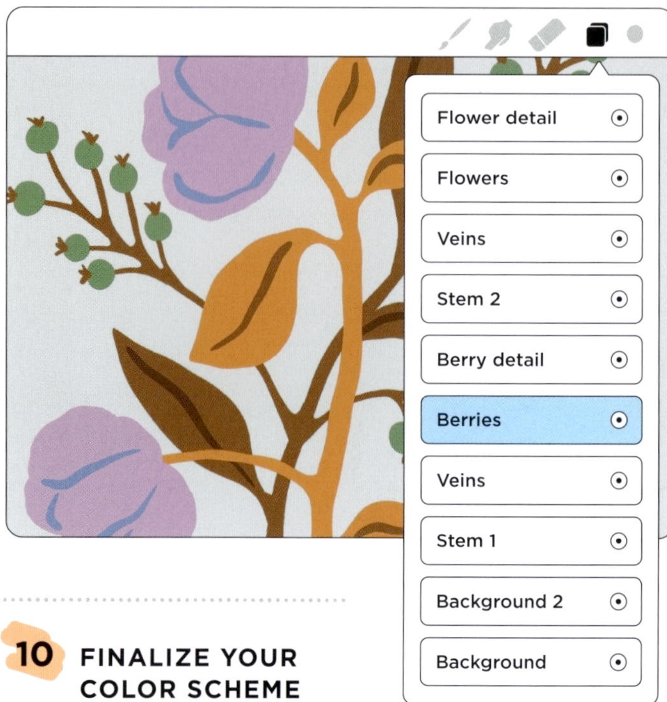

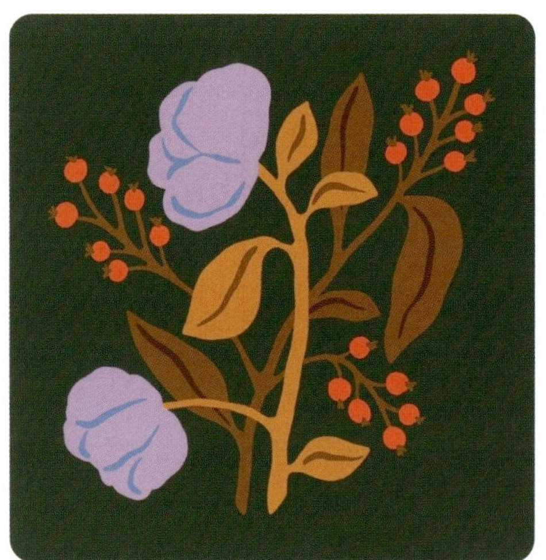

10 FINALIZE YOUR COLOR SCHEME

Repeat this step with all the elements in your composition until you get the colors how you like them.

Keep It Going

Go to your Gallery, tap Select, then tap Duplicate to duplicate the document. Now you can create a completely different color version of your composition—make at least three or four different color versions. Having a range of color versions on hand is helpful for sharing online, client work, and selling online and in stores.

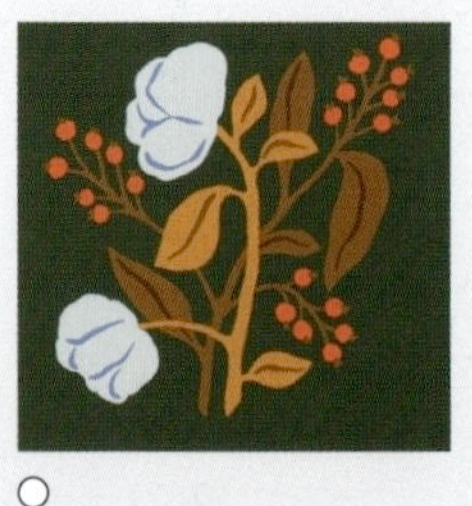

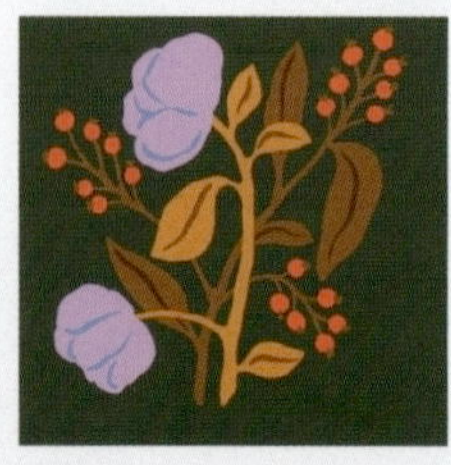

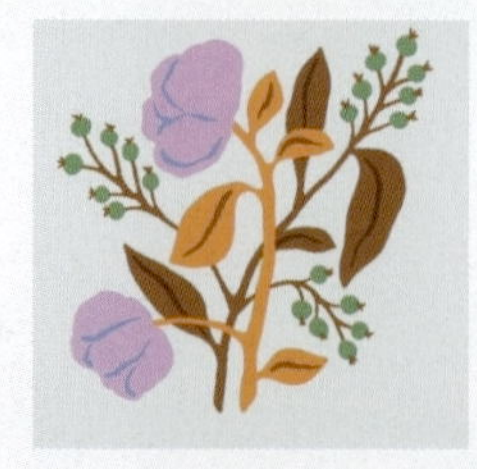

The End Result

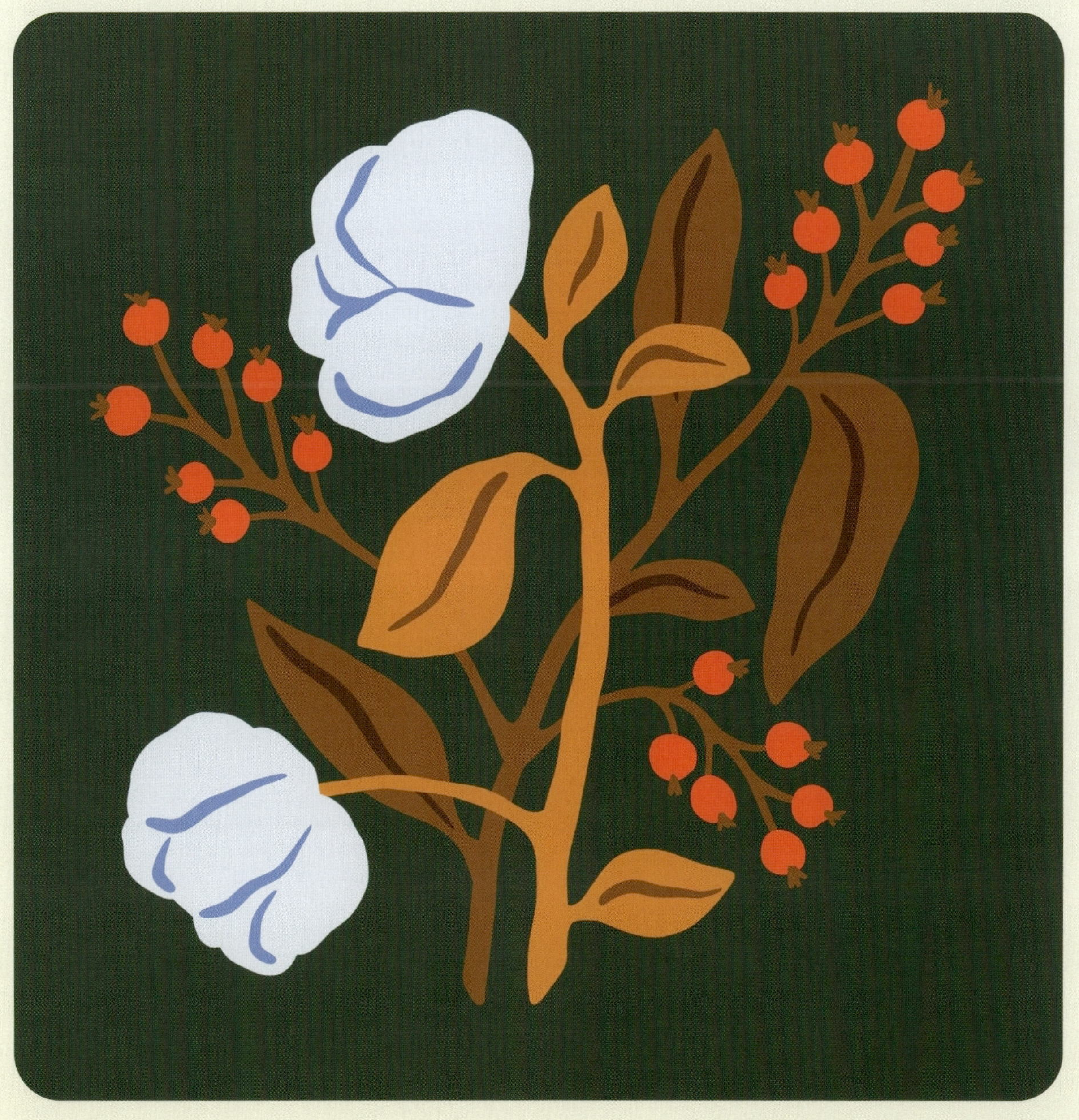

6

DESIGN A Textured Stamp

In this project, you'll go beyond using basic brushes and delve into realistic effects and brushstroke layering. You'll be designing a postage stamp. Choose something simple like a fruit branch as the image for your stamp so that you can focus your attention on understanding how brushes work.

What We're Learning:
Using realistic brushes

Brushes:

Dry Gouache Glaze

Dry Gouache

Palette:
50s Motel

Cotton Candy Pink #ff90be

California Neon Pink #ff005b

Mint Gum Green #34c494

Deep Sea Green #063420

Mustard Yellow #dbae00

Earthy Stone Yellow #917400

Vanilla Cream White #fff4d4

Pebble Path White #c0b28d

Lavender Haze #dad7e7

Mochi Purple #746a99

Creamsicle Orange #f9aa12

Burnt Toast Orange #9d6900

Lilac Purple #d9a9e3

90s Nails Purple #7e5884

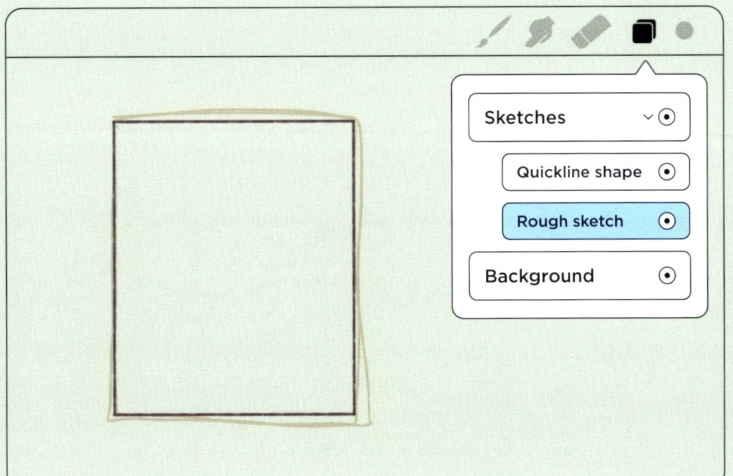

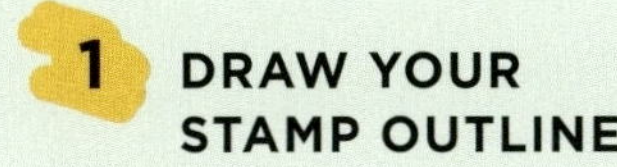

1 DRAW YOUR STAMP OUTLINE

Start by roughly sketching a rectangle that is the relative height and width of a standard postage stamp. Remember, you can start by looking at stamp reference images to get some inspiration for the border and orientation of your stamp. Then use **Quickline** to create a perfect rectangle.

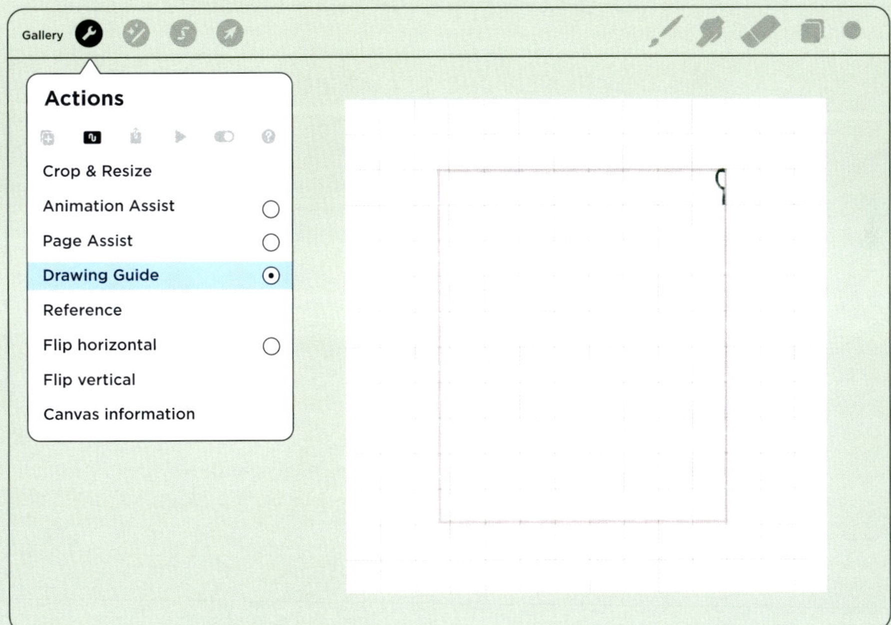

2 DRAW THE EDGE PERFORATION AND ACTIVATE THE GRID

Draw one part of the perforated stamp edge then, to make the perforated areas of your stamp even, activate the grid by tapping the **Actions Menu**, **Canvas**. Then turn on the **Drawing Guide** and tap **Edit Drawing Guide**.

3 ADJUST THE GRID

Using the **Grid Size Slider**, adjust the grid so that your perforated edge shape fits within one grid block. Adjust your perforated edge and/or rectangle size and placement if necessary, so that one perforation fits in one square and there are an even number of squares down the side of the stamp.

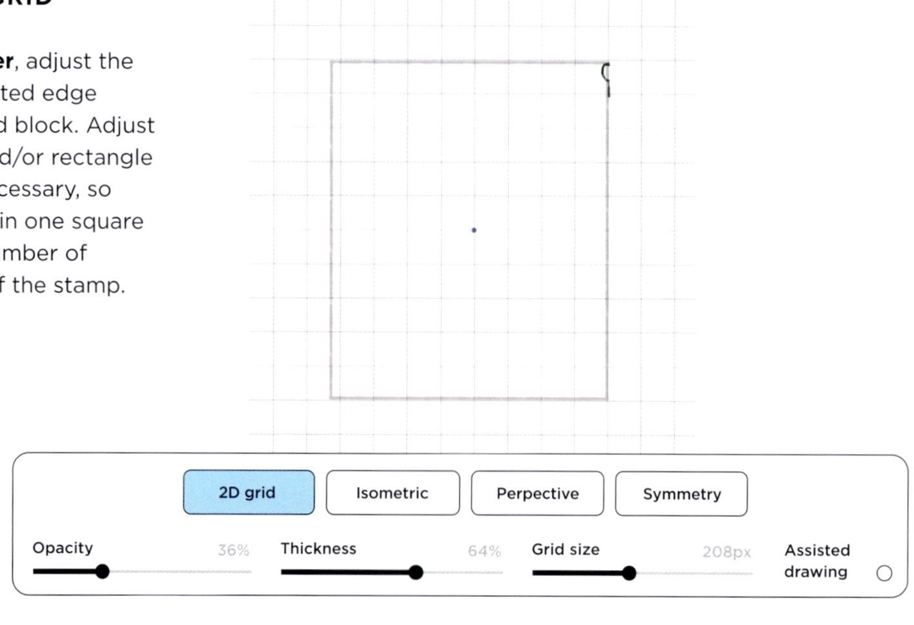

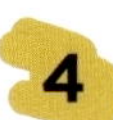

COMPLETE THE STAMP EDGING

Duplicate the perforation shape until it fills the whole side of your stamp. Turn off your grid by going to **Actions**, **Canvas**, and turn off the **Drawing Guide Slider**. Now duplicate the perforated edge and rotate it by tapping the **Move Tool** and tapping **Rotate**. Duplicate and position the perforated edge you have created to fill all four edges of your stamp, erasing extra parts if necessary. Remember, you can merge all those perforation layers together by pinching them in the **Layers Panel.**

ADD YOUR STAMP DESIGN

Use **Quickline** to create an inner box in your stamp, then draw your chosen design inside the stamp shape (a branch of lemons here). You could try going outside the box for a more experimental composition.

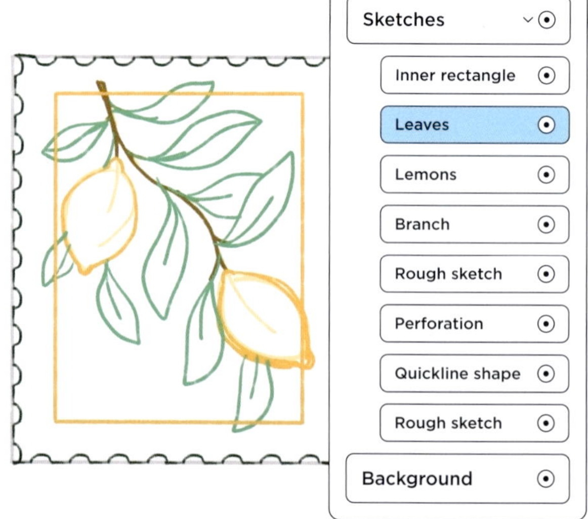

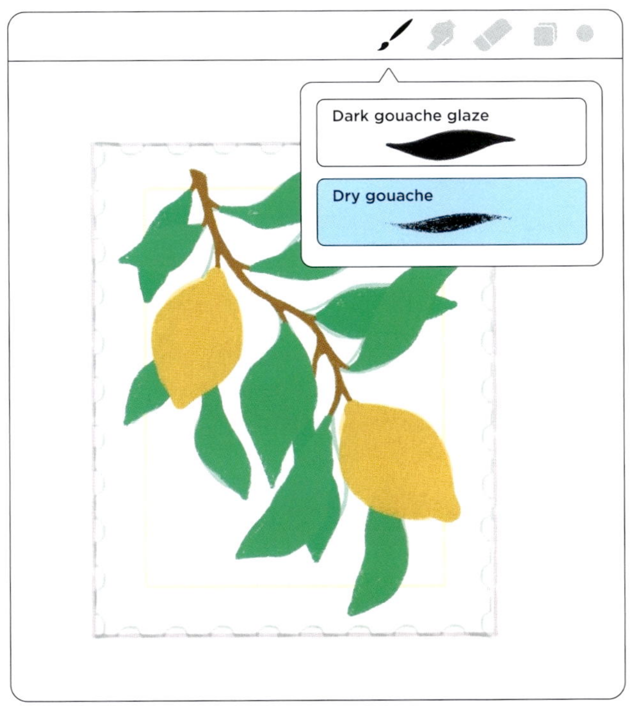

START ADDING COLOR

Tap on the Dark Gouache Glaze or Dry Gouache brush and start filling your shapes with color. A slightly darker shade of "gouache" has been used below the first layer of leaves, this is to get the same subtle color shifts you would see in a real gouache painting.

HIGHLIGHT THE LEMONS

Once you have filled all of your shapes, **Alpha Lock** each layer by tapping on the layer and tapping **Alpha Lock**. This prevents you from drawing outside the alpha-locked shape, so you can add layers of color without going outside the lemon shape. Select a lighter color than the original and brush it over the shape with the Dry Gouache brush. You can continue working with multiple layers of lighter/ darker colors, or choose a totally different color altogether for a two-toned look.

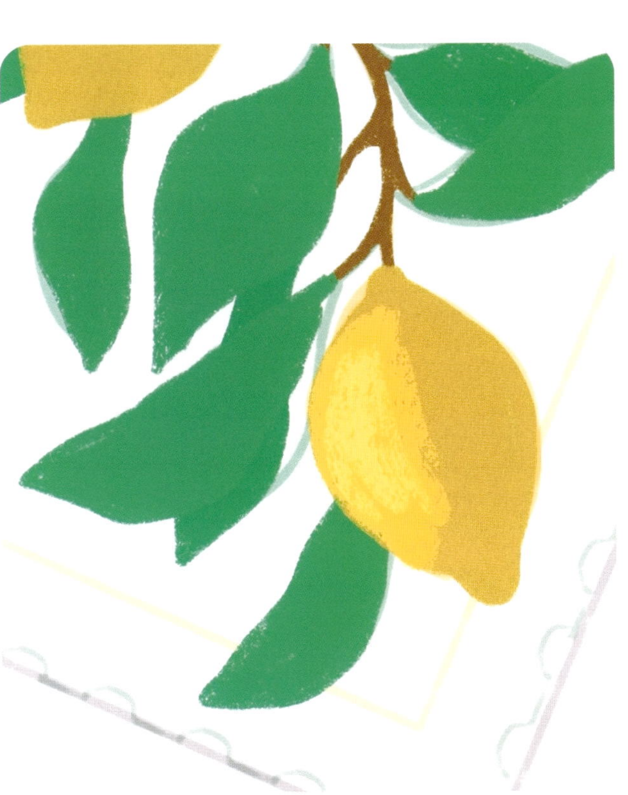

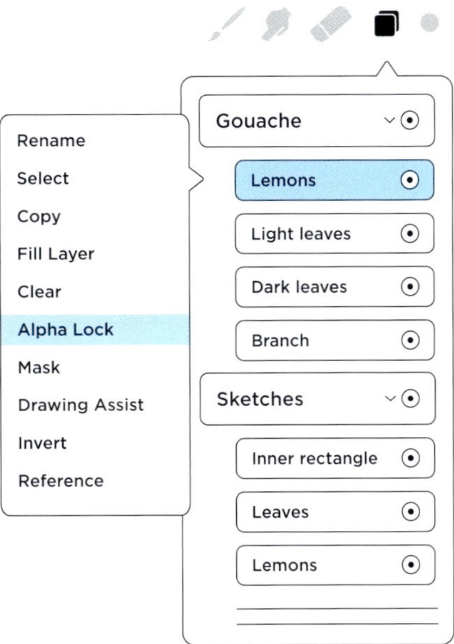

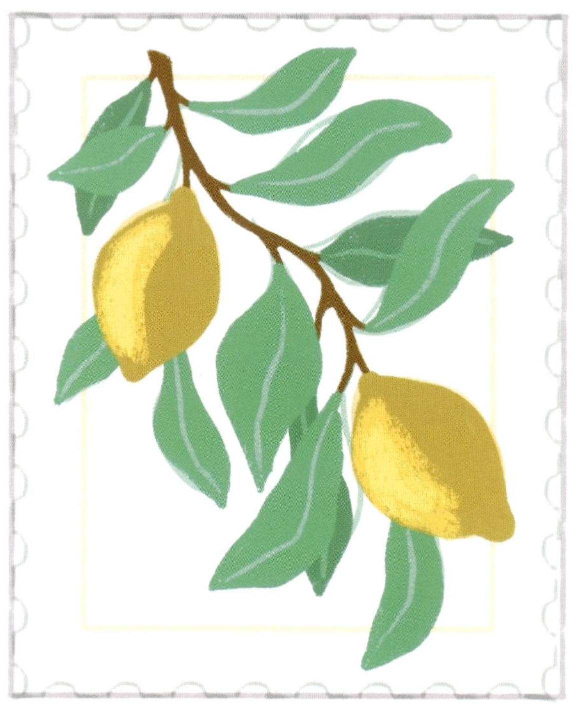

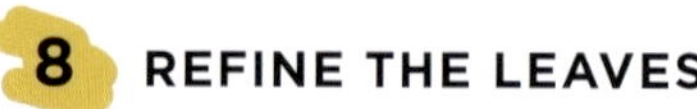

8 REFINE THE LEAVES

Either repeat the same process on your leaf shapes or you could just add some veins to your leaves using the Dry Gouache brush. Also, add some lighter shades to them using the same **Alpha Lock** method as for the lemons.

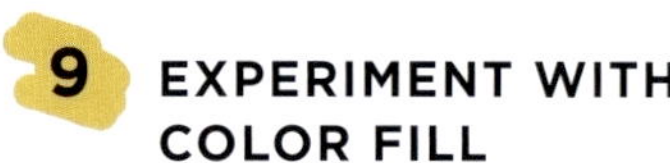

9 EXPERIMENT WITH COLOR FILL

Use **Color Fill** to change colors. Experiment to see what works. Remember, it can be really valuable to produce multiple color versions of your artwork. Continue the inking process by coloring the background and the rectangle behind your design to create a finished composition. You could choose to add a price on the stamp to give it an authentic feel, or just let it be a simple illustration on your stamp shape.

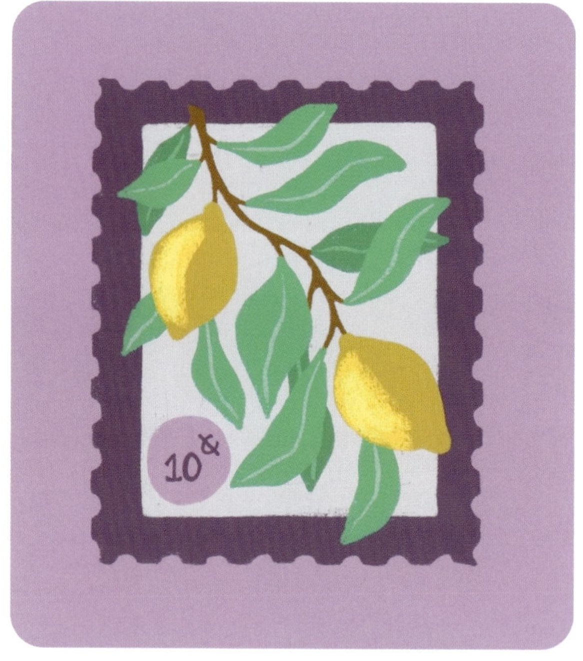

10 FINALIZE THE BACKGROUND

Try a variety of colors and numbers of gouache layers to see what fits your personal style. You might like subtle gouache strokes or extreme layering. In this example, I added a lighter color gouache stroke to everything, including the background and stamp border. Do you like the overall gouache look or do you prefer the subtle accents in the original composition? This is a great time to try it all so you can get a sense of what you like.

The End Result

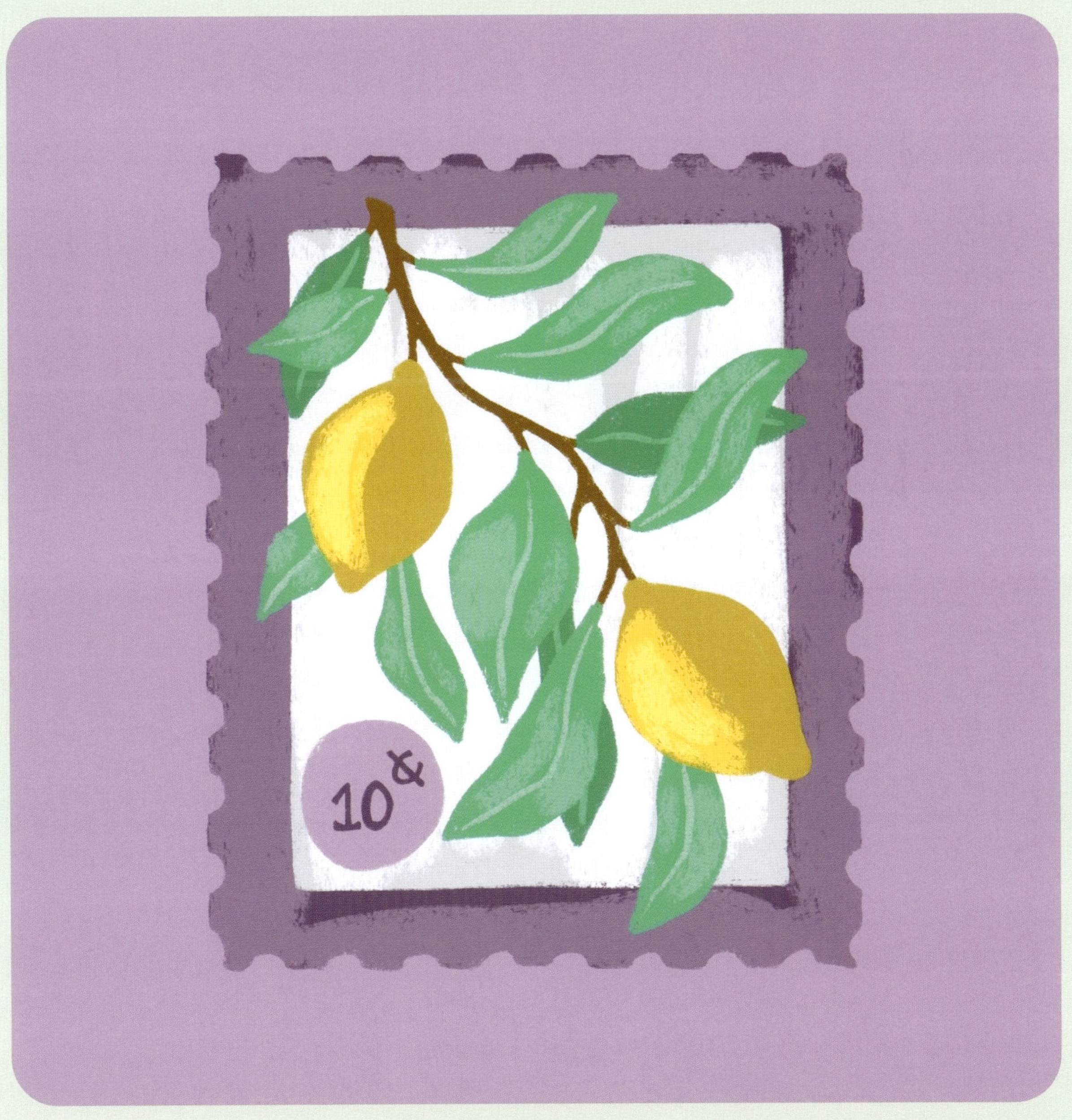

7

MAKE A Star Print

Making stamps in Procreate is a great way to save elements or shapes that you have drawn that you might want to use again—it means you can easily access "assets" that you made earlier. Here, you'll learn how to put together a simple composition built from stamps that you will create yourself.

What We're Learning:
Making stamp brushes

Brushes:

Fluid Ink

Dot Stamp

Pencil Taps Texture

Palette:
Poolside Paradise

Robin Egg Blue #98f2f4

Faded Jade #347373

Cherry Blossom #ffb9bd

Watermelon Pink #ff6472

Seafoam Green #77f0b5

Eucalyptus #3d845f

Pale Green #9cf08c

Astroturf Green #395f36

Butterscotch Orange #ffad56

Pumpkin Skin #ad5a00

Dawn Pink #ffebe2

Coral Pink #f4947c

Lavender Ice Cream #eea8f2

Dark Lilac #a465aa

1 SKETCH A SIMPLE MOON AND STAR COMPOSITION

Start by sketching out your composition. Consider where to place the moon. You could position it in the corner rather than the center to create an asymmetrical composition and then space the stars out around the canvas. Try to avoid having several stars lined up in a row, as that can lead to a boring composition. Rather, space the stars out randomly to give your drawing a feeling of fluidity.

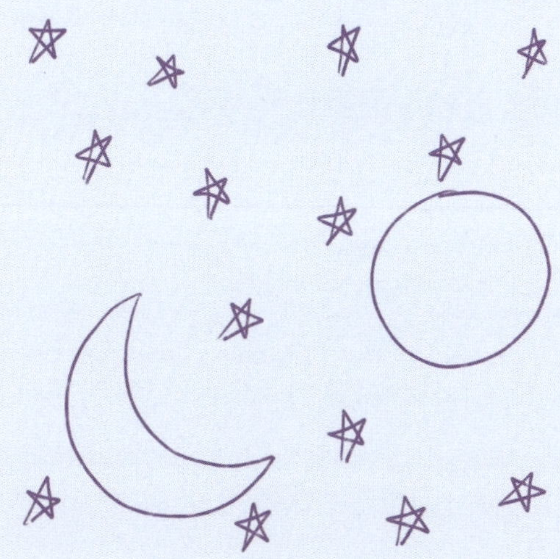

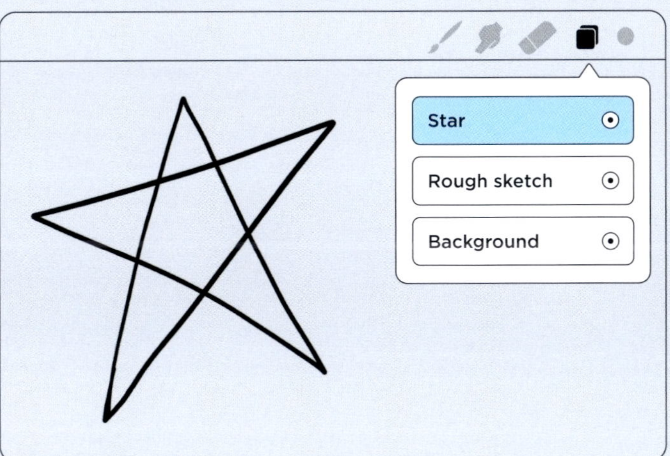

2 DRAW YOUR STAMP SHAPE

First, we'll make the stamp shape. Make your sketch layer invisible and select a pure black in the **Color Disc** by double-tapping in the black area. Stamps must be made with pure black and white on a square canvas to work properly. Using the Fluid Ink brush, draw a star shape that is as loose or refined as you'd like.

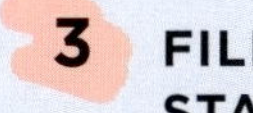

FILL AND SAVE THE STAMP IMAGE

Use **Color Drop** to drag the color from the **Color Disc** into the open space to create a fully filled shape. Save the image as a JPEG by tapping the **Actions Menu**, **Share**, then choose **JPEG** as the image type. Now your black star drawing is saved to the **Camera Roll** on your iPad, so you can head to the **Brush Library** to insert that drawing into a stamp brush.

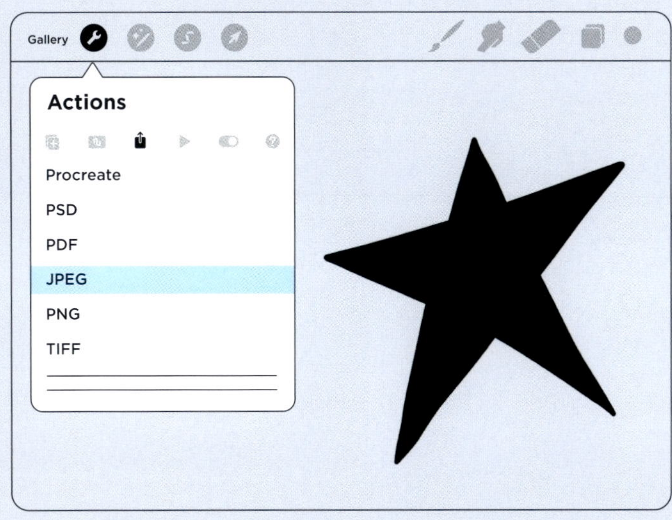

4 MAKE YOUR STAMP

To make your stamp brush, first tap on the Star Stamp brush that already exists in the **Brush Sampler**, then swipe left on it and tap **Duplicate** to make a copy of the stamp. The duplicate will become your custom star stamp and can be used over and over to insert different shapes on your canvas.

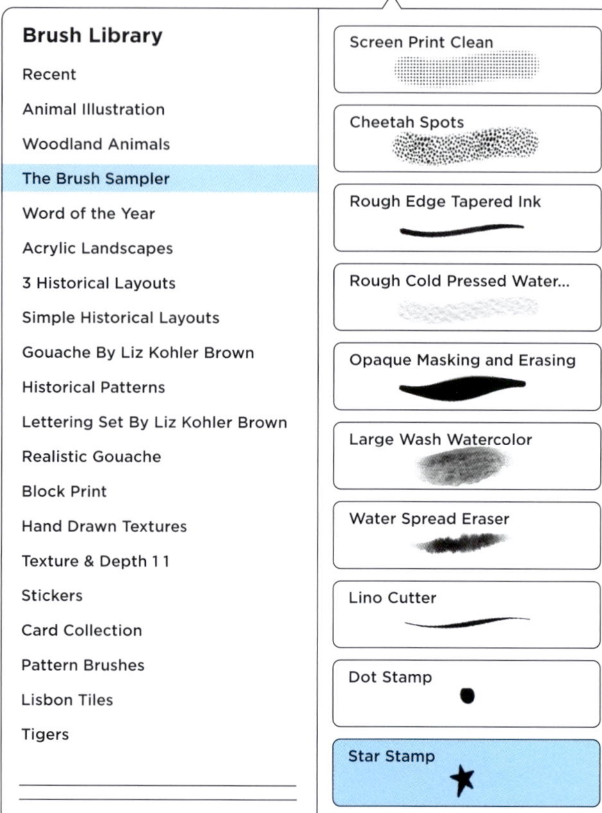

5 SELECT YOUR STAR

Next, tap on the brush in the **Brush Library** to open the brush settings menu. Tap on the **Shape** and then tap **Edit**. This will lead you to a menu where you can insert your own shape, in this case, a star.

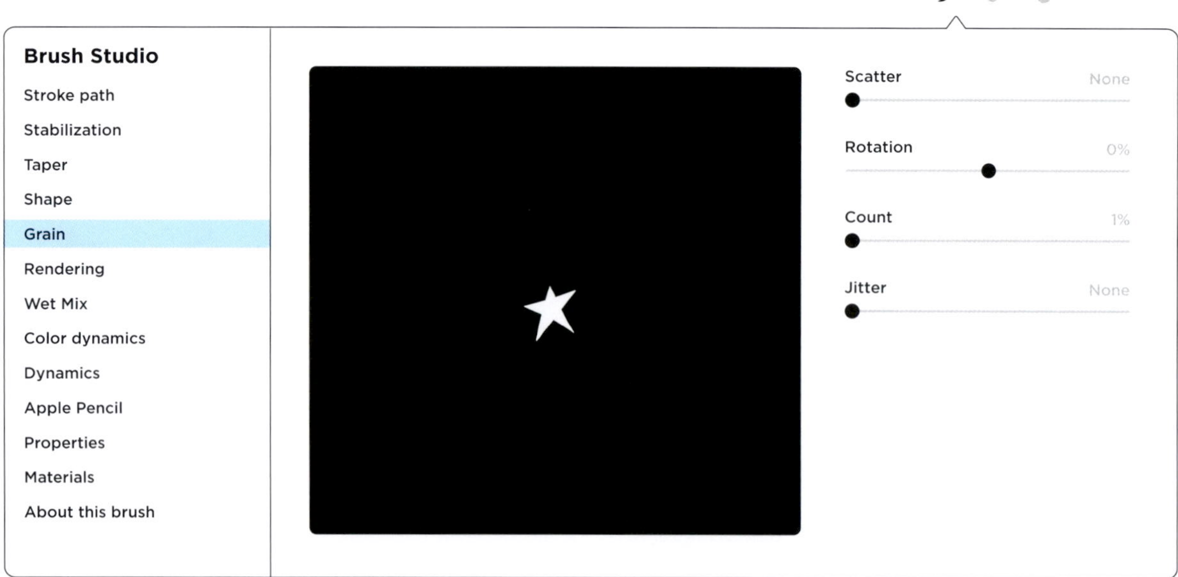

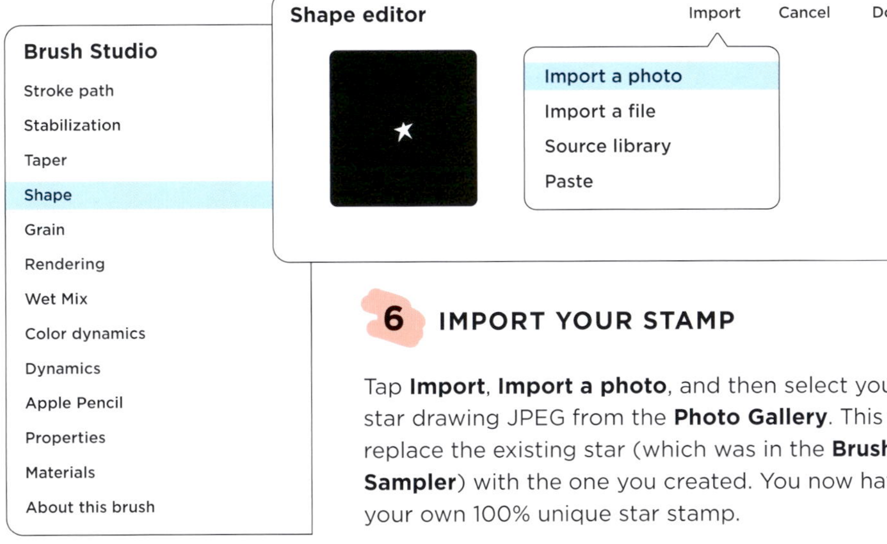

6 IMPORT YOUR STAMP

Tap **Import**, **Import a photo**, and then select your star drawing JPEG from the **Photo Gallery**. This will replace the existing star (which was in the **Brush Sampler**) with the one you created. You now have your own 100% unique star stamp.

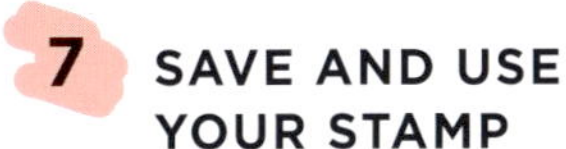

7 SAVE AND USE YOUR STAMP

Tap **Done** to save your brush and close the **Brush Library**, then choose a color and tap on the **Canvas** to see your stamp appear!

8 EXPERIMENT WITH YOUR STAMP

Play with changing the size of your stamp until it is the size you want for your composition, then use it to fill your rough sketch. You could place each star on its own layer so that you can resize, flip, or rotate each one as you choose.

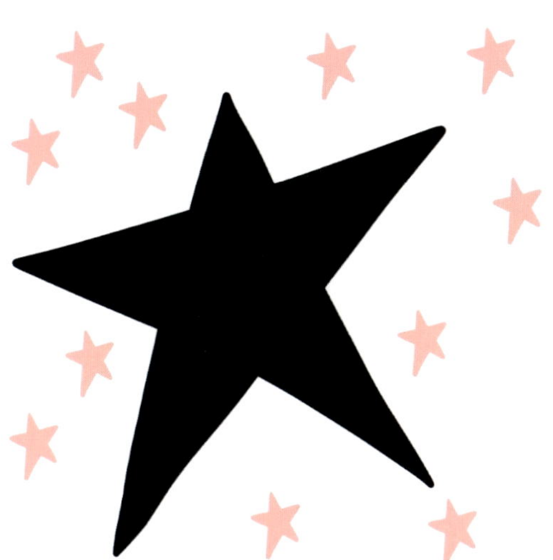

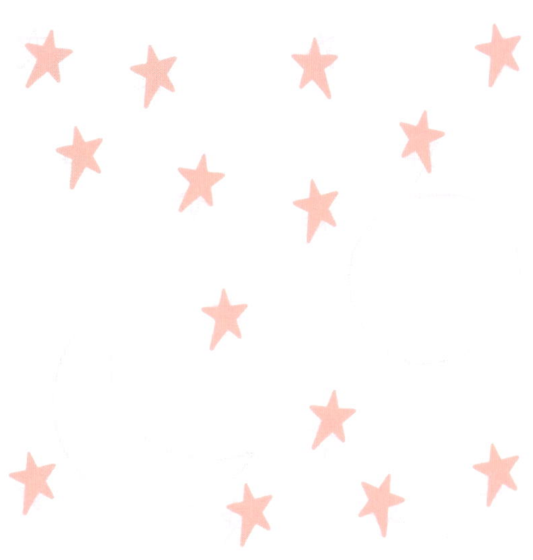

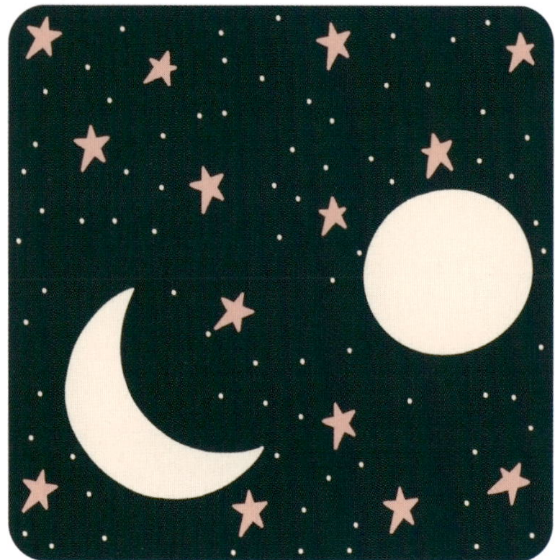

9 ADD THE FINISHING TOUCHES

Merge all your star layers together onto one layer by pinching them. Ink your moons and add a background color to finish the composition. You could use the Dot Stamp brush or make your own alternative star shape if you'd like to try filling your canvas with another shape.

10 ADD TEXTURE

If you wish, you could use the Pencil Taps Texture brush in the **Brush Sampler** to swipe over the whole composition to add some interesting texture to the background.

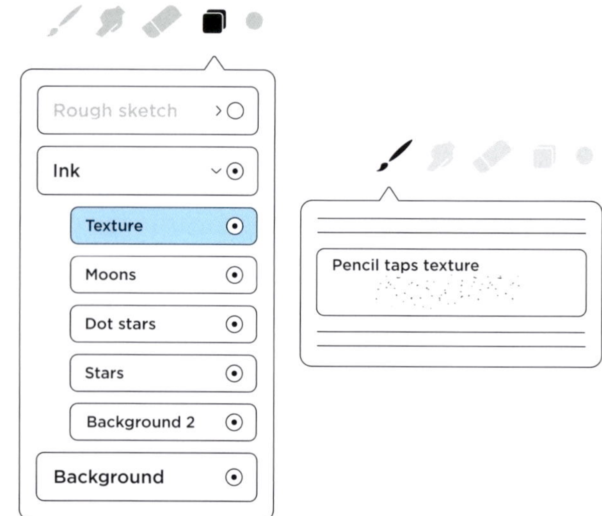

Keep It Going

Now that you know how to make stamps, why not make a selection featuring shapes that you love? This could include simple symbols like stars, dots, and hearts, but also more complex elements like your signature for your artwork or letters of the alphabet. Here are some of the stamps I've made. Stamps are not only something you could use in your illustrations but also sellable assets that you could build an entire business around. So, if you love making stamps, it might be time for a deep dive into the possibilities!

The End Result

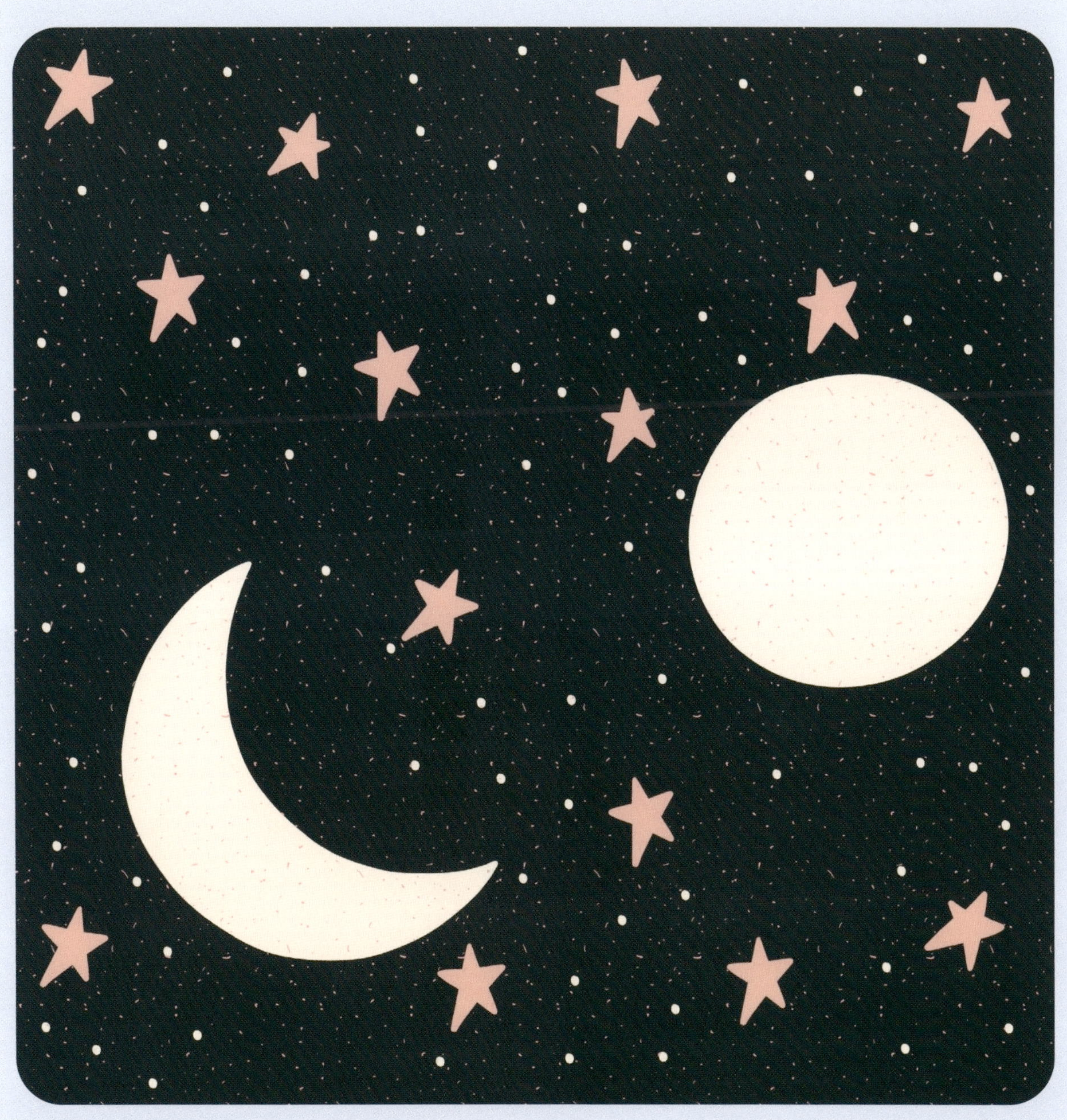

8

CREATE A Vintage Snapshot

Blend Mode settings allow you to mix and filter layers through each other in a way that creates interesting overlapping effects. In this project we'll experiment with layering color in a screen-printed style using Blend Modes.

What We're Learning:
Blend Modes and adjusting brushes

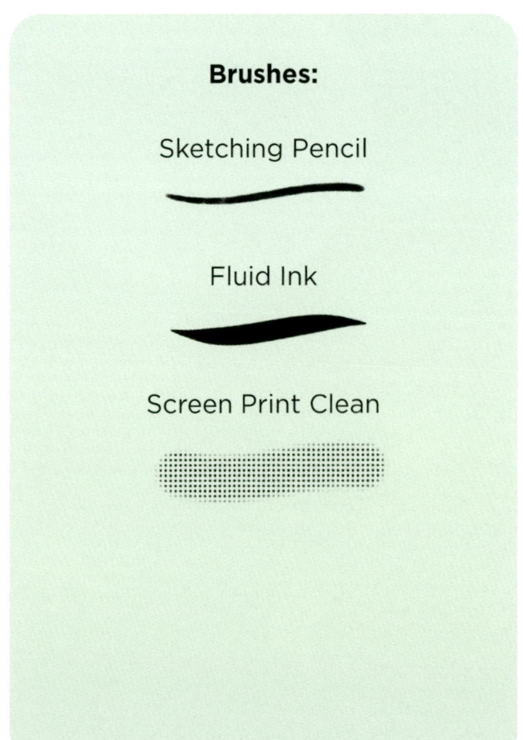

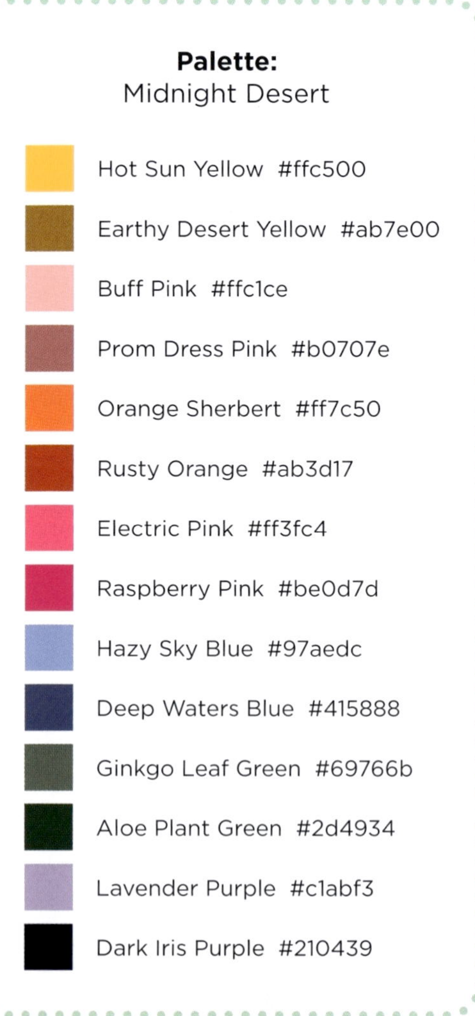

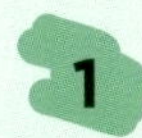

SETTING UP CROSSHAIRS

Make a rough sketch of the camera following a reference image. You can use **Quickline** to draw the straight edges of the camera for your refined sketch, but there is one part of the camera that requires guides to build correctly—the concentric circles on the lens. To get these circles lined up properly, first turn on the **Drawing Guide** in the **Canvas Menu**, then turn the **Grid size** all the way up to **Max**, so you just have crosshairs across your canvas.

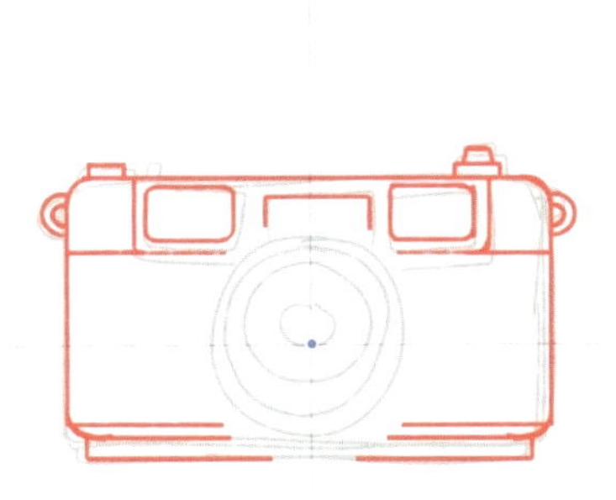

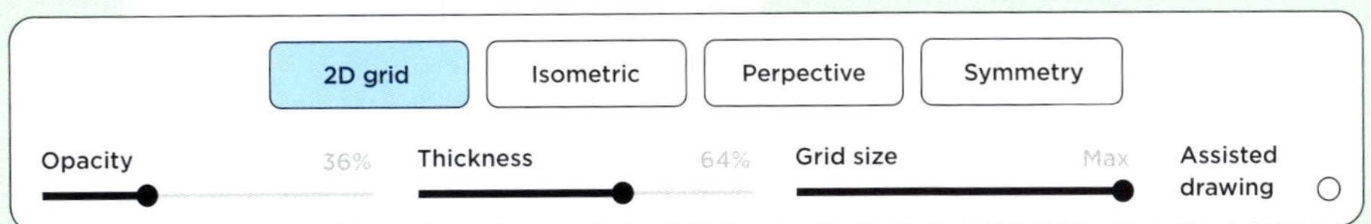

2 DRAWING CIRCLES

When you draw each circle on a new layer, use the crosshairs to ensure your concentric circles are aligned along the center axis of the lens. To draw a perfect circle, create a new layer then draw a circle as well as you can, but before picking up your stylus, hold for a moment while **Quickshape** improves your circle. If you hold down one finger while keeping your stylus on the screen, the circle will become a perfect circle.

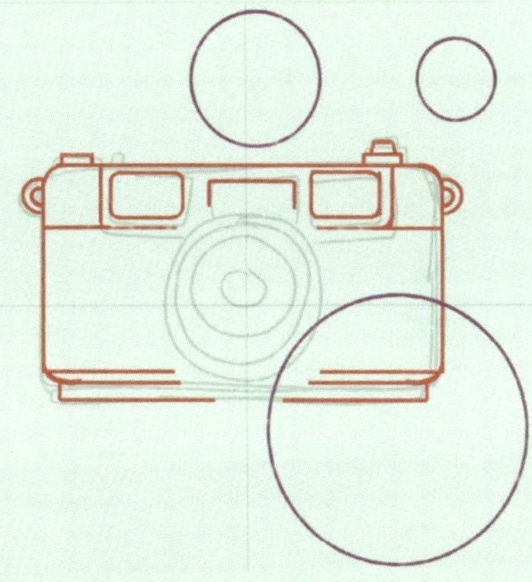

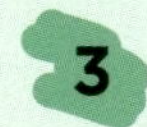

POSITION THE CIRCLES FOR THE LENS

Repeat the process for all of your circles, placing each on its own layer and using the **Move Tool** to resize or adjust the placement. Use the crosshairs of the guides to line up the little blue dots on each circle. Once you are finished, turn off your **Drawing Guide** in the **Canvas Menu** to avoid the distraction of the crosshairs on your artwork.

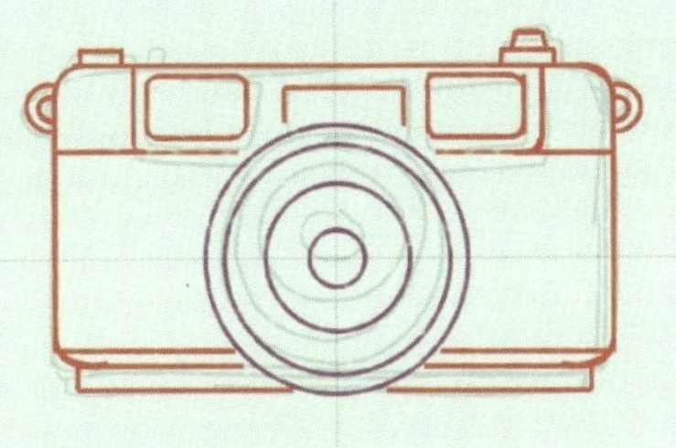

Freeform | Uniform | Distort | Warp

4 FINALIZE THE COMPOSITION

At this point you could choose to rotate your camera to make a slightly more interesting composition, or you could just leave it in the center of the canvas. You may also want to add a strap and merge all the layers of your refined sketch to keep your **Layers Panel** organized.

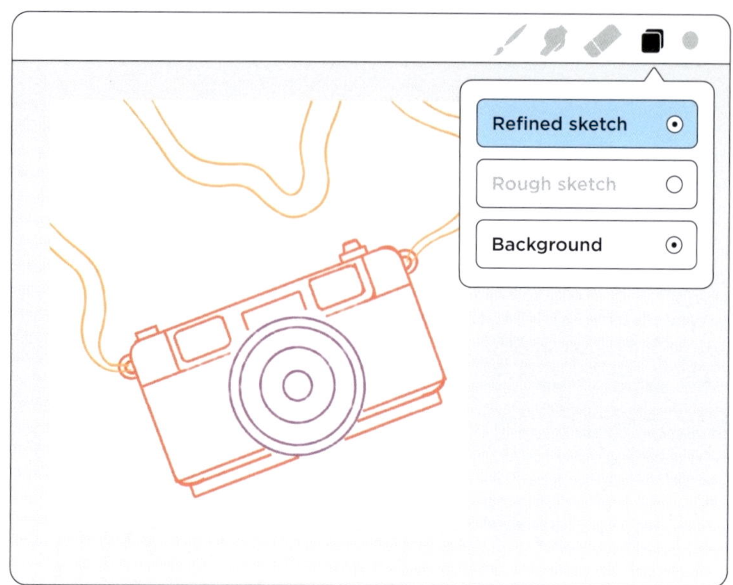

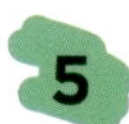

5 ADD THE COLOR

Next, use the Fluid Ink brush to ink color onto each part of your camera on its own layer. Remember not to worry too much about choosing colors at this stage because you can always experiment with the colors later.

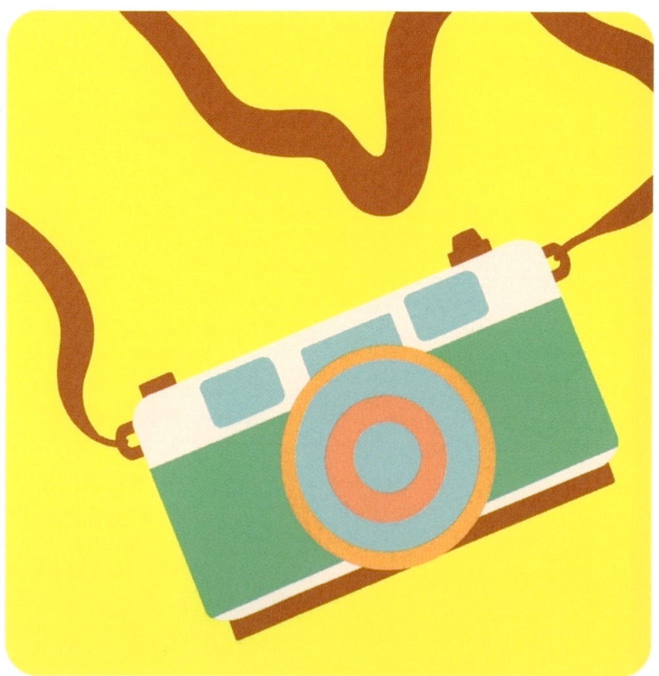

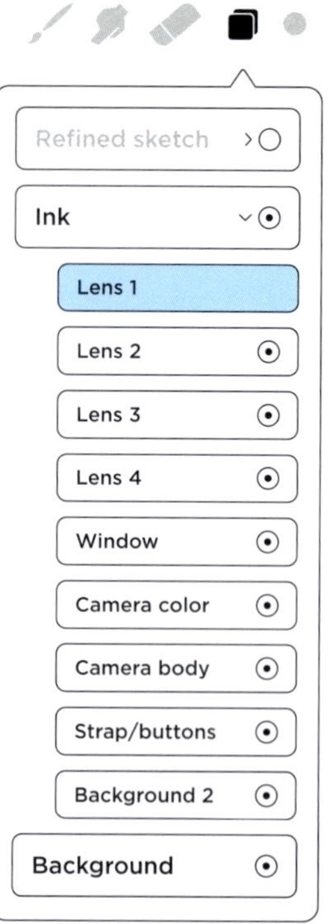

6 ADD THE SCREEN-PRINTED EFFECT

Open the **Brush Sampler** and choose the Screen Printed Clean Texture brush. On a new layer, swipe that brush over everything using any color. It's important that this layer is above all your other inked layers, so make sure to drag it to the top of your folder. Yes, it looks terrible now, but you'll see why this ugly phase is important in the next step.

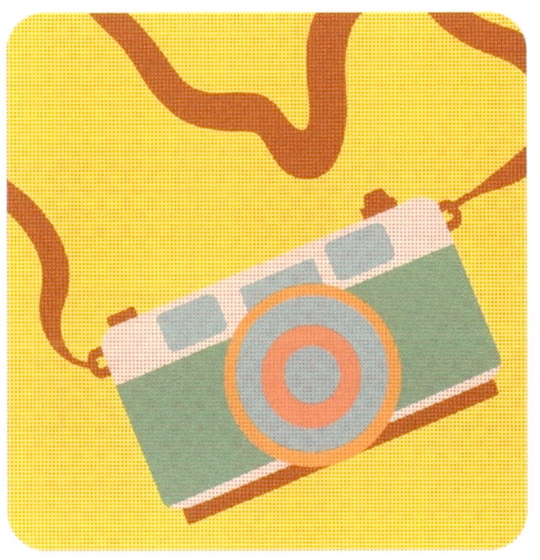

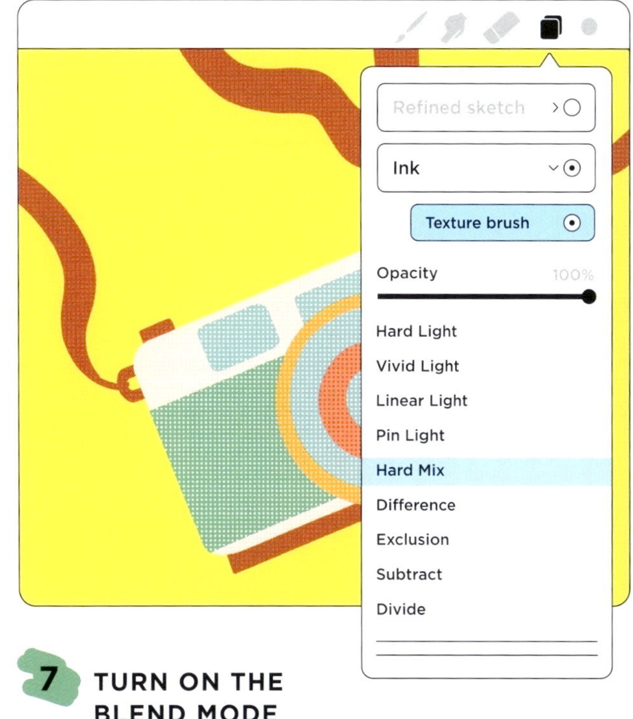

7 TURN ON THE BLEND MODE

Next, we'll use a **Blend Mode** on this layer to start changing the way it affects the layers below it. To turn on a **Blend Mode**, tap on the layer and then tap the **N** symbol beside the layer name.

8 CHOOSE YOUR BLEND MODE

The layer is currently set to **Normal** (that's what the **N** stands for) but you can slide your finger up and down to choose different **Blend Modes**. Try each one to see how it transforms your artwork. **Color Burn** has been used here, but use whatever works for your style, and keep in mind that the original color of your texture decides the color of the **Blend Mode** result, so you can play around with the color of your original texture to see even more options.

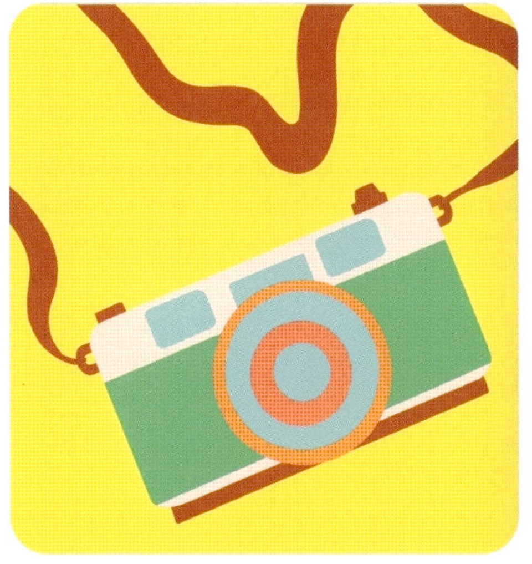

Multiply
Darken
Color Burn
Linear Burn
Darker Color
Normal
Lighten

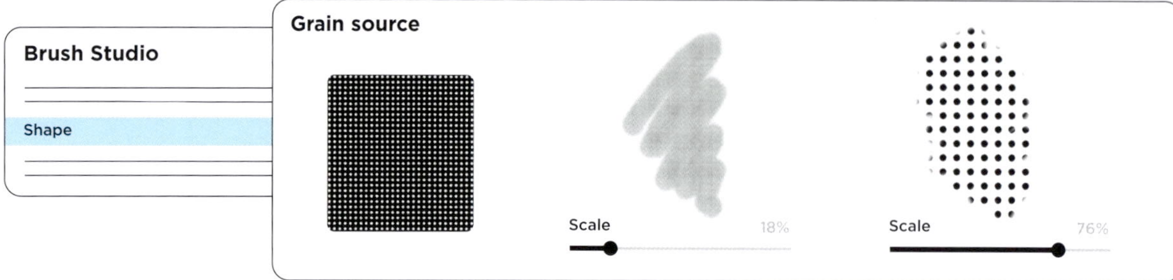

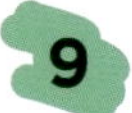

9 ADJUST THE TEXTURE

You can also adjust the scale of the texture, so if the dots are too big or too small, you can adjust that by tapping on the brush to open the **Brush Settings Menu**, tapping on **Grain**, and adjusting the **Scale Slider** before pressing **Done**. You'll see two very different scales in the examples here. Each scale will produce different results, and both are worth trying over your camera drawing.

Tip Duplicate your brushes before making changes to them to avoid losing the settings on the original brush. Play with brush settings as much as you'd like, but you don't want to lose the original settings in case you want to go back to them.

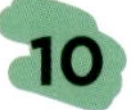

10 PUSH THE CONCEPT EVEN FURTHER

To push the "screen-print concept" even further, you can duplicate parts of your camera, then use the **Move Tool** to slightly offset them and use a **Blend Mode** on those as well (either the same one or a different one). When you combine the possibilities of color, texture, and **Blend Modes**, you literally have an unlimited number of styles at your fingertips.

Keep It Going

This is a great time to do a deep dive into layering screen-print textures and changing colors. Why not add another layer of the screen-print texture to see how it overlays the first one, and offset more layers of your camera to make it even more layered?

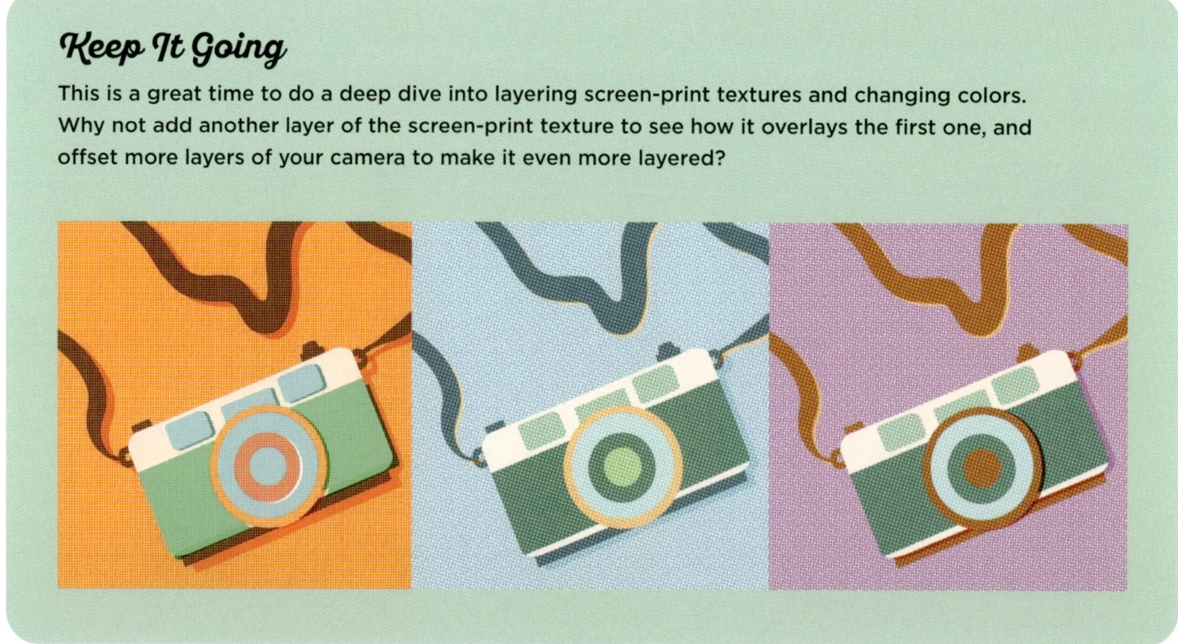

The End Result

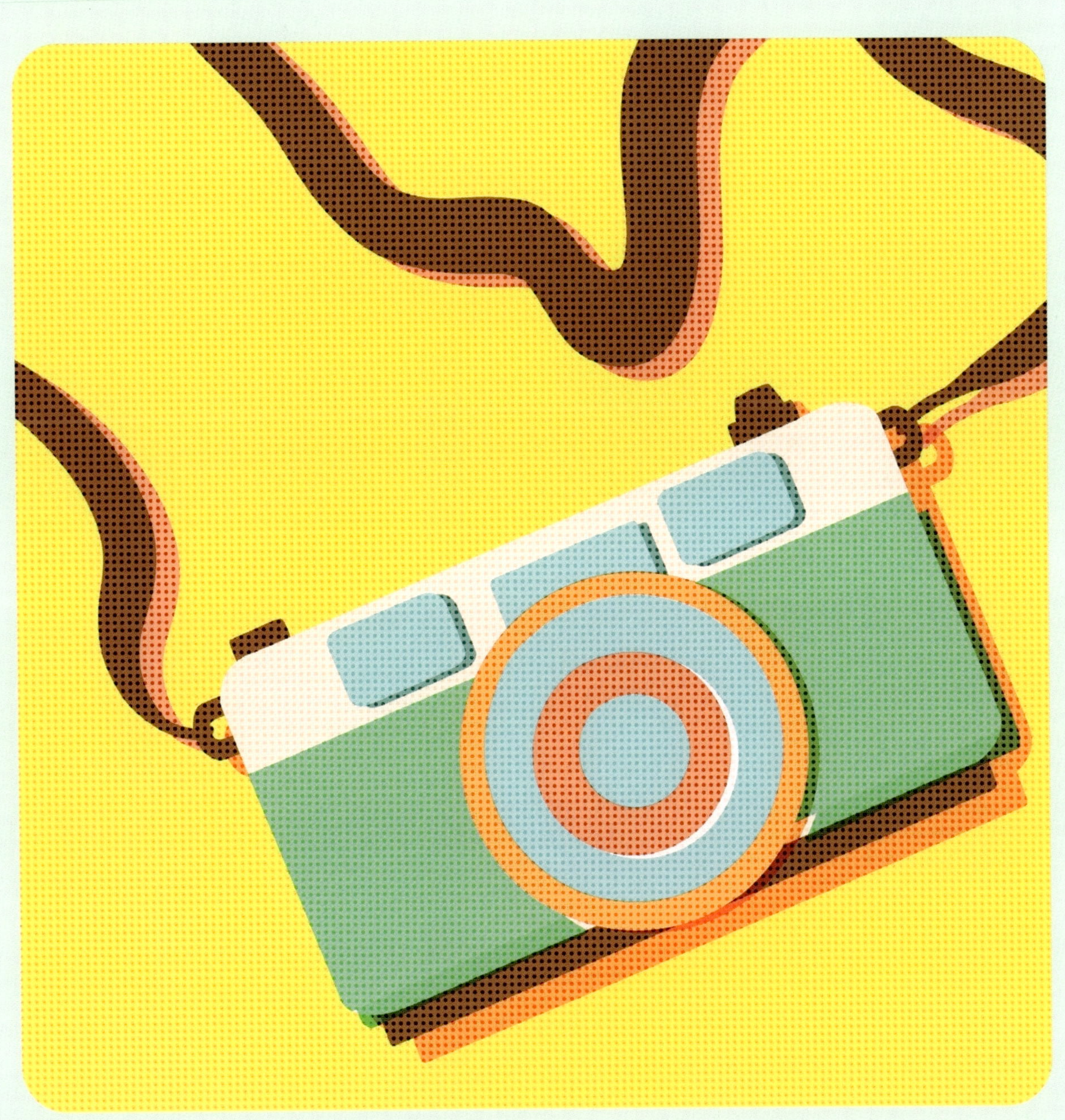

9

TOOLS FOR A Scenic View

In this project, we'll take a deeper look at the Procreate drawing tools that help build shapes quickly. These tools save time on the drawing process, leaving you able to focus your energy on creating more art!

What We're Learning:
Using **Quickshape** to build geometric-based shapes

Brushes:

Sketching Pencil

Rough Inking Worn Texture

Palette:
Muted Retro

Tomato Red #ff3100

Red Wine #981200

Cornflower Blue #597ce9

Blue Jay Blue #283c77

Glacier Blue #e0e4ea

Mountain Mist Blue #8799ad

Buttermilk Yellow #efb233

Oak Brown #916800

Dark Pastel Purple #917dbd

Plum Purple #493a62

Avocado Green #b1a450

Pickled Bean Green #595221

Flamingo Pink #f8abab

Valentine Red #e9605c

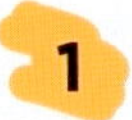

CREATE SOME THUMBNAILS

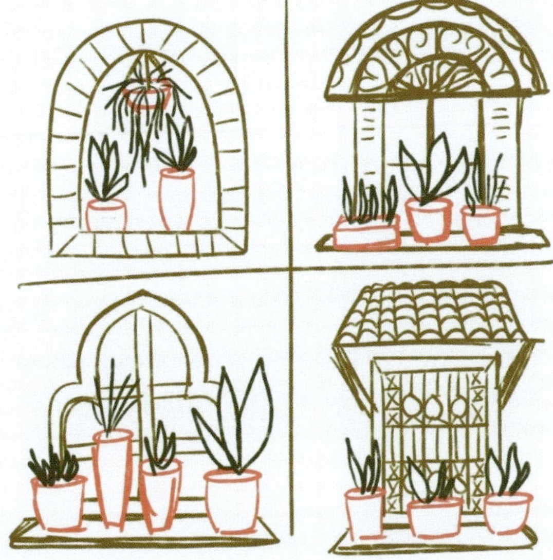

First, choose a location for your window. This could be the city you live in, or a place you've been dying to visit. Take screenshots of your favorites as a reference. Now move on to the rough sketch stage—this time we're going use thumbnails. Thumbnails are tiny sketches that are variations on a drawing idea, so you can explore a few options before committing to a drawing. Start by making a simple grid on your canvas, then fill each square with a different concept.

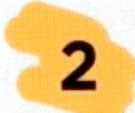

CHOOSE YOUR COMPOSITION

Which composition seems the most promising? If you're not sure, just choose the one you're most excited about. Go back to your **Gallery**, tap **Select** and then tap **Duplicate** to duplicate the document. Why not duplicate it three times so that you have canvases ready for all four options?

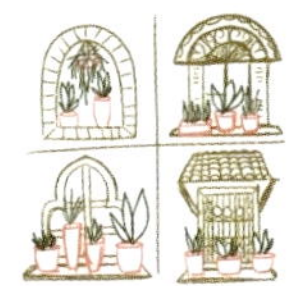

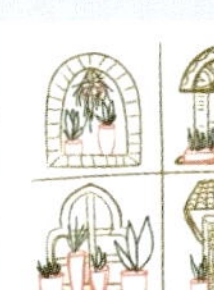

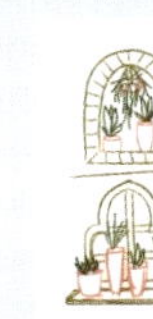

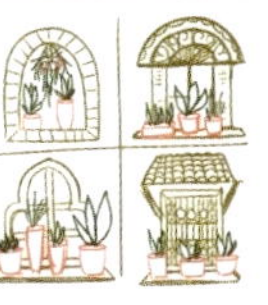

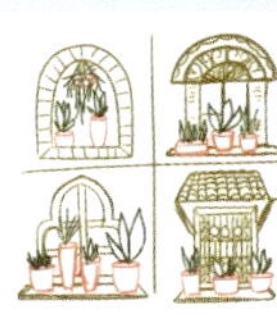

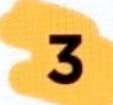

RESIZE YOUR THUMBNAIL

Open the original drawing, merge all your thumbnail layers onto one single layer by pinching them together, and use the **Move Tool** to resize your chosen composition. This thumbnail has now become your rough sketch, so you can check that off your to-do list!

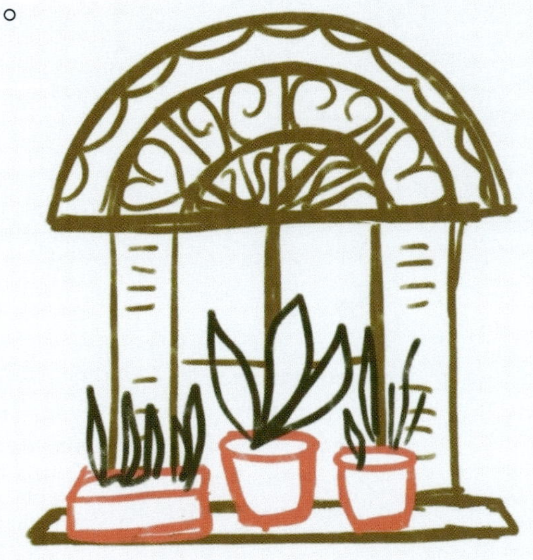

4 BUILDING THE DRAWING

Use **Quickline** and **Quickshape** to build the drawing, but rather than building the whole window, build only half of it, then duplicate it and flip it for the other half. **Quickshape** senses what you want to draw and helps you draw it faster and more accurately. You'll notice a text bar that pops up at the top of the screen when you invoke **Quickshape**. This menu allows you to choose from a variety of shapes. However, if **Quickshape** isn't working for you, use **Quickline** to build the shapes from scratch.

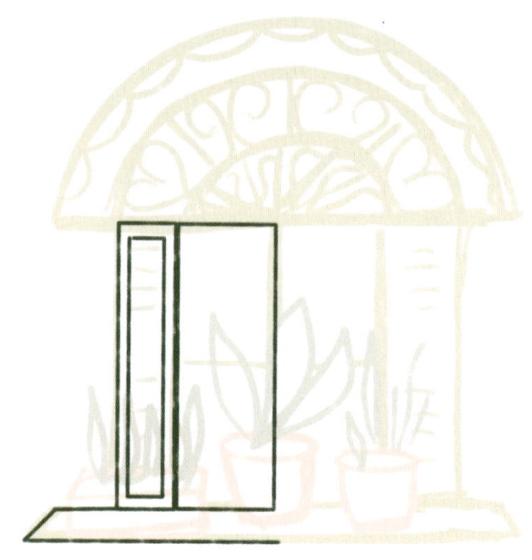

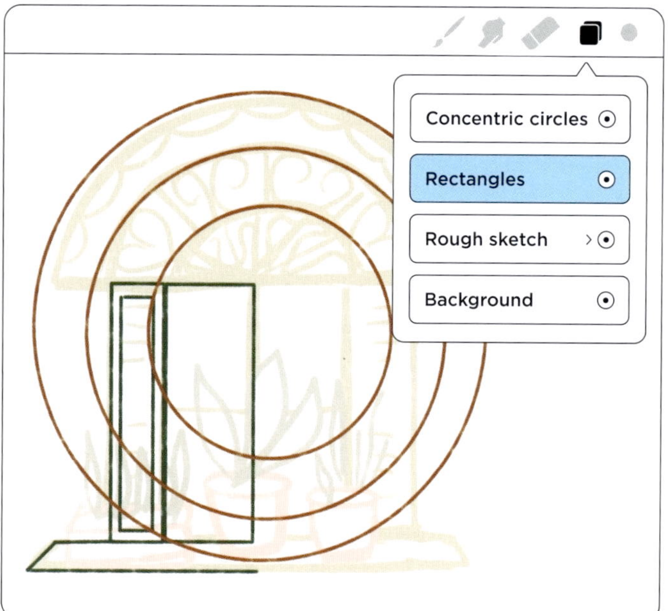

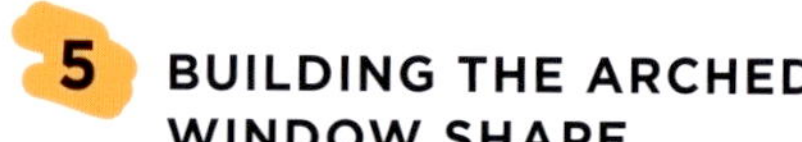

5 BUILDING THE ARCHED WINDOW SHAPE

The arched window in this example was built by drawing concentric circles using the same process as for the lens on the Screen-printed Camera project, the bottom half of the circles was then erased. If your window includes an arch, you may want to use that trick to speed up your work process.

Tip Another time-saving technique is duplicating elements that are repeated on the canvas. The sketch of the iron bars on this window is repeated four times in the arch, but it's only necessary to draw the shape once, then swipe left on the layer in the **Layers Panel**, tap **Duplicate**, then move the duplicate to its proper location.

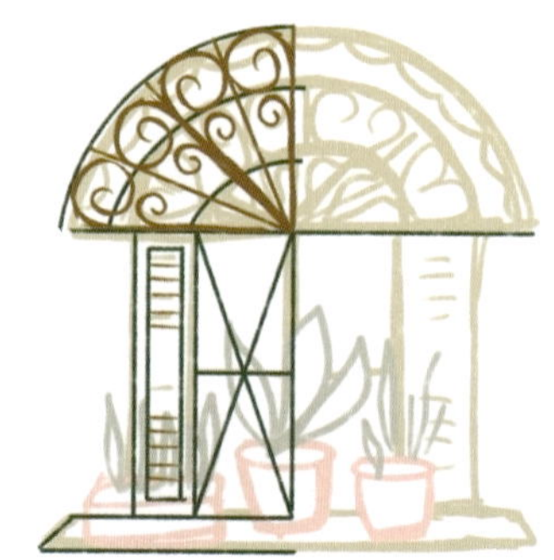

6 DUPLICATING THE HALF-WINDOW

Once half of your window has been sketched, it's time to duplicate it and position the duplicate. First, merge your sketch layers onto one layer, swipe left on the layer in the **Layers Panel**, and tap **Duplicate**, then tap the **Move Tool**. Before moving your object, turn on the **Magnetics** function on the the **Move Tool**. This "locks" your artwork along vertical and horizontal axis lines.

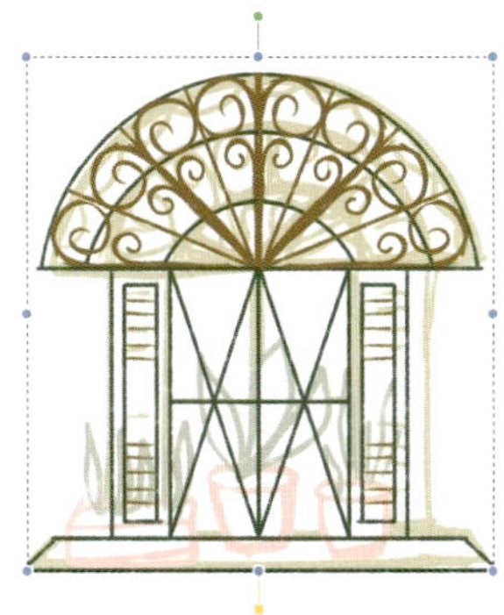

Settings
Magnetics
Snapping

Freeform
Uniform
Distort
Warp

Snapping
Flip ↔
Flip ↕
Rotate 45°
Fit to canvas
Bilinear
Reset

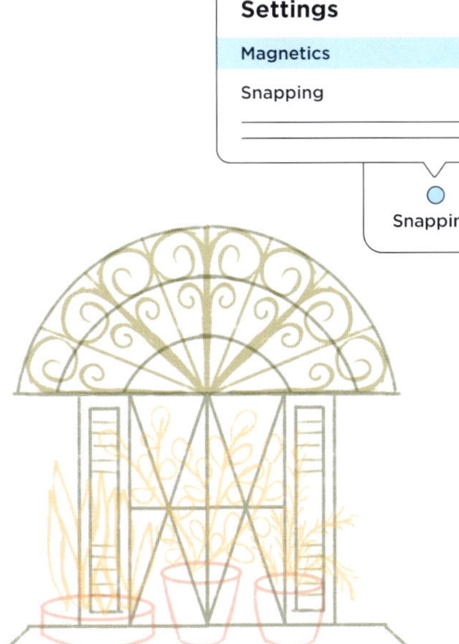

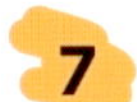

7 FINISHING THE SKETCH

Finish off your sketch with the pot and plant sketches, adding in any other details that you'd like to have on your windowsill. Then reduce the opacity of your sketch layers so you can move on to the inking stage.

8 ADDING COLOR

Ink your drawing using any brush you'd like (the Rough Inking Worn Texture brush was used in this example), and experiment with different inking techniques and color versions. You could leave your window at this point or add something to give it more life, like a bird, animal, or even a person peeking through the window. Here, we'll add a cat sitting on the ledge. To do this, find an image to use as a reference, then create a rough sketch using big geometric shapes to block out the cat shape.

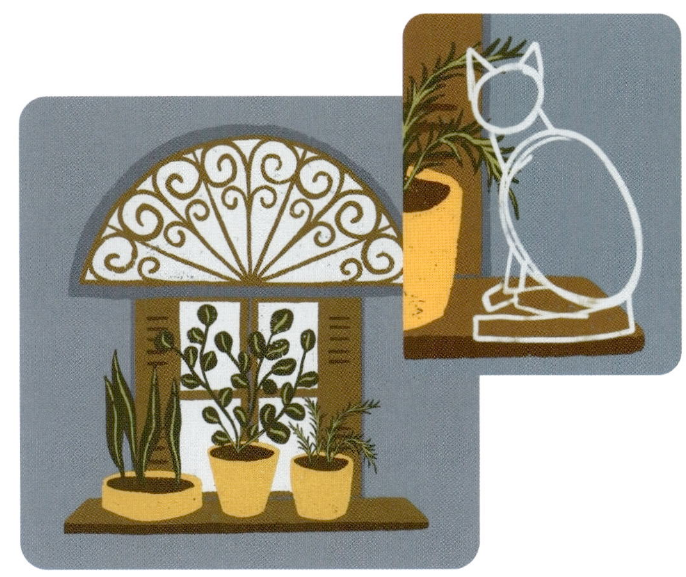

9 REFINE THE CAT SKETCH

Create a refined sketch layer to add more detail to the cat's body, and if you're having trouble working out the details of the features or proportions of the body, create a few more sketch layers until you're happy. Drawing animals is a skill that takes time, so don't be surprised if it takes you longer than expected to get it right.

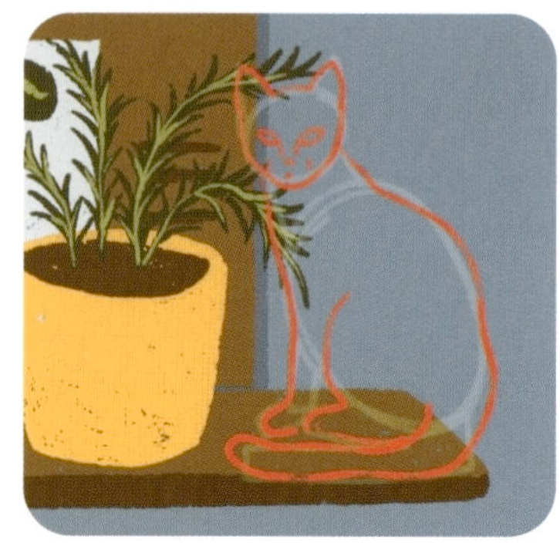

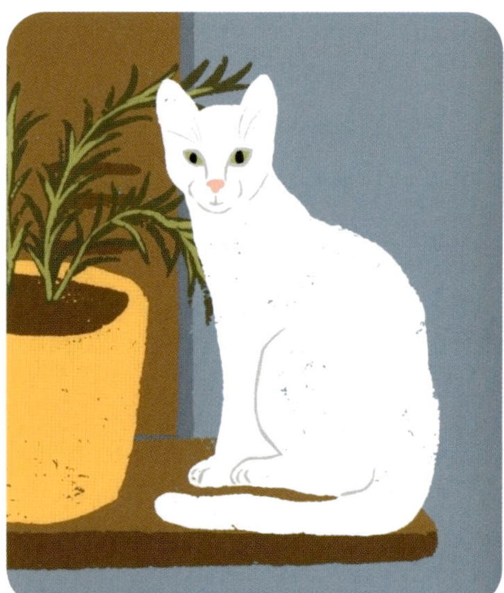

10 INK THE CAT

Finally, ink the cat, keeping each color on its own layer in case you want to change the color of the cat, eyes, or detail lines. Zoom out to be sure the scale of the cat is proportional to the pots and remember that you can resize the whole cat group if you realize it is too large.

Tip When drawing extra elements like the cat, it's best practice to draw them at the right scale or larger than they need to be. You can always size an element down, but if you size it up, you will create a blurry object since you can't add more pixels to a drawing after it's been created. A good mantra to remember this concept is "blowing up is blurring up."

Keep It Going

There are a variety of special touches you could add to this illustration to give it more character. What about adding some brick or stone lines to the wall? In this example, I created a new layer just above my background layer, then drew in some brick lines using the **Drawing Guide** to measure the bricks. Then I created a new layer below the brick lines to add various brick colors.

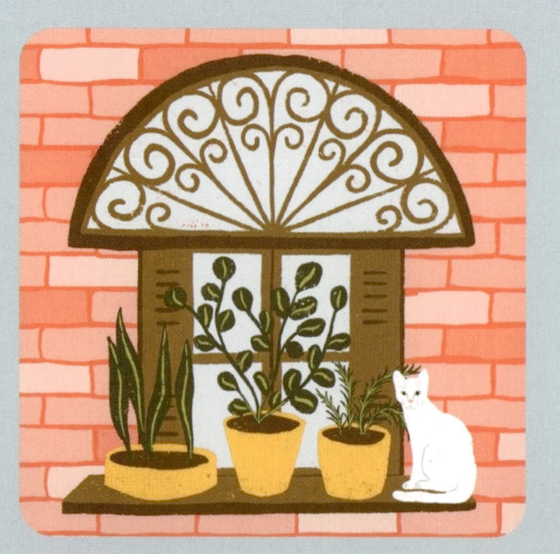

The End Result

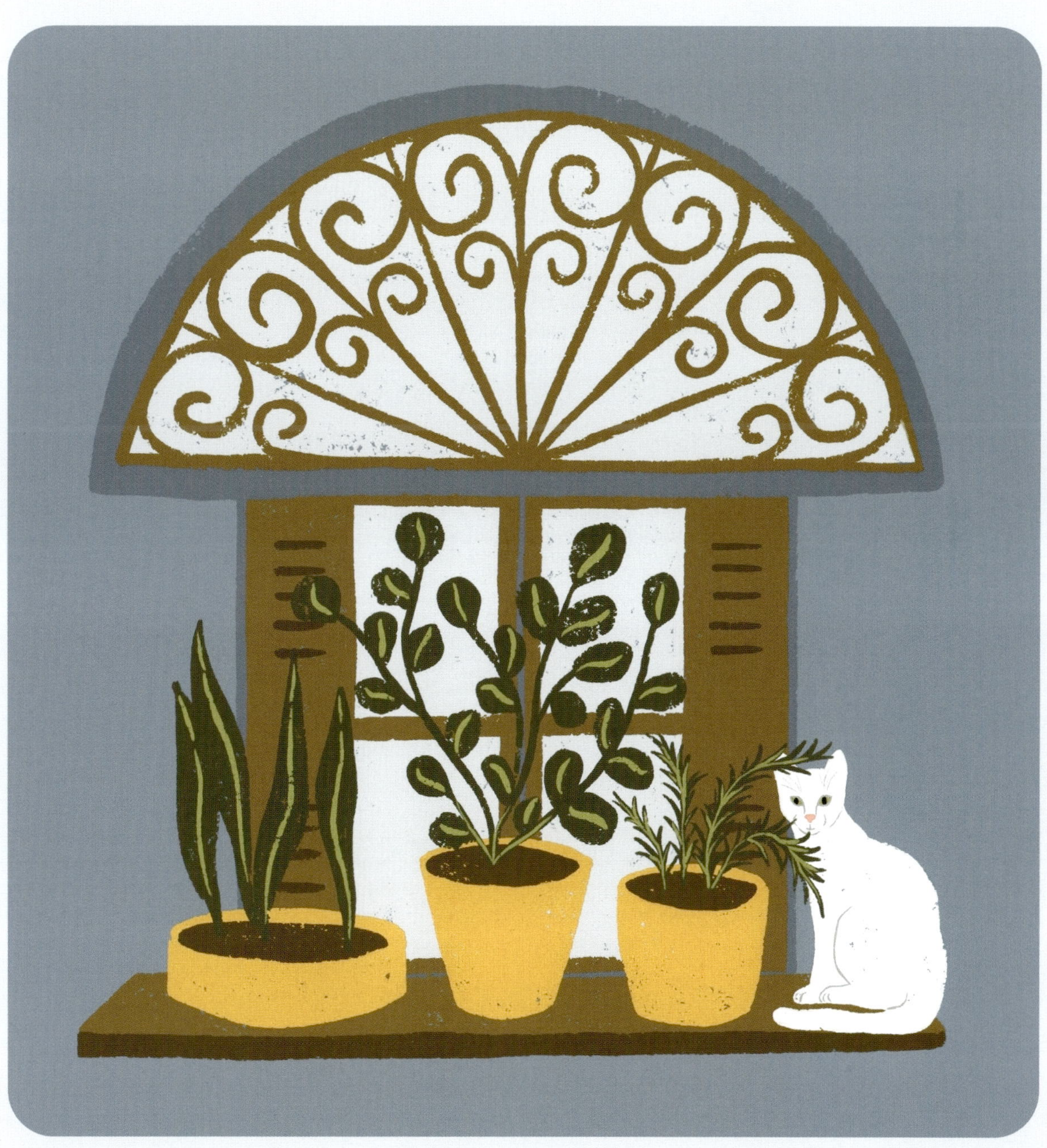

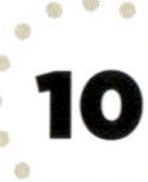

SKETCH PERSPECTIVE AT *Your Desk*

The Procreate Perspective Guides allow you to accurately draw in perspective, showing the depth and angle of an object. In this project, you'll practice using Perspective Guides to draw your dream studio space.

What We're Learning:
Using **Perspective Guides**

Brushes:

Sketching Pencil

Rough Inking Worn Texture

Rough Inking

Palette:
50s Motel

- Cotton Candy Pink #ff90be
- California Neon Pink #ff005b
- Mint Gum Green #34c494
- Deep Sea Green #063420
- Mustard Yellow #dbae00
- Earthy Stone Yellow #917400
- Vanilla Cream White #fff4d4
- Pebble Path White #c0b28d
- Lavender Haze #dad7e7
- Mochi Purple #746a99
- Creamsicle Orange #f9aa12
- Burnt Toast Orange #9d6900
- Lilac Purple #d9a9e3
- 90s Nails Purple #7e5884

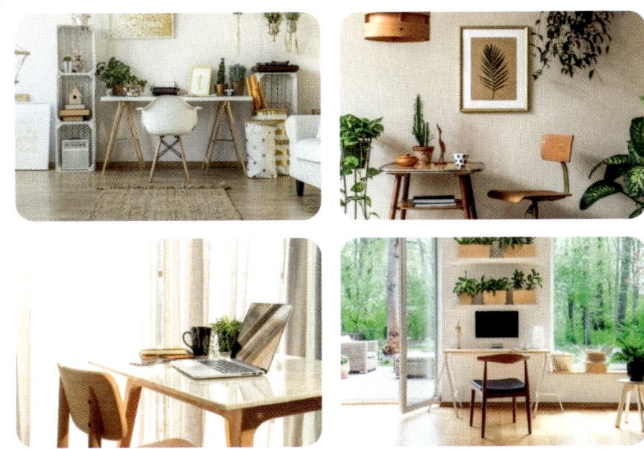

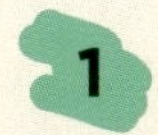

1 FINDING INSPIRATION

Find some reference images featuring workspaces that you love. You could even make a Pinterest board of studio spaces, offices, and maybe even office sheds that inspire you. That way you'll have a lot of furniture, wall art, plants, and colors to choose from as you draw.

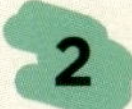

2 CREATING A "SUPER ROUGH"

Start by creating what I call a "super-rough" sketch of your table, chair, and some artwork on the wall. The super-rough sketch will help you to determine the angle of the table. If you aren't sure what angle you want to use, copy the angle used here and then next time you'll be able to jump right in and choose one for yourself. The angle of the perspective is indicated in the image so you can see the kind of angle you are determining as you make this initial sketch.

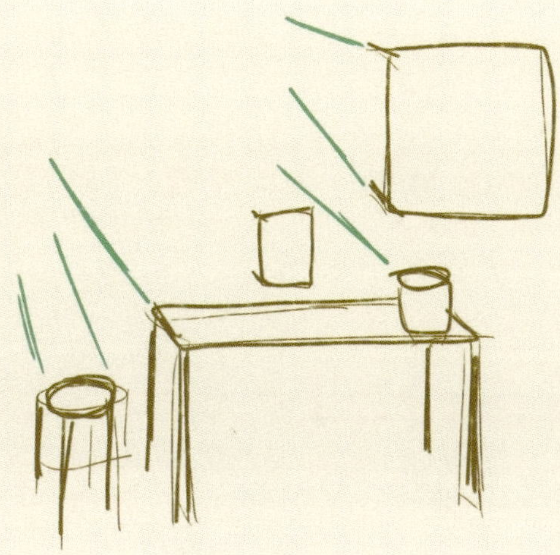

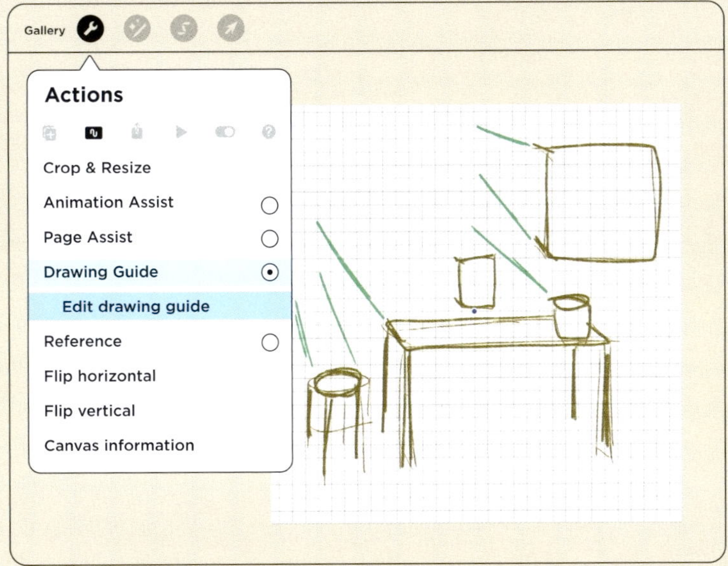

3 TURN ON THE PERSPECTIVE GUIDES

Next, turn on the **Perspective Guides** by going to **Actions**, then **Canvas**, turn on the **Drawing Guide**, and then tap **Edit Drawing Guide**.

4 BRING UP THE GUIDES ON YOUR CANVAS

On the **Edit Drawing Guide** screen, you'll see **Perspective** as one of the options at the bottom. Tap on that option, then tap somewhere on your canvas. It's worth noting that if you tap multiple times on the canvas you will accidentally create multiple points, but you can tap on the point again to delete it!

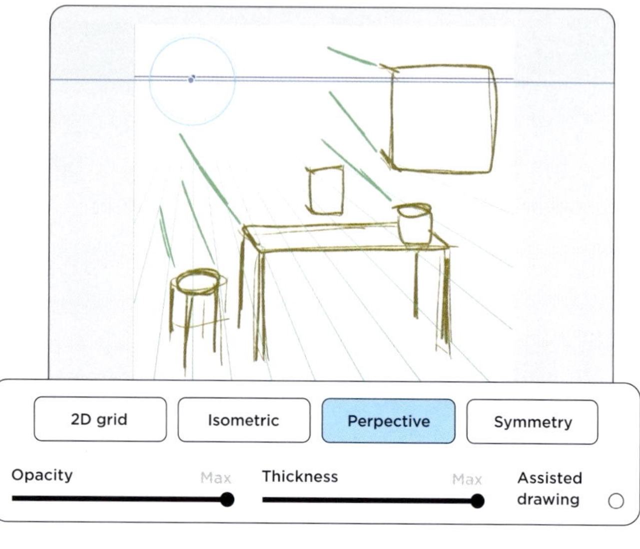

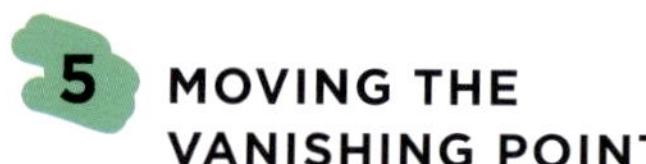

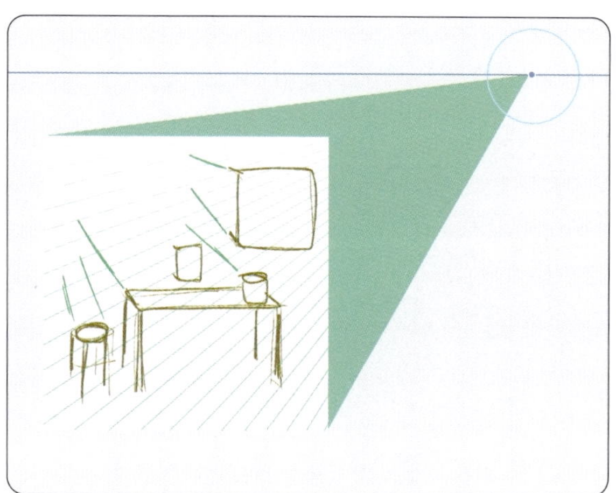

5 MOVING THE VANISHING POINT

Hold your finger on the blue dot that appears, and you'll find that you can move it around the page to adjust the perspective's "vanishing point" (the place where the horizon of your drawing ends).

6 ESTABLISH YOUR CHOSEN VANISHING POINT

Adjust the vanishing point (the blue dot) until it lines up with your original plan. The vanishing point can go off the canvas to make for a less extreme perspective drawing, or you can keep it on the canvas to show an extreme perspective (or a sideways angle).

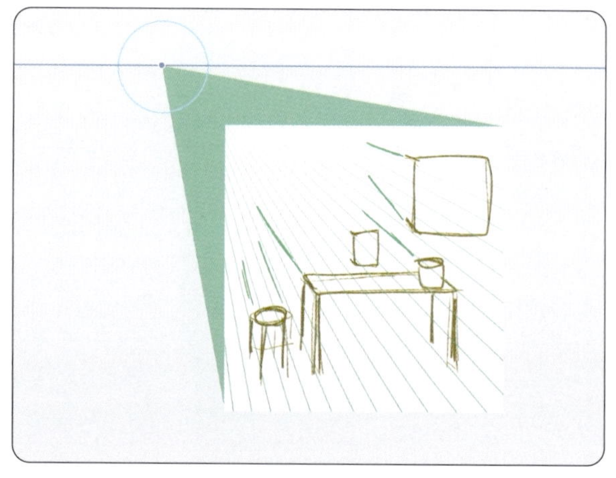

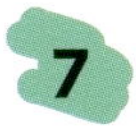

7 DRAW THE BASIC ELEMENTS OF YOUR COMPOSITION

Now that you have the overall perspective structure of your drawing, you can sketch the table and artwork frames, keeping all the angles aligned with the **Perspective Guides** you have turned on. Notice how horizontal lines are straight and aligned with the floor, while vertical lines follow the **Perspective Guides**. This includes the sides of the table, and even the sides of the artwork frames.

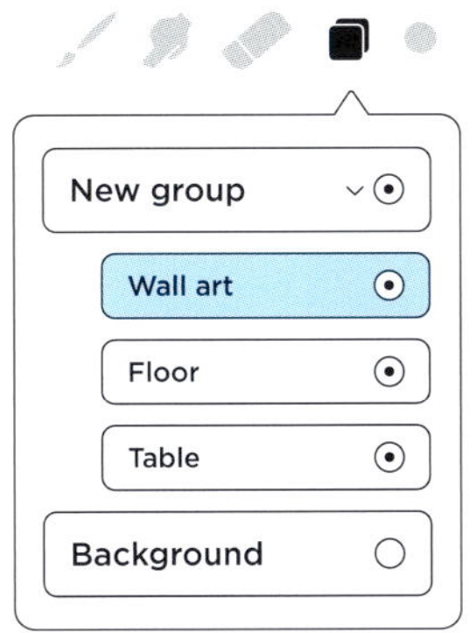

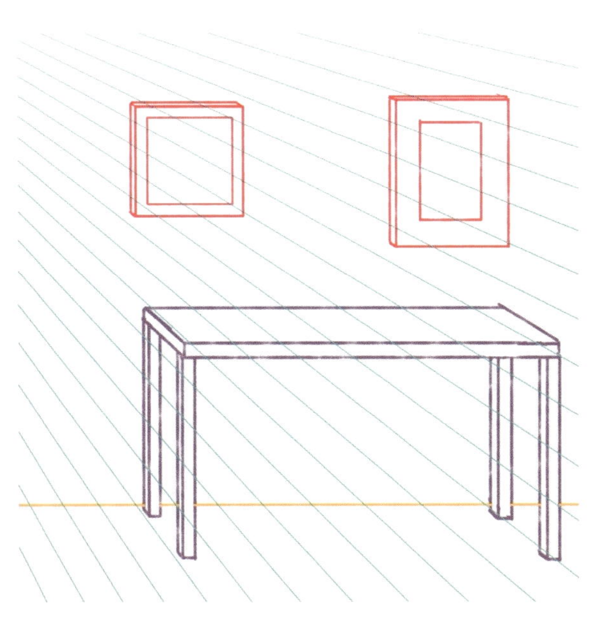

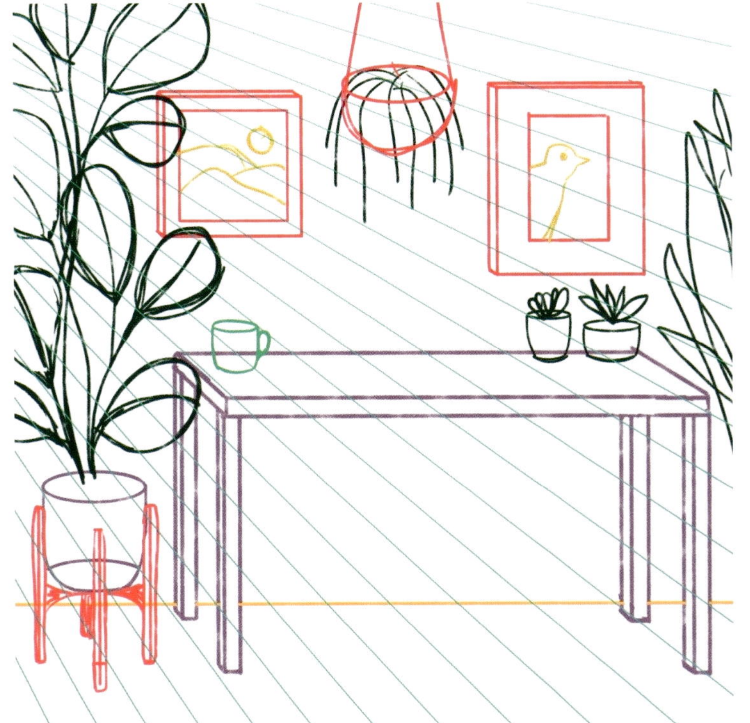

8 ADD MORE ELEMENTS

Sketch all the other objects in your composition, like some plants on the table, artwork inside the frames, and a drink on the table. Add any items that show your personality and reflect what you like to have on your desk when you work.

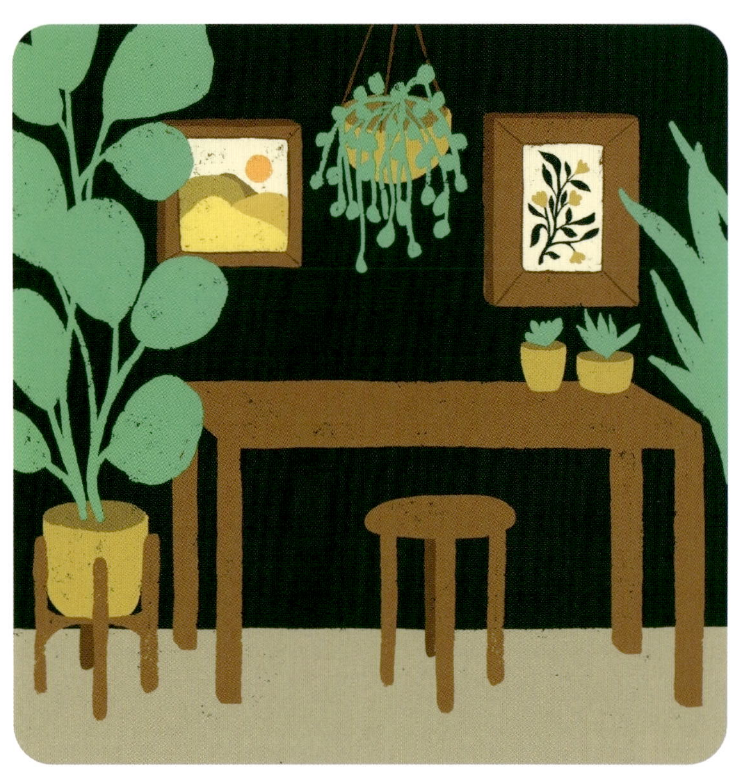

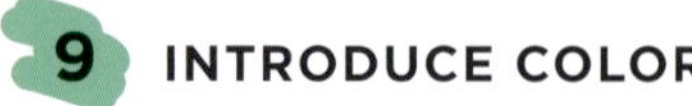

9 INTRODUCE COLOR

Ink each layer using the brush of your choice (the Rough Inking brushes are used in this example) and try a few different color versions for each item in your drawing. You'll notice that quite a large number of layers has been built up in the **Layers Panel**, so this is a good time to start grouping and naming parts of your drawing to help you stay organized. This will make creating color versions much easier later on.

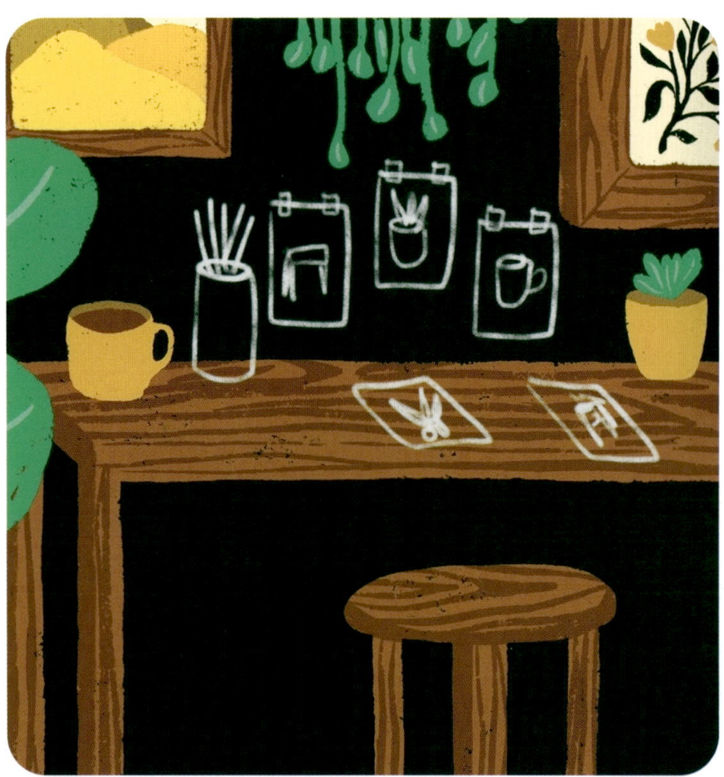

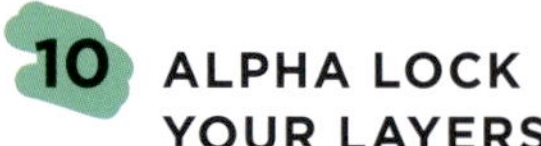

10 ALPHA LOCK YOUR LAYERS

Alpha Lock all your layers and add some details to each layer, like wood grain using some simple wavy lines, veins on the plant leaves, or any other tiny details that will add personality to your objects. In this example, I added some of the items that are usually on my desk—a cup with pencils in it and some sketches on the desk and taped to the wall. To add these objects, just sketch right on top of your inked drawing on a new layer, then repeat the same inking process that you used for the other objects.

The End Result

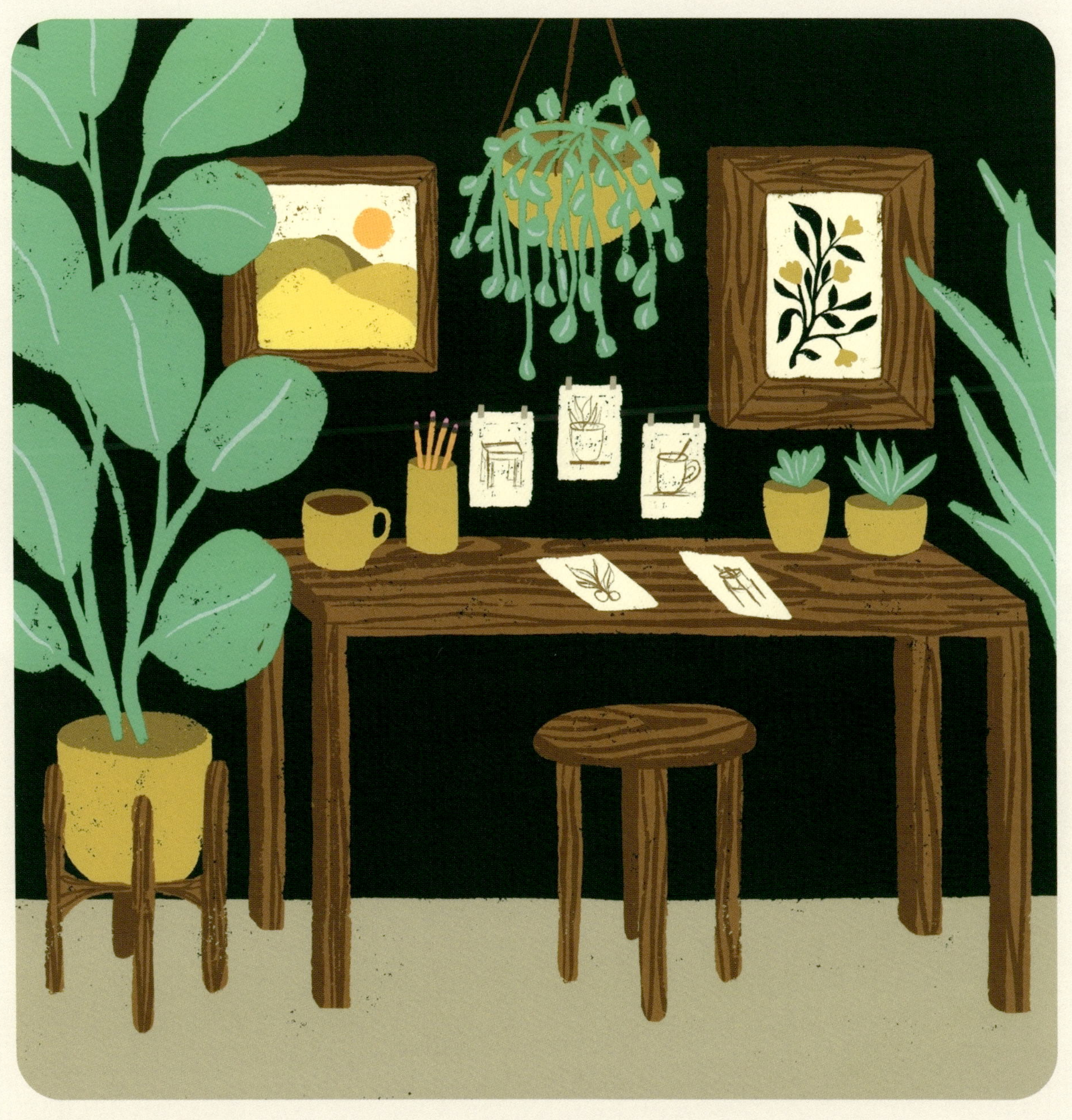

11

ERASE the Sun

The technique of "carving" away ink from a solid block of color can be used to create bold and interesting drawings that resemble block-print artwork. In this example of that technique, we'll be lettering a phrase in the center of a sun.

What We're Learning:
Drawing by erasing

Brushes:

Sketching Pencil

Fluid Ink or Lino Cutter

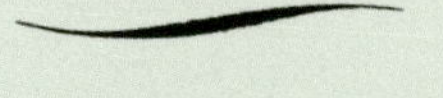

Pencil Taps Texture

Super Subtly Scuffs Texture

Palette:
50s Motel

Cotton Candy Pink #ff90be

California Neon Pink #ff005b

Mint Gum Green #34c494

Deep Sea Green #063420

Mustard Yellow #dbae00

Earthy Stone Yellow #917400

Vanilla Cream White #fff4d4

Pebble Path White #c0b28d

Lavender Haze #dad7e7

Mochi Purple #746a99

Creamsicle Orange #f9aa12

Burnt Toast Orange #9d6900

Lilac Purple #d9a9e3

90s Nails Purple #7e5884

1 SELECT A PHRASE

Choose a short, three- or four-word phrase you would like to letter inside your sun shape. Here, we're adding "Don't worry be happy" but you could choose your name, your city, or anything else. Starting with something short is a good way to ensure your project is readable. You can always try longer phrases later, and even fill up a whole canvas with block lettering.

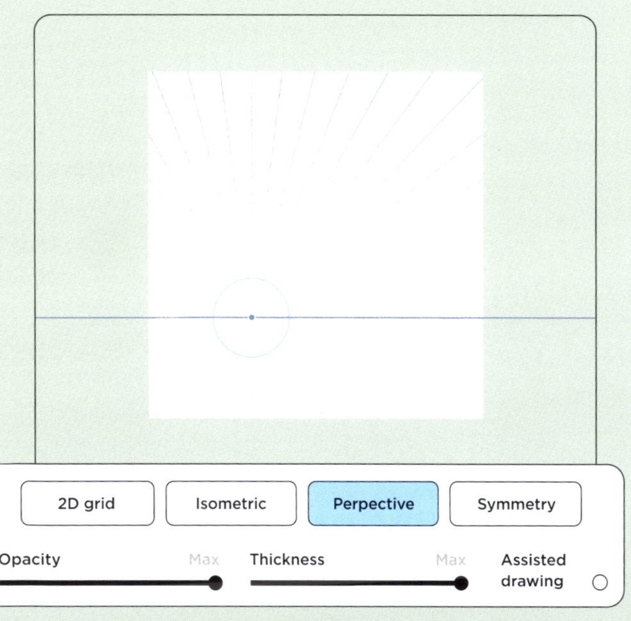

2 SET UP THE PERSPECTIVE GUIDES

Turn on the **Perspective Guides** to make radial marks on your canvas by going to **Actions**, **Canvas**, turning on the **Drawing Guide**, and tapping **Edit Drawing Guide**. Then, choose **Perspective** as the type and tap on the canvas once to create a perspective guide. You can adjust the opacity and color of your guides to make them easier to see if you'd like.

3 ESTABLISH THE RADIAL MARKS

Next, draw your radial marks using the Sketching Pencil, and **Quickline**. Follow the **Perspective Guides** to help you keep them in a radial pattern. These will be your sun's rays.

4 DRAW THE SUN

On a new layer, draw a circle using **Quickshape**, then make sure the circle is in the center of your radial marks. Erase the lines that are inside the circle, then merge the circle and line layers together to keep your **Layers Panel** tidy.

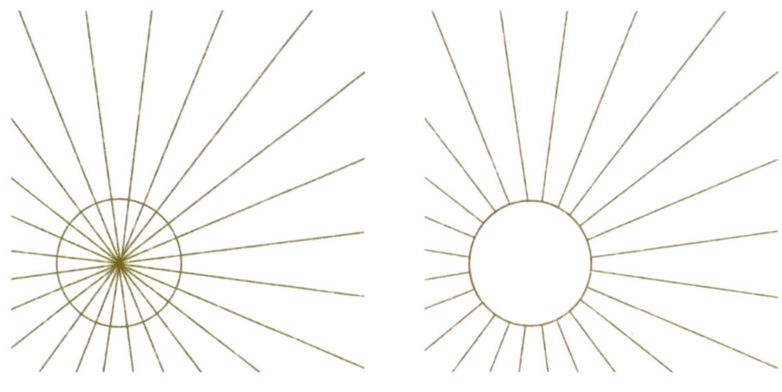

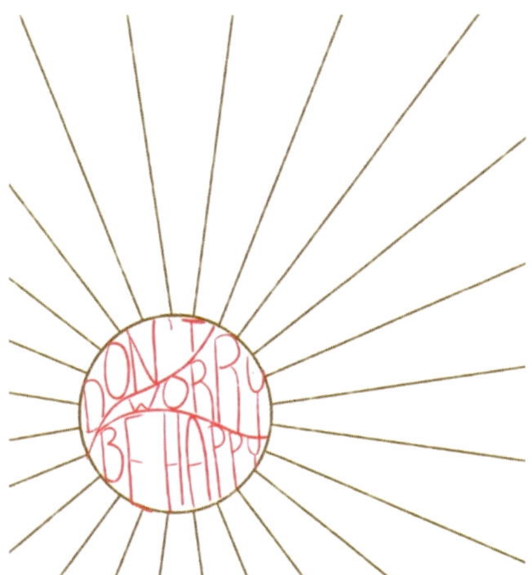

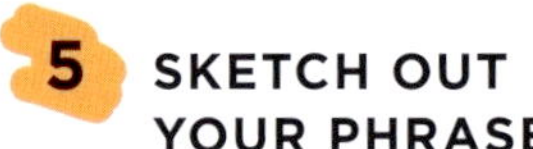

5 SKETCH OUT YOUR PHRASE

Using the Sketching Pencil, draw some wavy lines to mark out areas where you will draw your letters. Keep these lines fluid and consider the length of the words when choosing how large to make each space. Next, write your letters and if needed, adjust the lines to fit all the words of your phrase. It may take a few sketch layers to get this right!

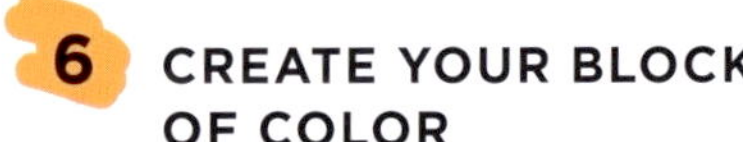

6 CREATE YOUR BLOCK OF COLOR

Create a new layer and fill it with a solid color by dragging and dropping color from the **Color Disc** to your canvas or tap on the layer and tap **Fill Layer**. This will be the "block" that you carve from as you create your block lettering composition.

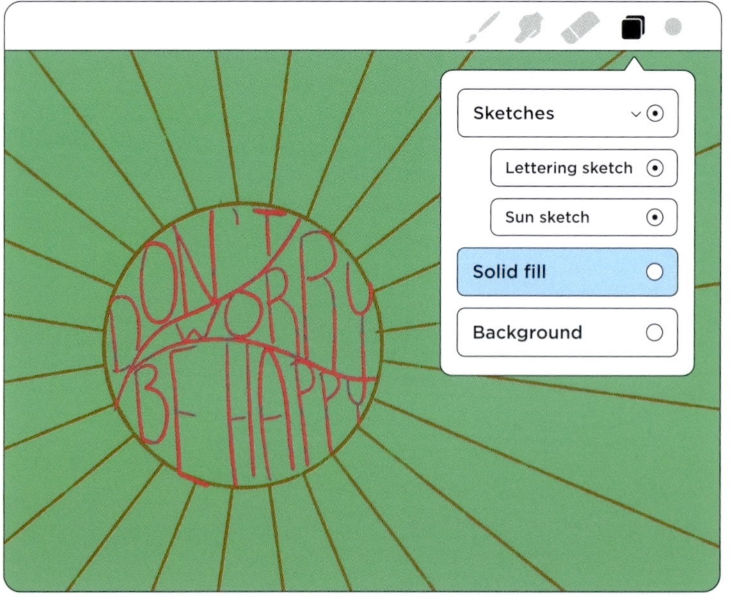

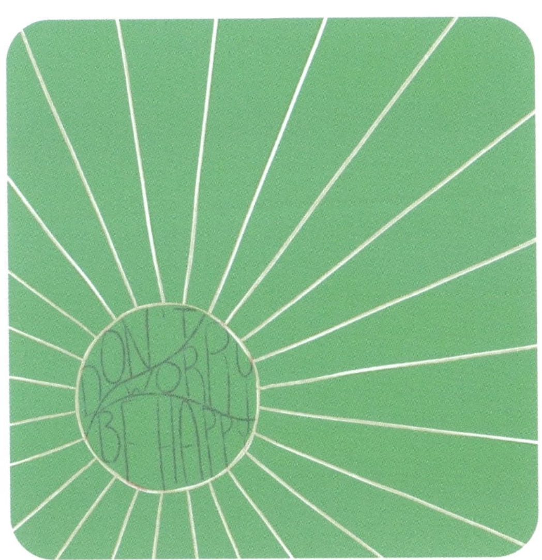

7 ERASE THE LINES OF YOUR SUN RAYS

Using the Fluid Ink brush, brush lines out of the solid color layer following the radial marks you sketched for your sunrays. These don't have to be perfect; in fact a bit of inconsistency will help give your composition a handmade look. You may even want to try the Lino Cutter brush in the **Brush Sampler** as your eraser if you'd like to create a rough, linocut feel for your lines.

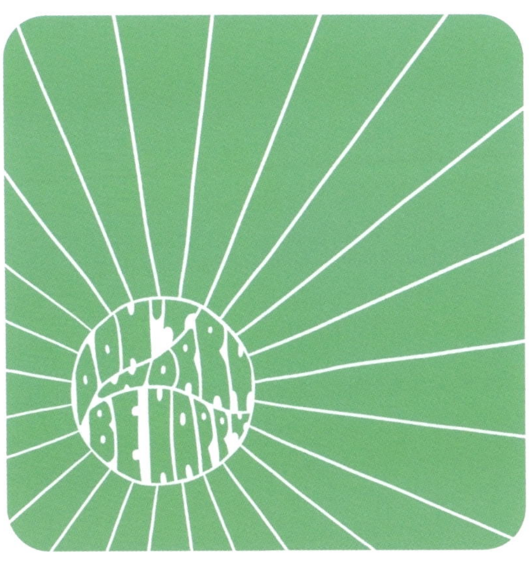

8 ERASE THE SHAPES OF YOUR TEXT

Repeat the same process for your letters by erasing parts of the solid layer to reveal the text. Try to erase as little as possible for each letter. For example, for the D, removing a tiny hole in the center of the letter and a small amount of ink on the front of the letter to make it curved was all that was needed. The less you take away, the more it feels like a block-print composition.

9 ADD COLOR

Next, we'll add some color to the spaces that you cut apart by dragging color from the **Color Disc** onto the space. If multiple sections fill with color at once, that means that you did not fully separate the shapes. Even one pixel of material can "connect" shapes and prevent them from being filled with color separately.

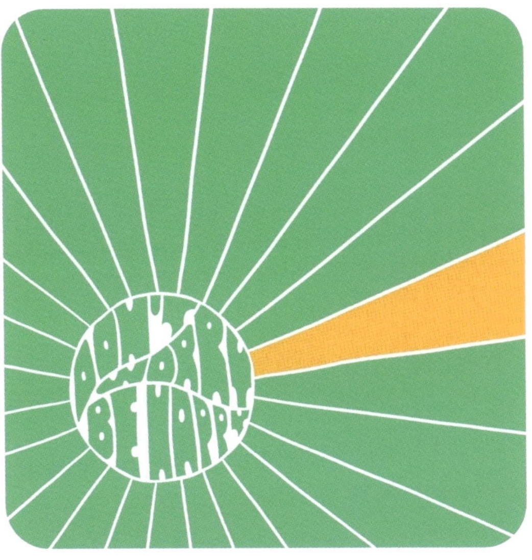

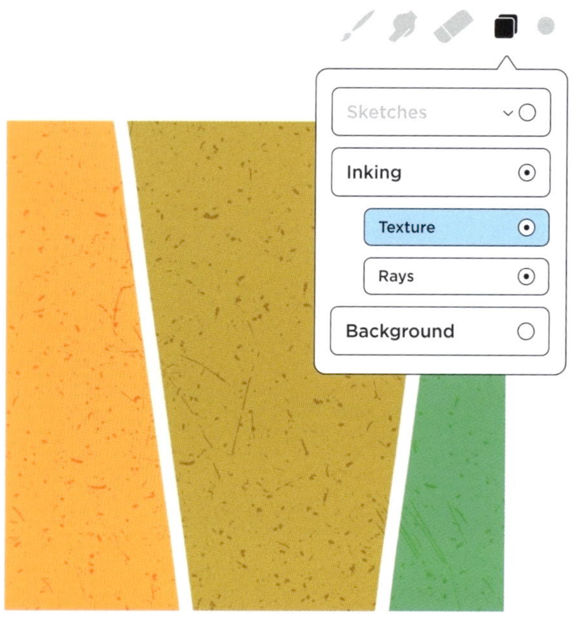

10 ADD SOME TEXTURE

You may want to add some texture to your composition. To do this, create a new layer above all your other layers, swipe one of the texture brushes in the **Brush Sampler** set over your canvas, then set it to a **Blend Mode**. In this version, both the Pencil Taps Texture brush and the Super Subtle Scuffs Texture brush were used, and the layer was set to the **Overlay Blend Mode** to achieve a vintage, grungy feel.

Tip If you're creating block lettering, ask a friend to read it to you without telling them what it says. Block lettering can be unreadable if some letters are not erased properly, so be sure that a non-artist friend can read it before calling it done.

Keep It Going

Now that you have a created a sun composition, why not try putting some other things inside it? You could duplicate the canvas, then erase the letters and try other things inside your sun. Why not try a face in a few different color versions?

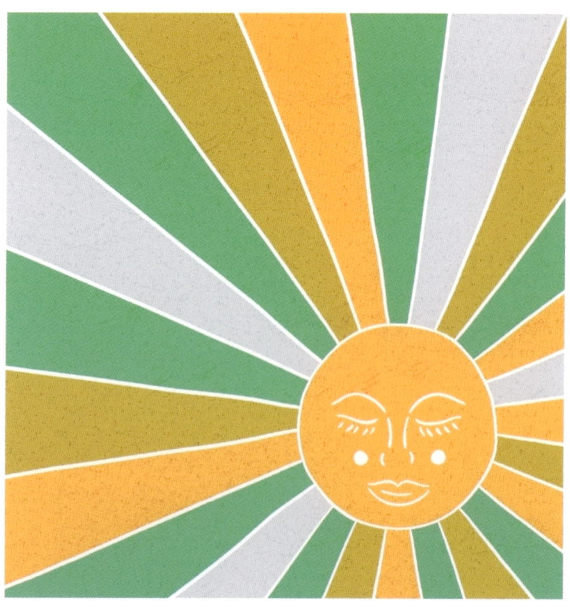

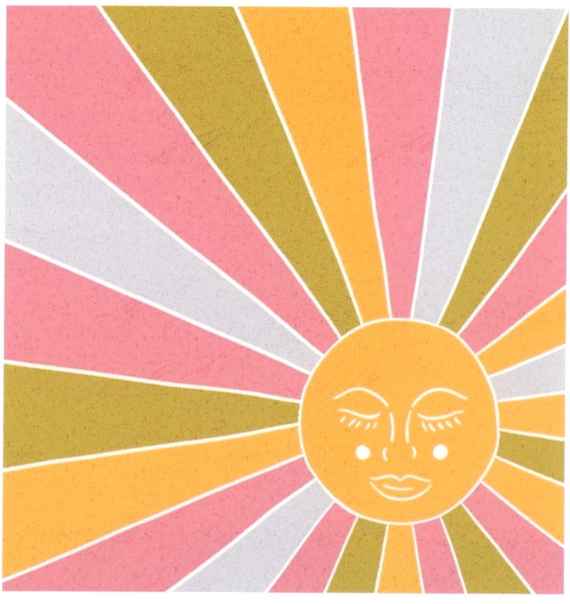

The End Result

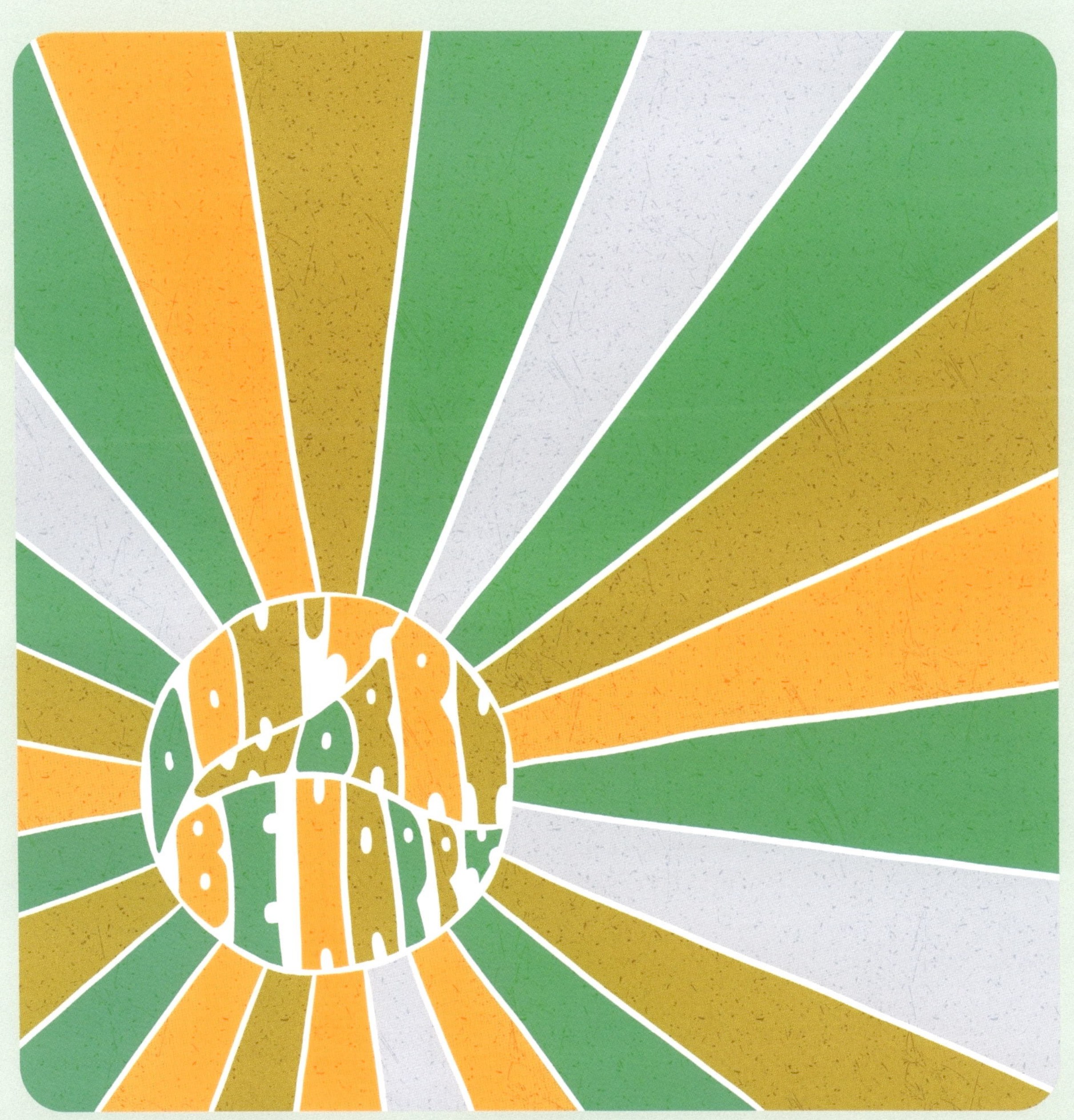

12

MIRROR *Nature*

Through this simple, moth illustration project, you'll learn how to use Procreate's Symmetry Tool, which works by mirroring your drawing vertically, horizontally, or in all four corners depending on the desired result. Choose a simple winged insect like a dragonfly, moth, or butterfly to draw.

What We're Learning:
Using Procreate's
Symmetry Tool

Brushes:

Sketching Pencil

Rough Inking

Palette:
Funky Modern

- Reddish Orange #ff4b18
- Red Fox #d34925
- Rose Bud #ffb09b
- Dark Peach #d1725f
- Mango Orange #df8000
- Ginger Brown #9f5d00
- Pink Pearl #ff9ce2
- Neon Fuschia #ff54c2
- Lake Mist Blue #d7dce7
- Steel Blue #7297c9
- Aqua Forest Green #6b9b78
- Pine Green #3a5a44
- Pale Violet #eda7fc
- Amethyst Purple #ac4cc1

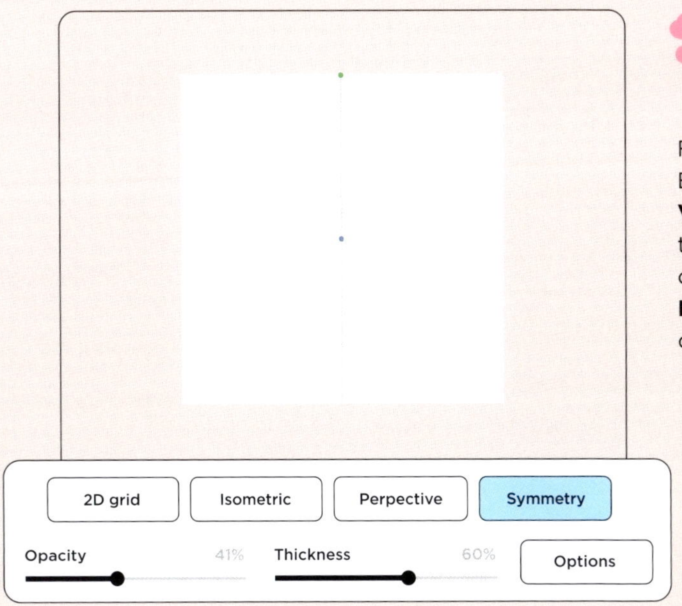

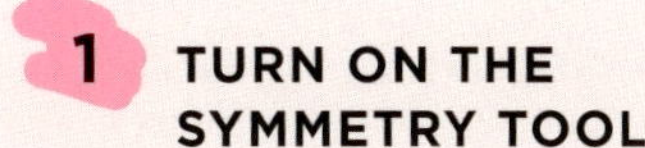

1 TURN ON THE SYMMETRY TOOL

Find some reference images of moths. Before you start sketching, turn on the **Vertical Symmetry Tool**. Do this by tapping the **Actions Menu**, then **Canvas**, then turn on the **Drawing Guide** and tap **Edit Drawing Guide**. Now tap the **Symmetry** option at the bottom.

2 SELECT VERTICAL SYMMETRY

Tap **Options** to see the settings for symmetrical drawing. In this example, we'll be using vertical symmetry, but it's a good idea to try all of the symmetry options at some point so that you can see how they help you save time on the drawing process.

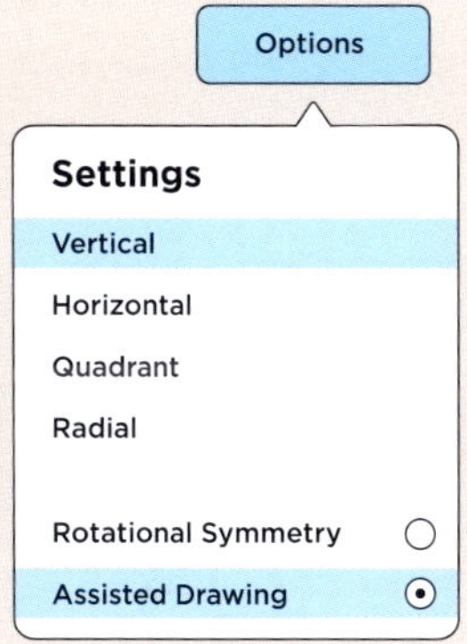

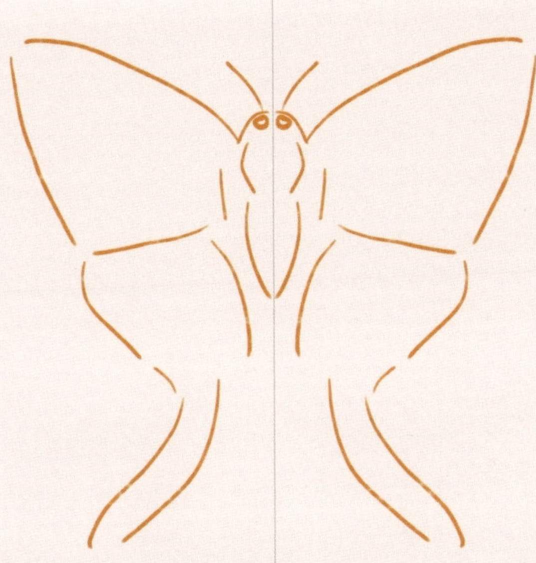

3 CREATE A ROUGH SKETCH

Tap **Done** to save the vertical symmetry setting and start sketching on one side of the canvas. You'll notice that anything you do on the left, is replicated on the right and vice versa (lefties rejoice!). Complete your rough sketch using this helpful tool, then continue with your refined sketch on a new layer.

4 TURN ON DRAWING ASSIST IN THE NEW LAYER

When you create a new layer, you'll notice that it is not set to "**Assisted**" in the **Layers Panel** (i.e. the **Vertical Symmetry** function is not on), so you will have to tap on the layer, then turn on **Drawing Assist**. The layer will remember the symmetry you chose last time and repeat it. If you need a different type of symmetry, you will have to go back to the **Symmetry Menu** to access the other symmetry types.

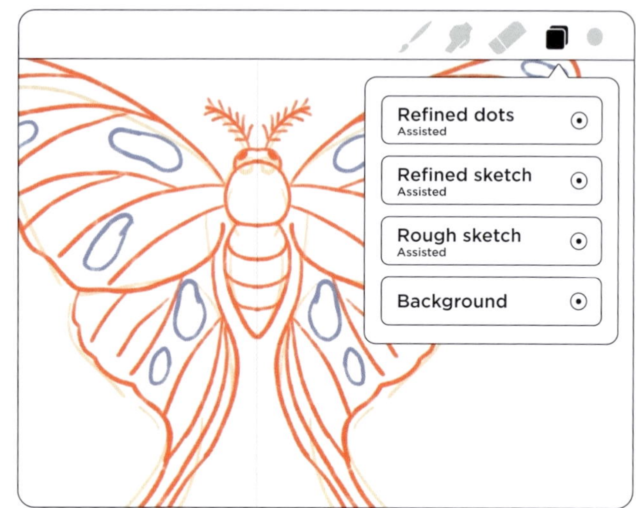

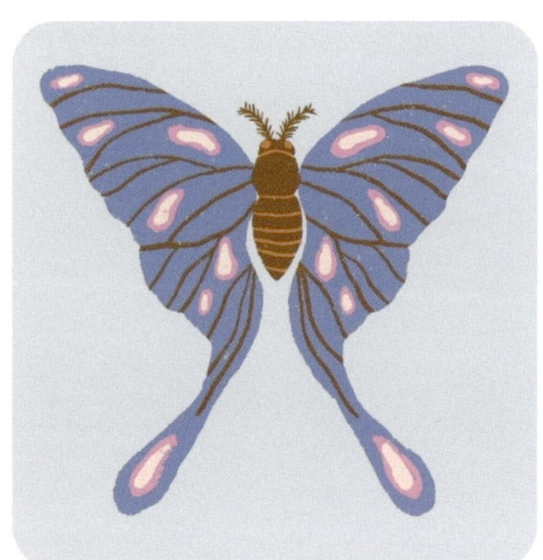

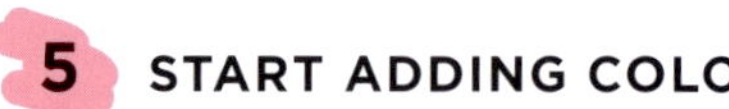

5 START ADDING COLOR

It's time to start inking your drawing. Choose your favorite inking brush and remember to turn on **Drawing Assist** as you create each new layer.

Tip You can save some time by creating layers that already have **Drawing Assist** activated. To do this, create a new layer, turn on **Drawing Assist**, then duplicate the layer a few times—each duplicate will already be in **Drawing Assist** mode!

6 DRAW MORE MOTHS

Now that you have experience of working in symmetry, try repeating the process with several different types of moths to create a series or a single illustration featuring four moth types. Do this on four different canvases so that you can choose to either present them as four different drawings or combine them onto one canvas.

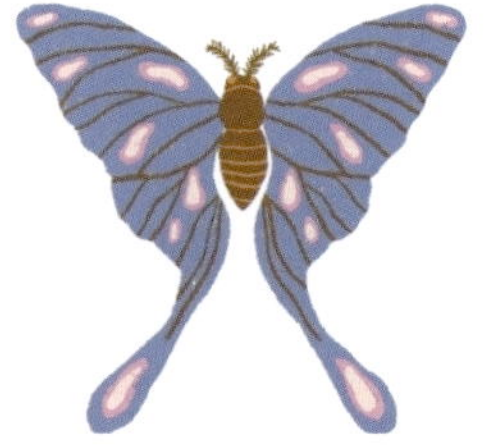

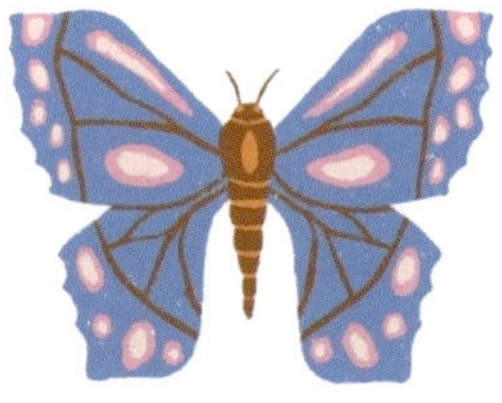

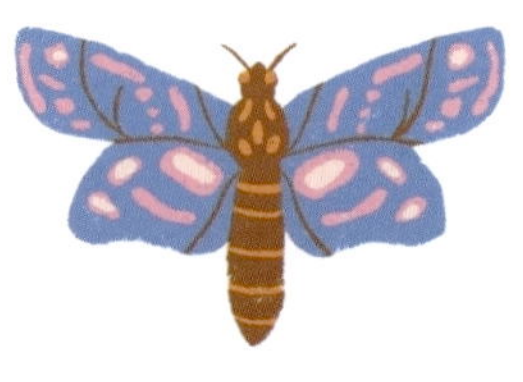

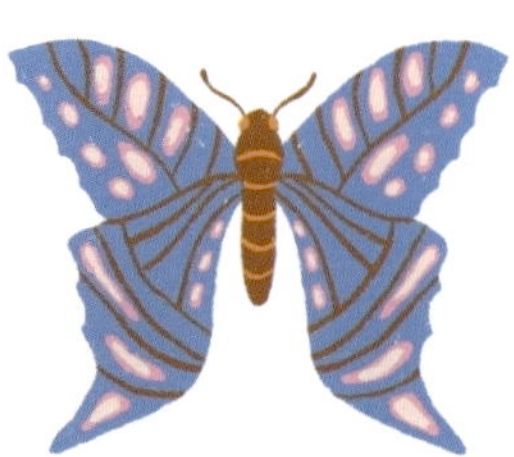

7 REMOVE BACKGROUND LAYERS

To combine the drawings on one canvas, first save them with no background. To do this, turn off the background layers on each drawing by tapping the check mark on the layer. This includes the layer you created called Background and the Background color layer that is always present when you create a new document. After turning off these layers, you should see the gray background of Procreate's interface.

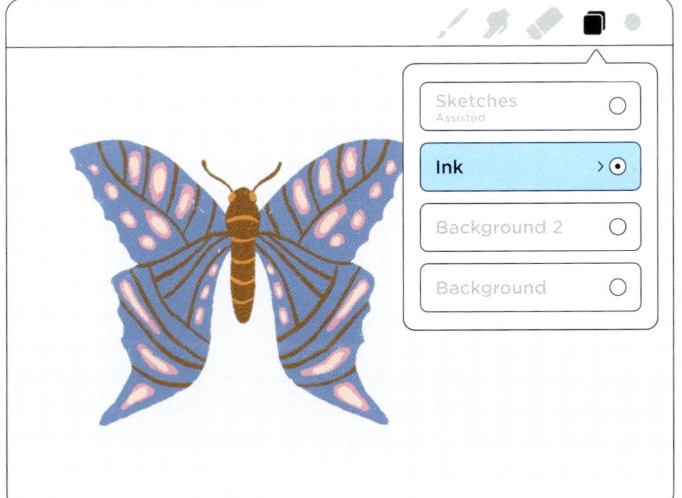

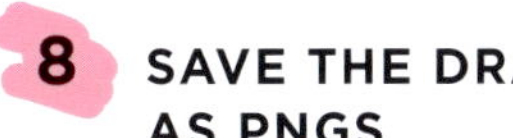

8 SAVE THE DRAWINGS AS PNGS

Go to the **Actions Menu**, tap **Share**, and save as a **PNG** file. A **PNG** is a file type that allows you to save transparent backgrounds, whereas other file types like **JPEG** do not allow transparent areas.

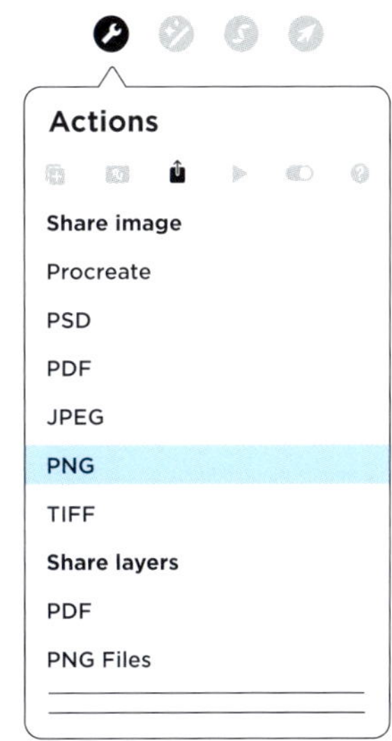

9 CREATE YOUR BASE CANVAS

Create a new canvas at the size you want for your finished image (8 x 10in [20 x 25cm] is a common art print size) and tap **Add**, **Insert a Photo**. Add all four **PNG** files using this method and use the **Move Tool** to resize and move them into the location you prefer. Try out different compositions, stacking them or putting them beside each other. You could make an image invisible to leave more room on the canvas for the remaining insects if you wish.

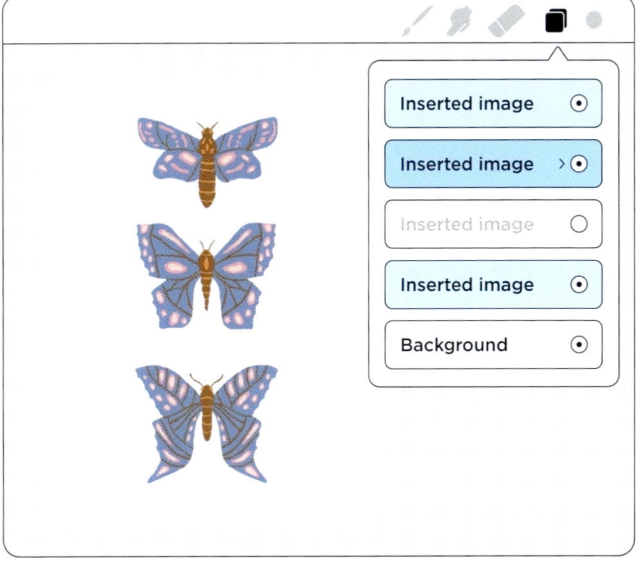

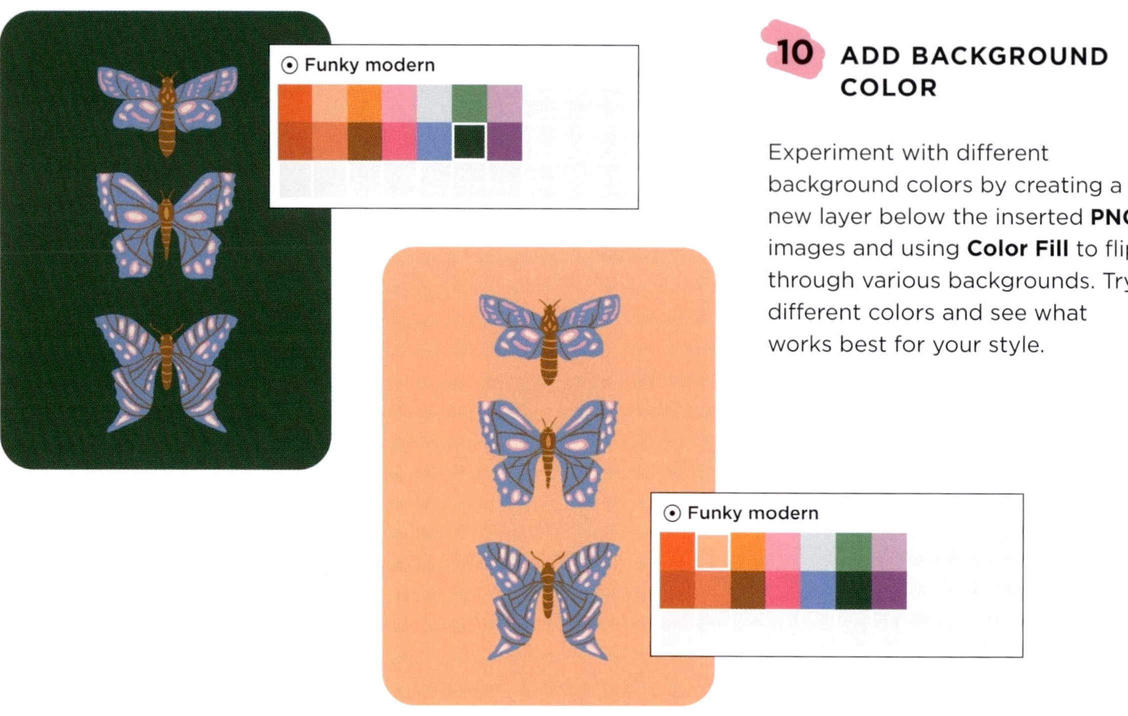

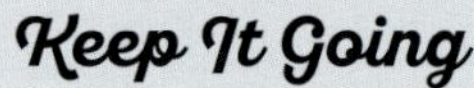

10 ADD BACKGROUND COLOR

Experiment with different background colors by creating a new layer below the inserted **PNG** images and using **Color Fill** to flip through various backgrounds. Try different colors and see what works best for your style.

Keep It Going

Why not offer your insect illustrations as stickers, phone wallpapers, or art prints for download or sale in a range of color versions? You can put your moths onto any canvas size so you can distribute and share them in a variety of ways.

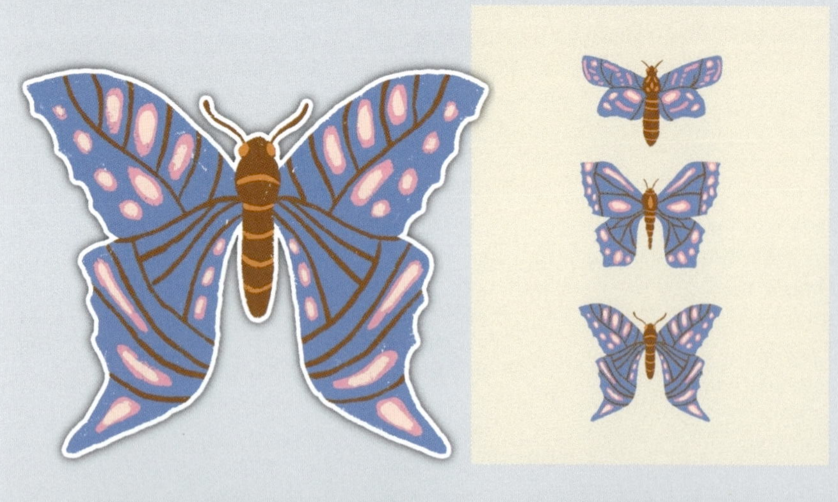

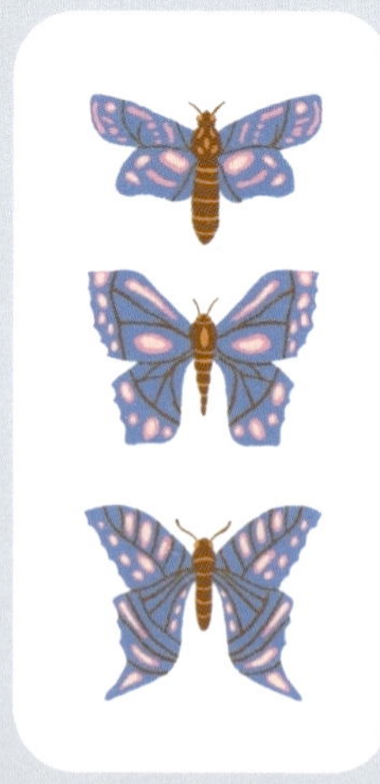

Stickers, upload to any site that sells printable stickers

8 x 10in (20 x 25cm), a standard art print size

1080 x 1090px = phone wallpaper

The End Result

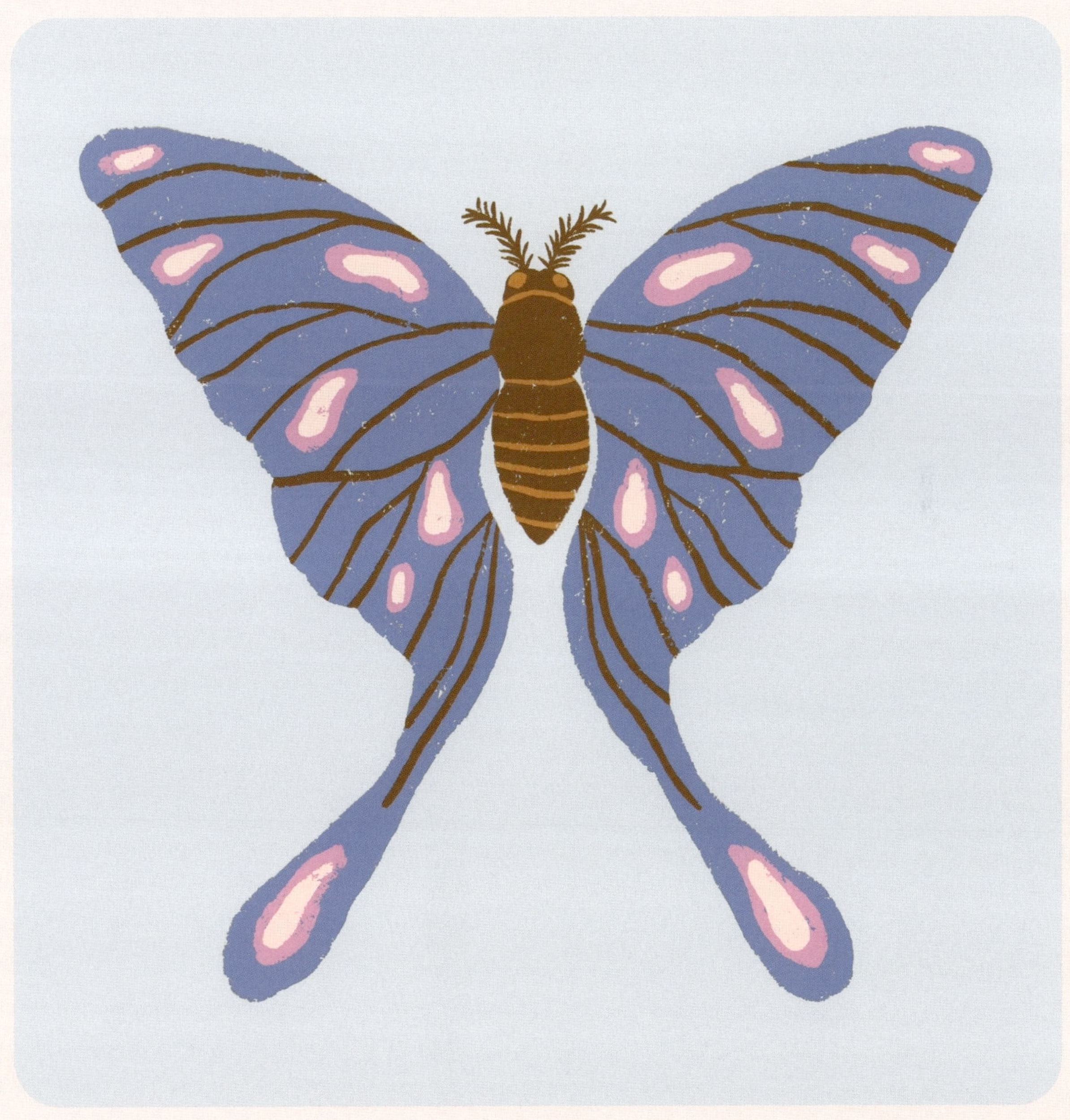

13

BUILD A LAYERED *Landscape*

Explore the process of illustrating a landscape using layering to build up depth on the canvas. This illustration is presented inside a circular shape, to give the viewer the feeling of peering through a telescope at an interesting view.

What We're Learning:
Creating depth through layering

Brushes:

Sketching Pencil

Fluid Ink

Tree Stamp

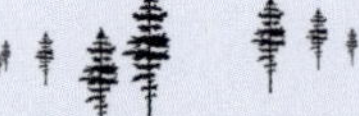

Palette:
Funky Modern

Reddish Orange #ff4b18

Red Fox #d34925

Rose Bud #ffb09b

Dark Peach #d1725f

Mango Orange #df8000

Ginger Brown #9f5d00

Pink Pearl #ff9ce2

Neon Fuschia #ff54c2

Lake Mist Blue #d7dce7

Steel Blue #7297c9

Aqua Forest Green #6b9b78

Pine Green #3a5a44

Pale Violet #eda7fc

Amethyst Purple #ac4cc1

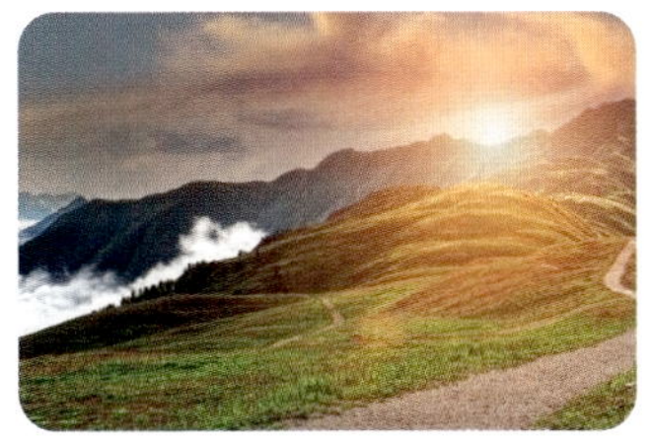
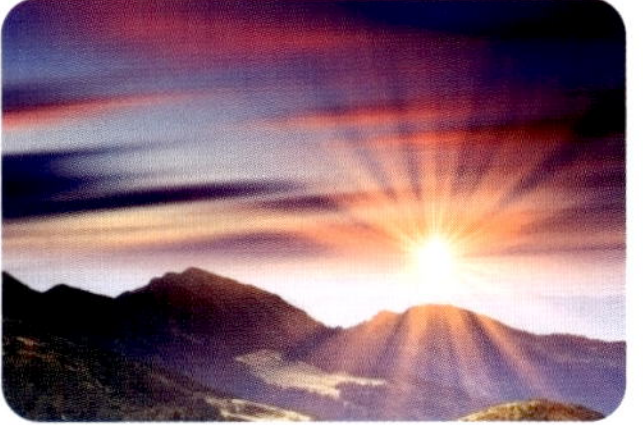
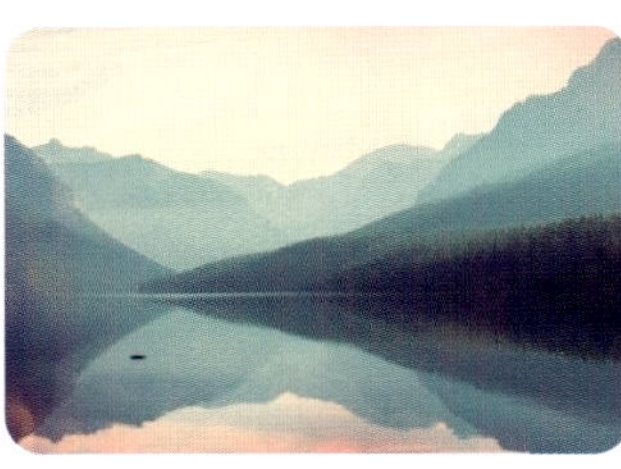
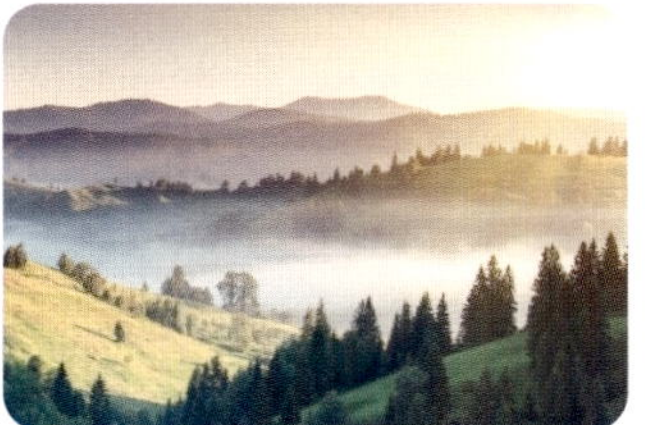

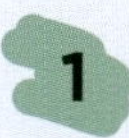

FINDING INSPIRATION

Look for ideas for your landscape illustration by searching for a location you'd like to depict + landscape (for example "montana + landscape"). Save a variety of images displaying the landscape features from that area so you have a lot of inspiration to draw from.

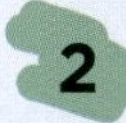

DRAW THE CIRCLE

The landscape illustration will be framed inside a circle, so start by drawing a large circle on the canvas, and then use **Quickshape**, plus one finger down on the canvas, to make a perfect circle. Remember that you can use the **Drawing Guide** to position the circle perfectly in the center of the canvas.

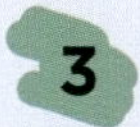

ADD FEATURES TO YOUR COMPOSITION

Sketch the various elements of your landscape, which might include mountains, rolling hills, rocks, trees, and a sun or moon in the sky. Keep in mind that each element you include will add to the overall depth of your composition, so play around with adding features to increase the depth of your drawing.

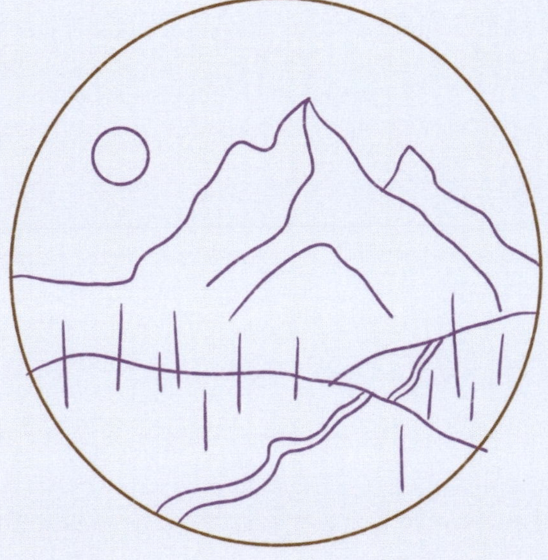

4 REFINE YOUR CIRCLE

Now let's create the circular frame that will mask out the borders of your landscape, and create an interesting shape that draws the viewer in. Black is the ideal color for creating your border, since the high contrast between black and white will make it easy to see if you have created a perfect circle. Draw the circle using the Fluid Ink brush, then use **Quickshape** to make the circle perfect. Use the **Drawing Guides** to make sure it's in the center of the canvas.

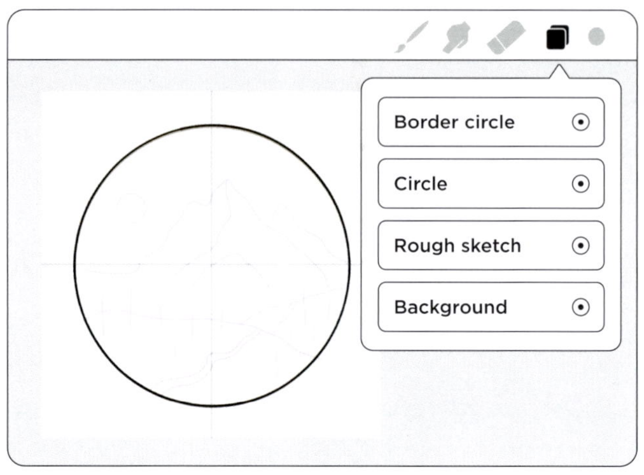

Tip **Some artists ink everything in black, then change the colors at the very end of their process. This is because black on white is the best contrast for spotting errors or inconsistencies in your inking. Give this a try on your next drawing to see if it makes it easier for you to spot errors.**

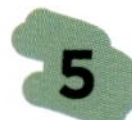

COLOR THE OUTER EDGES

Use **Color Drop** to fill the area outside the circular frame with black, and then change the black to a lighter color or white. Now anything you draw under this layer will be hidden behind the circular frame.

INK YOUR DRAWING

Start the inking process, working from back to front, top to bottom. Each layer you draw adds a level of depth to the composition. Adding small details, like the shadows on the mountains, can also give the composition an added level of interest.

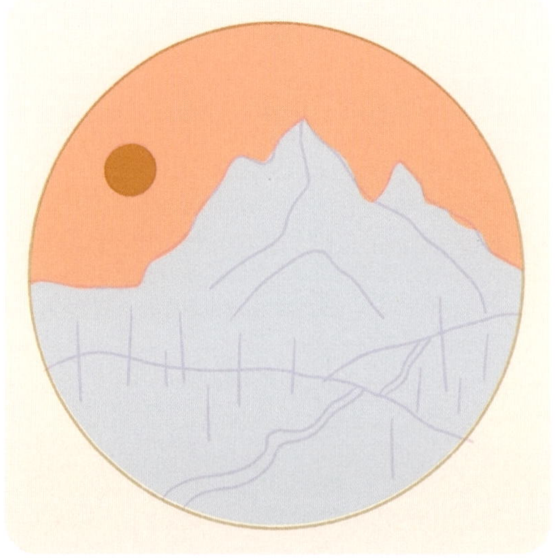

7 USE COLOR TO INDICATE DEPTH

When looking at a landscape, you'll notice that colors of features that are farther away tend to be lighter than those in the foreground. In this composition, the hills at the front are a darker green than the ones behind them, which helps to create a sense of depth. Follow this rule for your illustration if you are depicting multiple levels of mountains—or any other type of feature.

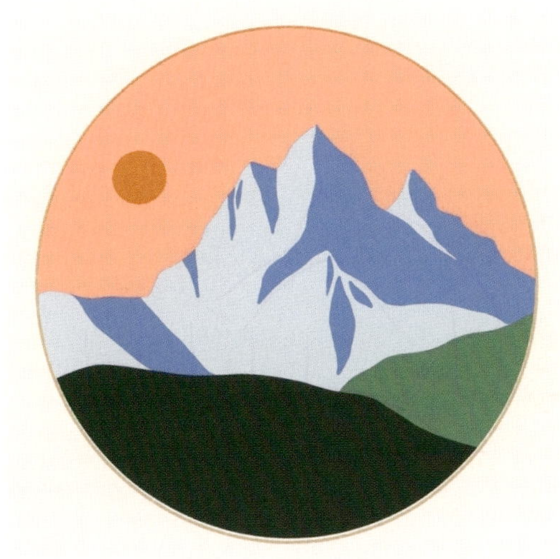

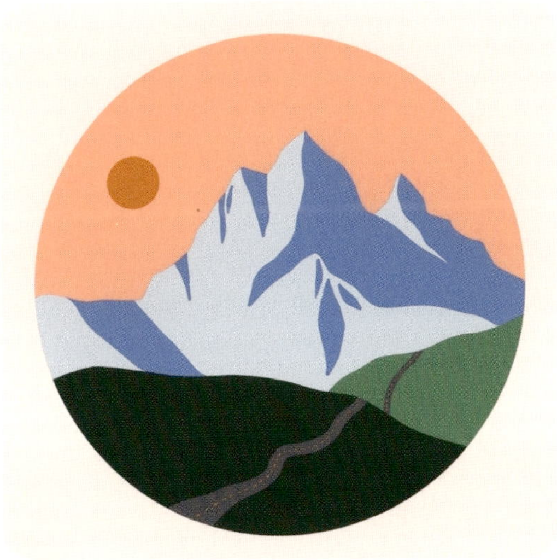

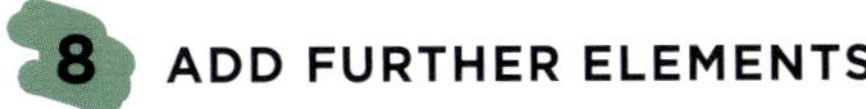

8 ADD FURTHER ELEMENTS

Next, add some features that will draw the viewer's gaze into the composition, like a path or road that winds through the landscape, or even a vehicle or cabin to show the scale of the mountains. If you want to add a road, to keep it within the bounds of the hills, you can tap on the Hill layer, tap **Select** (making sure **Color Fill** is off), then create a new layer for the road with the hill selection still active.

9 ADD TREES

Finish by adding some trees that are native to the area you are depicting. You can do this either by drawing each tree by hand or by using the stamp-making process described in the Star Print project (see page 58). If you choose the stamp option you can follow the steps in that lesson exactly, but rather than stars you can create stamps featuring trees. Then stamp those around the canvas in varying sizes to show the depth and distance in your landscape.

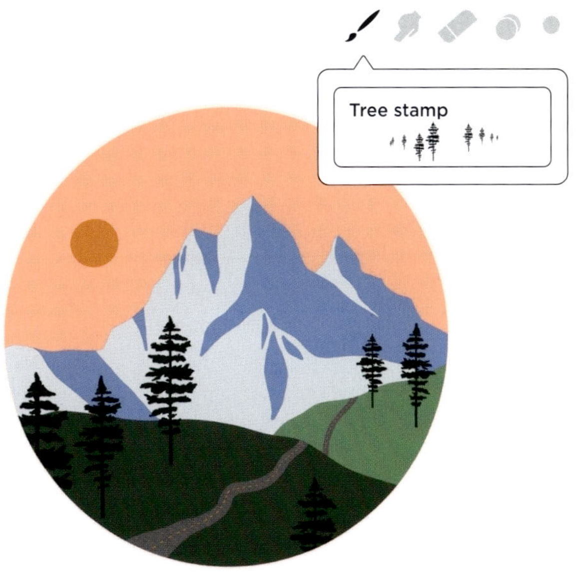

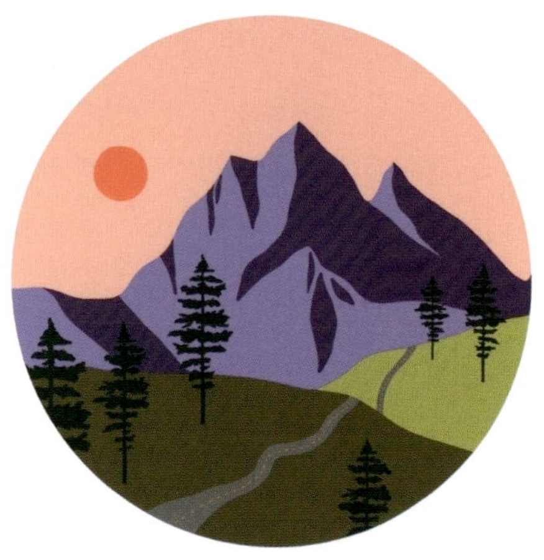

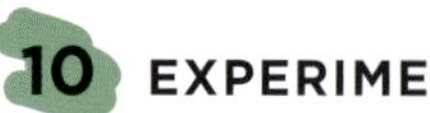

10 EXPERIMENT WITH COLOR

Finish off by trying a variety of color versions, changing the color of the border. You could also try changing your landscape color scheme from day to night or vice versa.

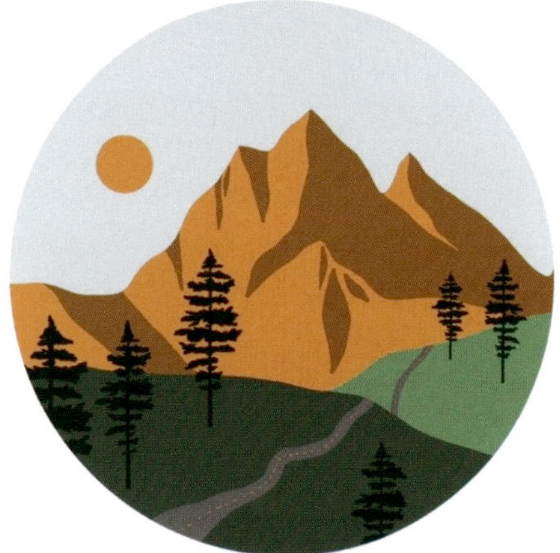

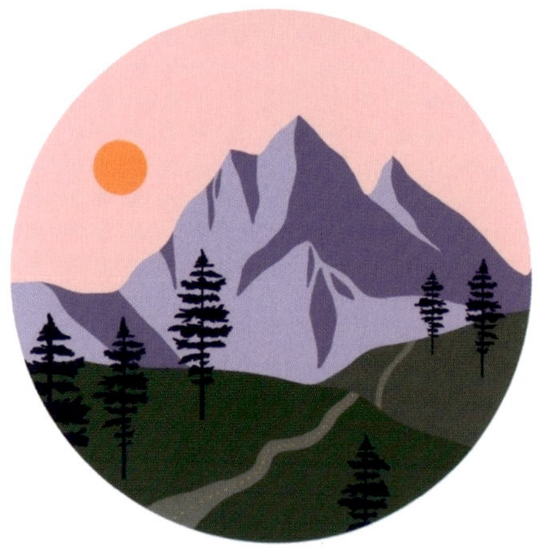

Keep It Going

If you enjoy drawing landscapes, this is a great time to consider a location-specific series. What if you drew a scene from every national park, or a scene from every state or province in your country? In this example, I drew an Arizona desert landscape because after taking a trip to Arizona I feel forever connected to the desert. Anyone who loves Arizona would feel connected to this scene, so they would be a potential buyer for an art print, sticker, or shirt featuring this design.

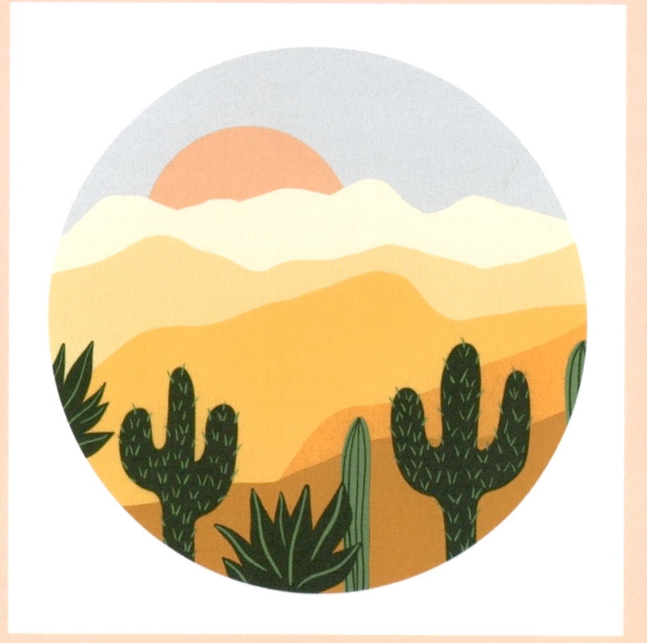

The End Result

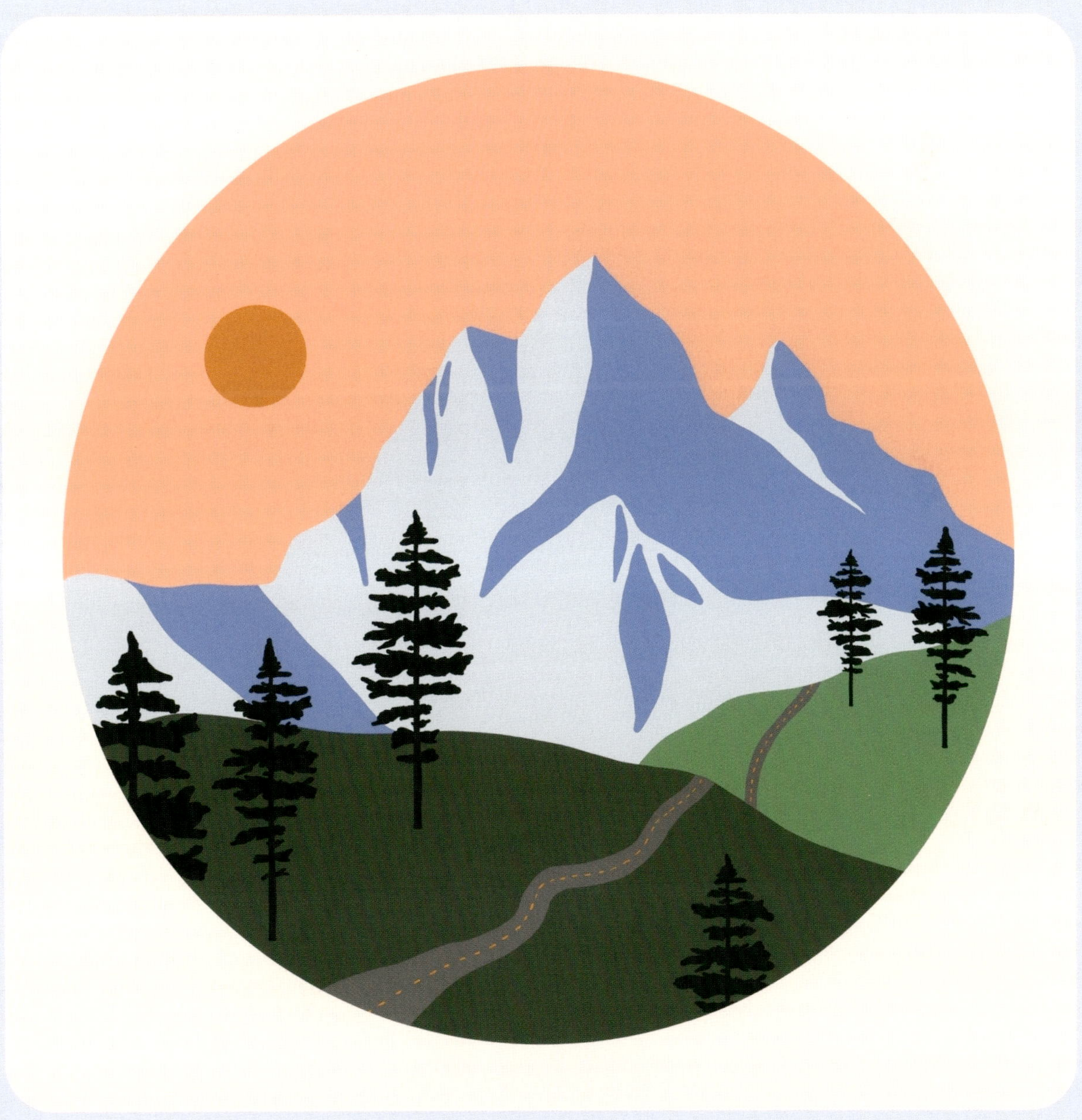

14

PAINT A Cityscape

Watercolor-effect brushes can be combined with layering and erasing to produce a realistic watercolor look in Procreate. Real watercolor paints can be expensive, so this technique is perfect for anyone who wants to create artwork in this style without the need for lots of equipment.

What We're Learning:
Layering and erasing to create texture.

Brushes:

Sketching Pencil

Rough Cold Pressed Watercolor Paper

Fluid Ink

Large Wash Watercolor

Water Spread Eraser

Palette:
Muted Retro

Tomato Red #ff3100

Red Wine #981200

Cornflower Blue #597ce9

Blue Jay Blue #283c77

Glacier Blue #e0e4ea

Mountain Mist Blue #8799ad

Buttermilk Yellow #efb233

Oak Brown #916800

Dark Pastel Purple #917dbd

Plum Purple #493a62

Avocado Green #b1a450

Pickled Bean Green #595221

Flamingo Pink #f8abab

Valentine Red #e9605c

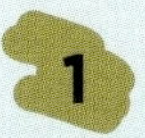

FIND YOUR INSPIRATION

Find a location somewhere in the world that has row houses. Good examples are London, New York, Boston, Amsterdam, Dublin, San Francisco, Paris, or Glasgow. Choose one of those well-known cities or a more "niche" location that you love. Gathering inspiration from the architectural features found in your chosen city, create a rough sketch of three to four row houses within a loose, hand-drawn square shape. Then create a refined sketch using **Quickline** to straighten the lines for the windows and doors.

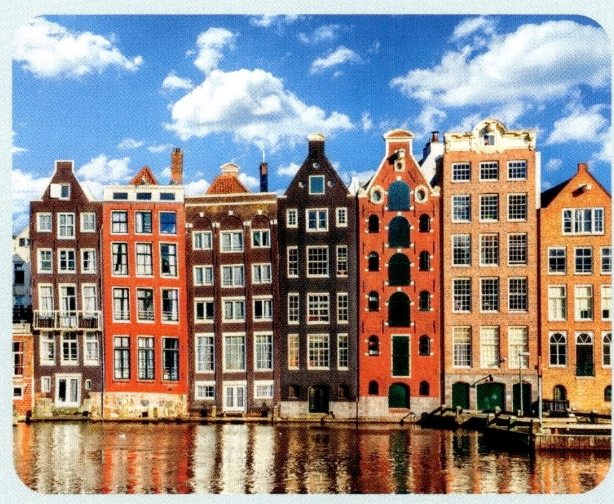

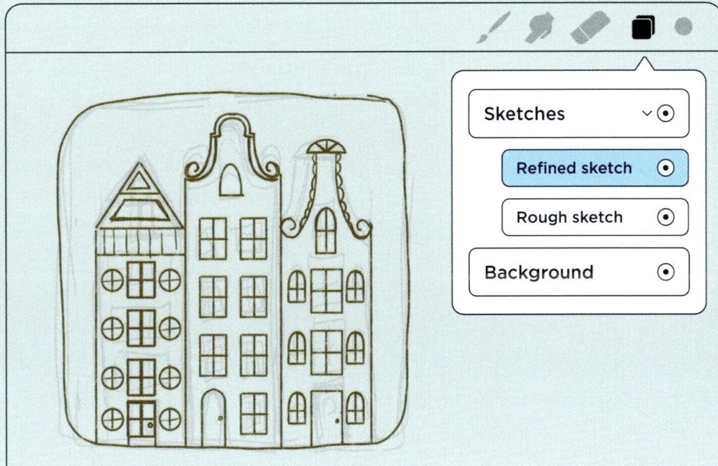

Tip In Procreate, there is no need to redraw the same object (like the windows) over and over. You only need to draw one of each window on a separate layer, then duplicate it multiple times and put it in place. Start with a large **Layers Panel** of unnamed layers featuring various parts of the architecture, then merge them all onto one neat layer at the end.

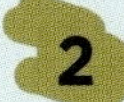

ADD TEXTURE TO YOUR CANVAS

Create a new layer beneath your sketch layers and select a light gray. Select the Rough Cold Pressed Watercolor Paper from the **Brush Sampler**. Swipe the texture all over your canvas without picking up your brush. If you want to change the scale of the brush, you can tap on the brush, then tap **Grain** and reduce or increase the scale. The darker the gray you use, the more intense your paper will look. If it's "too intense," you can use the **Opacity Slider** on that layer to tone it down.

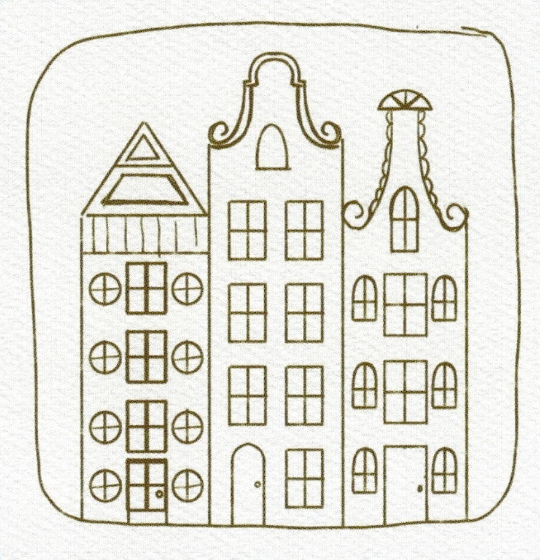

3 CREATE A MASK

Next, you're going to create a "mask" for the areas of the sketch that will be filled with watercolor, using the sketch as a guide. With real watercolors, you mask areas that you want to remain white; with digital watercolors, it's the opposite! Use the Fluid Ink brush to mask out the areas you want to contain watercolor. Try leaving a little bit of white space between the colors to give a real watercolor masked-out feel.

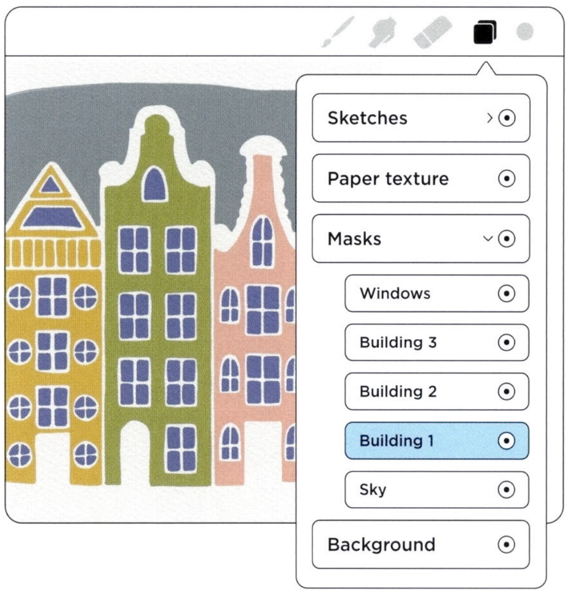

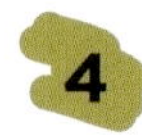

4 SELECT A MASKING LAYER

First, make all your masking layers invisible, then tap on one of them in the **Layers Panel** and tap **Select** on the flyout menu. Make sure that **Color Fill** is off. Once your masked layer is selected, you can tap on the **Layers Panel** and tap the **+** symbol to create a new layer. At this point, you should see all areas except the inked portion from your mask covered in gray slashed lines.

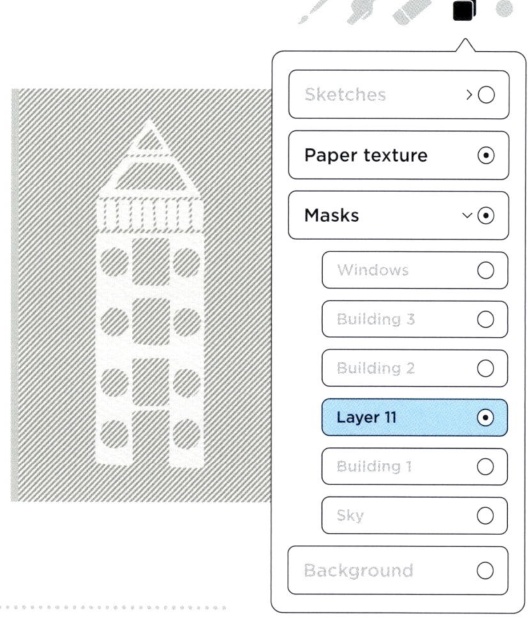

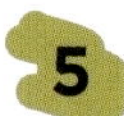

5 ADD WATERCOLOR

Create a new layer and add some watercolor to it using the color of your choice and the Large Wash Watercolor brush. Add just one layer of watercolor as layering this brush over itself will dull the watercolor texture. You can intensify and deepen the shade of the color later, for now just focus on selecting and filling your masked areas with watercolor. Once you finish the first mask, move on to the others so that all of the masked areas are filled.

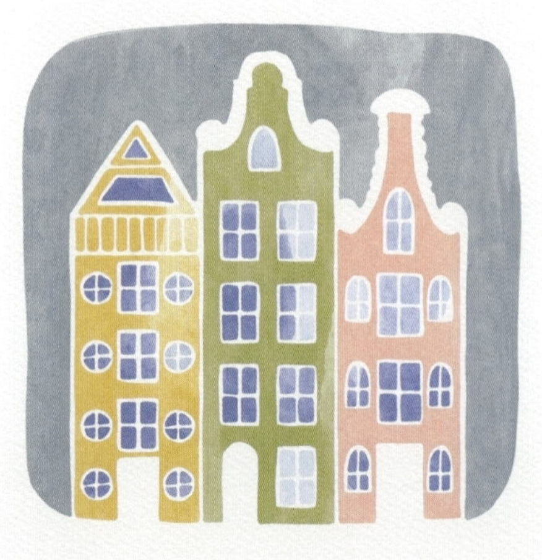

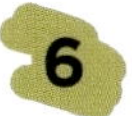

6 DUPLICATE SOME OF THE WATERCOLOR LAYERS

Once all your masked areas are filled with watercolor, try duplicating some of the layers to see how their intensity changes. You may want to duplicate some and leave others as a single layer. Once you duplicate a layer a few times, merge it with its duplicates so you end up with one layer for each color.

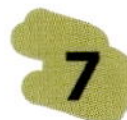

7 ERASE SOME AREAS OF WATERCOLOR

Select the **Eraser Tool** in the **Tool Menu** and choose the **Water Spread Eraser** as your brush. Carefully start erasing areas of your layers to reveal more paper and create that real watercolor look. The amount you erase is a personal choice, so this is a good time to try different levels of erasure to see what you prefer. On the left, small areas were erased all over the composition. On the right, big chunks were erased out of each shape.

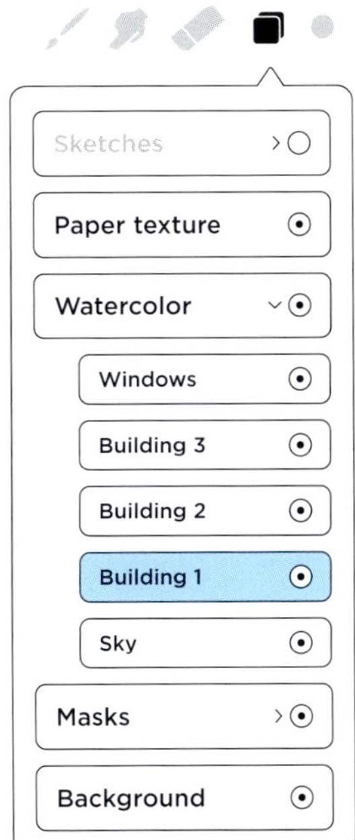

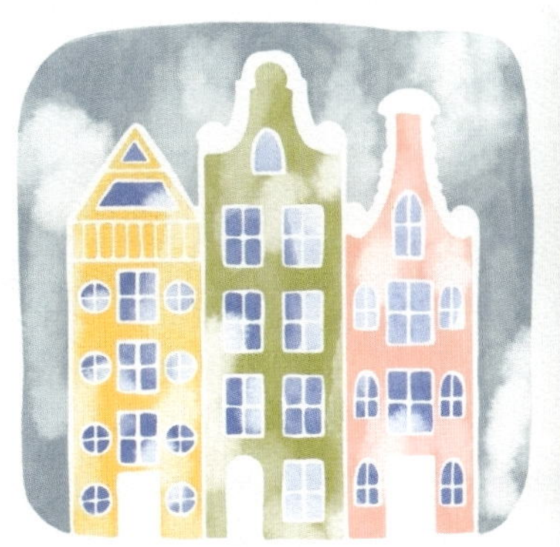

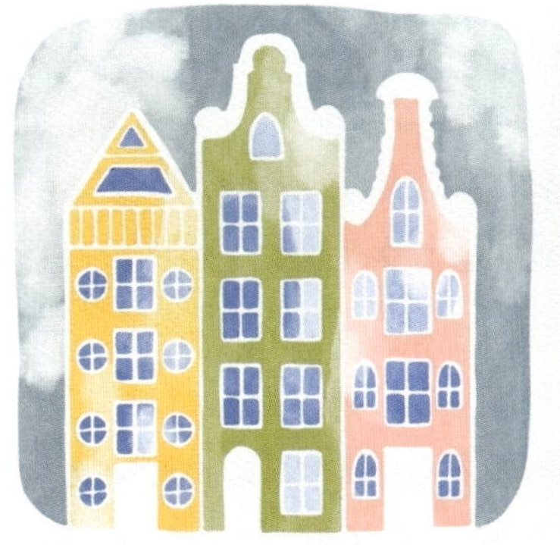

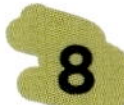

8 USE A BLEND MODE

To take the watercolor effect even further, set your layers to a **Blend Mode**. **Multiply** works well for watercolor, but try everything to see what happens. You'll notice that both the color and the way that the paper filters through the color will change. Some **Blend Modes** will emphasize the paper, whereas others will make it more subtle. Choose a level that you like or skip using **Blend Modes** altogether if you prefer your original.

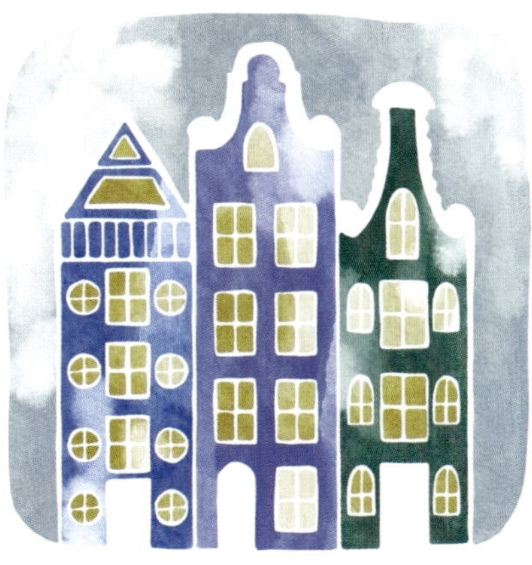

9 ADJUST HUE, SATURATION, AND BRIGHTNESS

To change the shade or intensity of a watercolor layer, select the layer in the **Layers Panel**, tap **Adjustments**, then tap **Hue**, **Saturation**, **Brightness**, and adjust the sliders to play around with those values for each color. Here, the pink was changed to a dark purple by adjusting the **Hue** and **Brightness**.

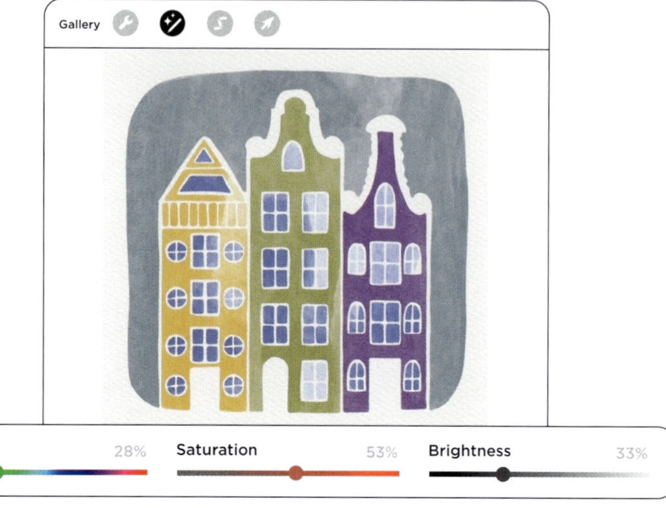

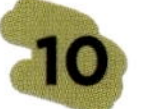

10 FINISHING TOUCHES

Why not create some new layers and add subtle color differences, like a hint of red or blue in certain areas to give that multicolored, watercolor effect? Try putting down a blob of color, then use the **Water Spread Eraser** to remove the harsh edges around the shape, so it looks like the new color is spreading into the original one. This is also a great time to add details like the decoration on the roofs or the wooden doors.

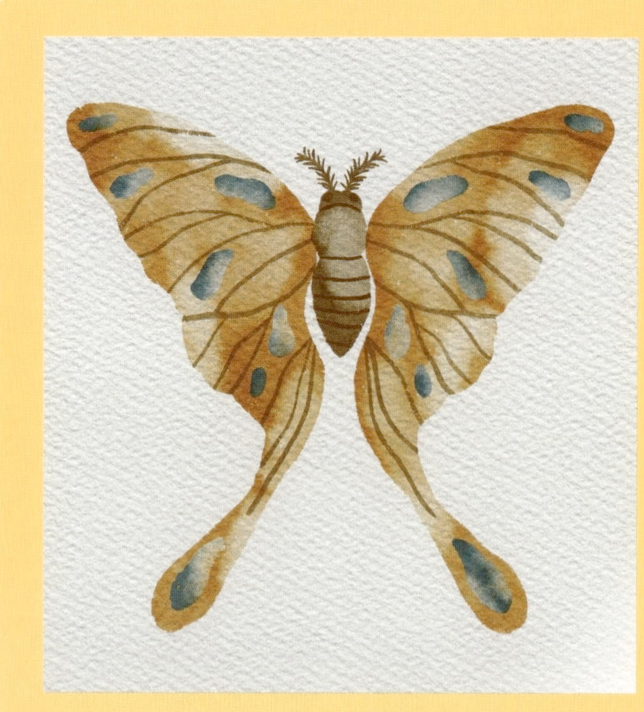

Keep It Going

Now that you understand how the watercolor process works, why not go back to one of the artworks you have already created (and perhaps didn't like) and turn it into a watercolor? Sometimes your original sketch is great, but the final treatment isn't quite right, so go back into your **Gallery** and try this style on some old artworks.

In this moth illustration, I used the existing inking layers as "masking layers" to create this watercolor composition. It was originally inked with the Rough Inking brush (rather than the Fluid Ink), so it has a slightly rougher feel than the row houses.

The End Result

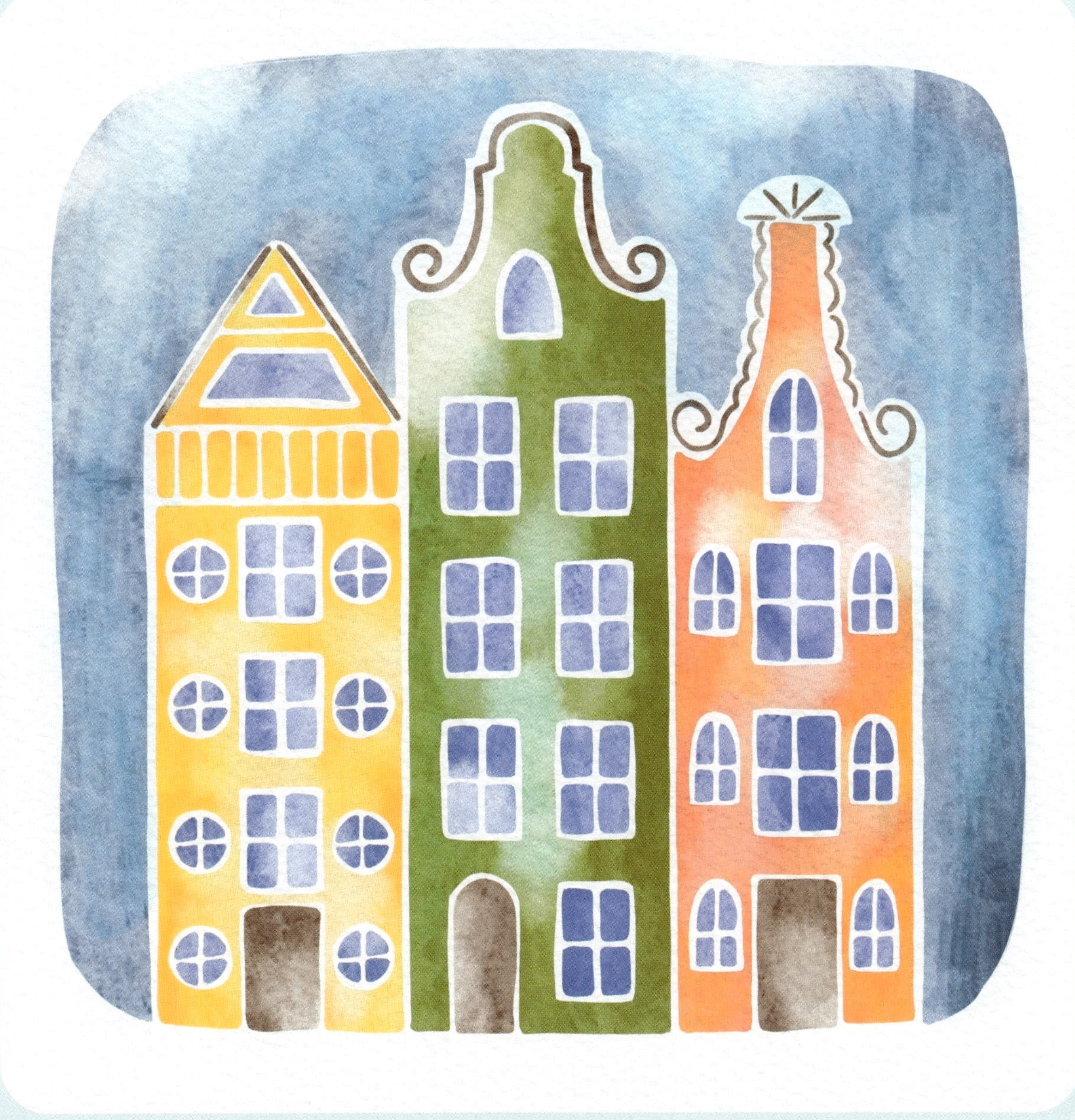

15

DRAW Your Avatar

In this project, you'll be drawing a self-portrait that you can customize to represent your personal style through color, accessories, and clothing. We'll practice using the Freehand Selection Tool, so that rather than erasing and redrawing things, you can move them around as needed.

What We're Learning:
Using **Freehand Selection Tools**

Brushes:

Sketching Pencil

Fluid Ink

Palette:
Poolside Paradise

Robin Egg Blue #98f2f4
Faded Jade #347373
Cherry Blossom #ffb9bd
Watermelon Pink #ff6472
Seafoam Green #77f0b5
Eucalyptus #3d845f
Pale Green #9cf08c
Astroturf Green #395f36
Butterscotch Orange #ffad56
Pumpkin Skin #ad5a00
Dawn Pink #ffebe2
Coral Pink #f4947c
Lavender Ice Cream #eea8f2
Dark Lilac #a465aa

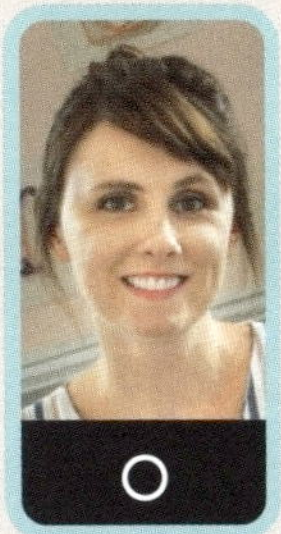

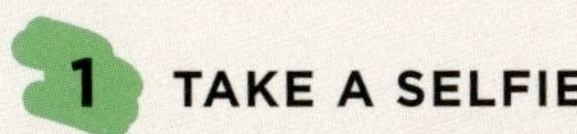

1 TAKE A SELFIE

Take a picture of yourself looking straight at the camera in bright light (ideally daylight). You'll be using the **Symmetry Tool** to draw both sides of the face, so looking directly at the camera, and not tilting your head, is important. Try different expressions and perhaps change your glasses, hair, or outfit to give the composition your personal flare.

2 SET UP YOUR CANVAS

Create a new layer and name it "Sketch," then turn on **Vertical Symmetry** by going to **Canvas**. Then turn on the **Drawing Guide**, tap **Edit Drawing Guide**, tap **Symmetry**, and under options, choose **Vertical**.

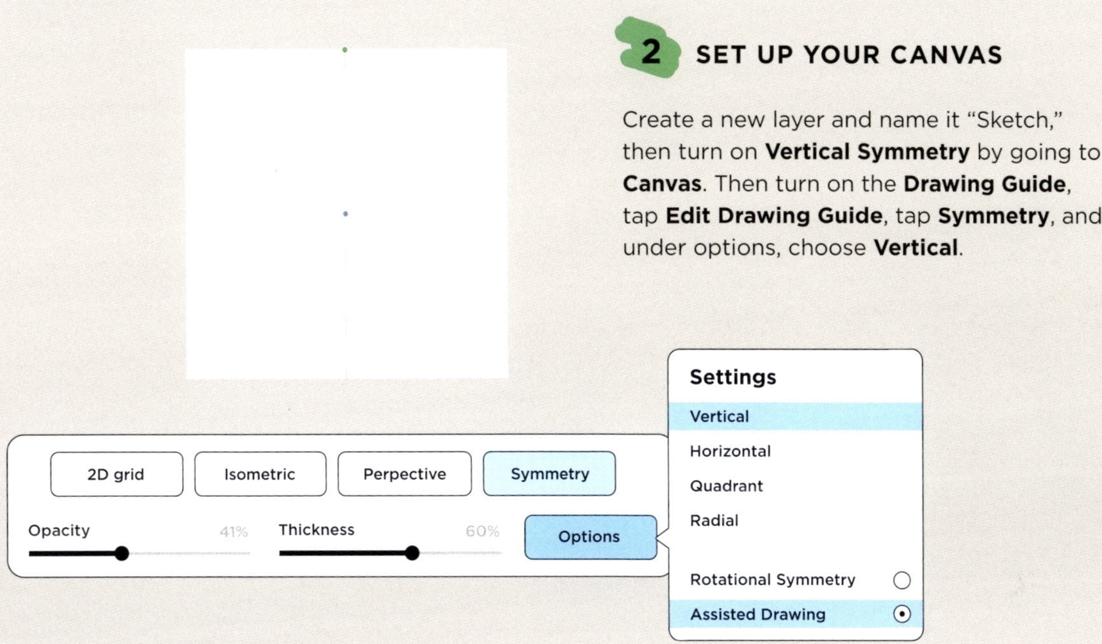

3 PLACE YOUR PHOTOGRAPH ON THE CANVAS

Create a new layer for your reference photo, then place it on the canvas by tapping **Actions**, **Add**, **Insert a Photo**. Resize your photo to fit the page, then tap the **N** symbol and reduce the opacity using the **Opacity Slider**. Adjust your photograph to make sure your nose and lips are centered along the horizontal line in the middle of the canvas. If your photo isn't symmetrical, just draw on one side of your face in the next step so that the features will look the same on both sides.

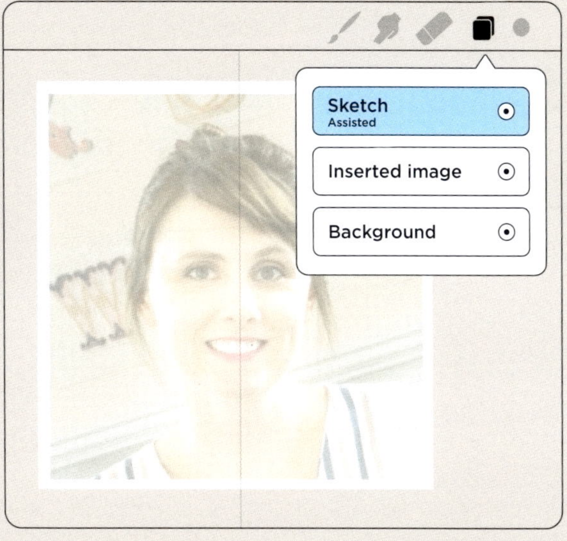

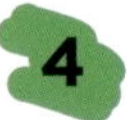

TRACE YOUR PHOTOGRAPH

Trace the main features of your photograph, focusing on subtle gestures and ignoring tiny wrinkles. Remember that avatars are typically simplified versions of the subject, so there's no need to draw in small details like the tiny creases beside your eyes or the pores on your cheeks.

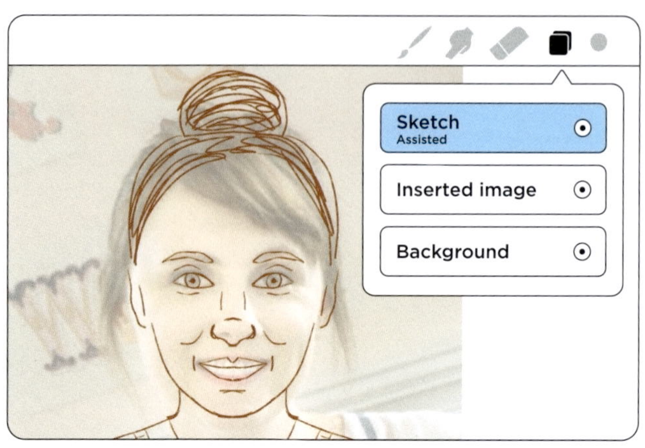

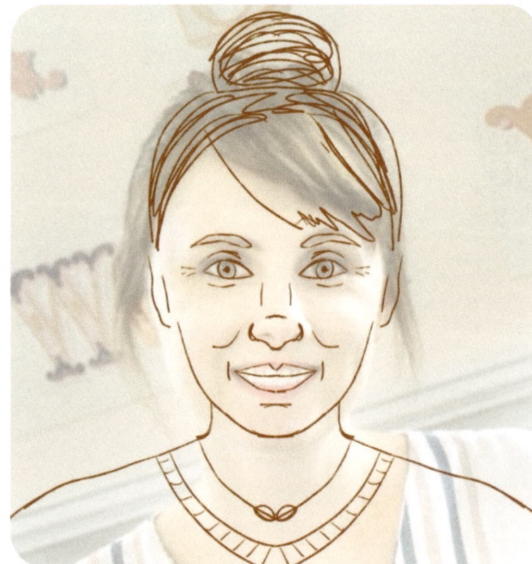

5 ADD NONSYMMETRICAL DETAILS

Turn off **Symmetry** at this point, so that you can add in some details that are nonsymmetrical. In this case, my bangs are on one side of my face, so symmetry isn't needed to sketch those in.

ADD MORE DETAILS

You could also take some time to sketch in some other elements like accessories or headwear, glasses or jewelry perhaps. Take this opportunity to create an avatar that reflects your personality.

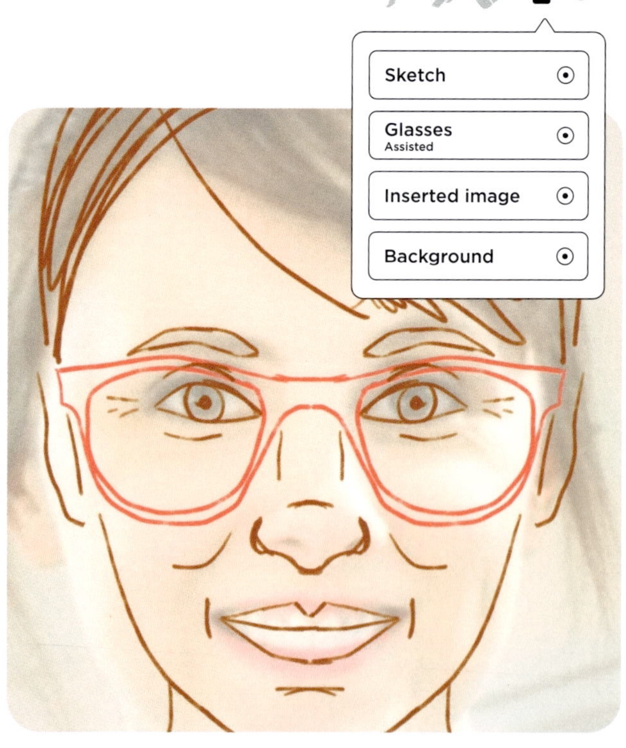

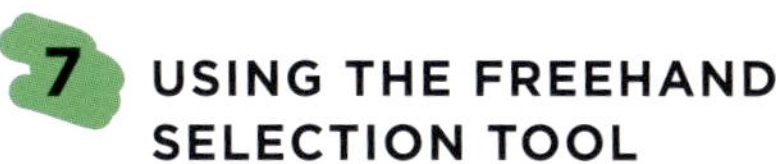

7 USING THE FREEHAND SELECTION TOOL

Now use the **Freehand Selection Tool** to make some subtle tweaks to your drawing. First, turn off your photograph layer so that all you can see is your sketch, then tap on the **Selection Tool** and tap **Freehand** on the bottom menu. Use your stylus to circle something in your drawing (like the line on the top of your chin for example) then tap the **Move Tool** so you can move it up and down slightly.

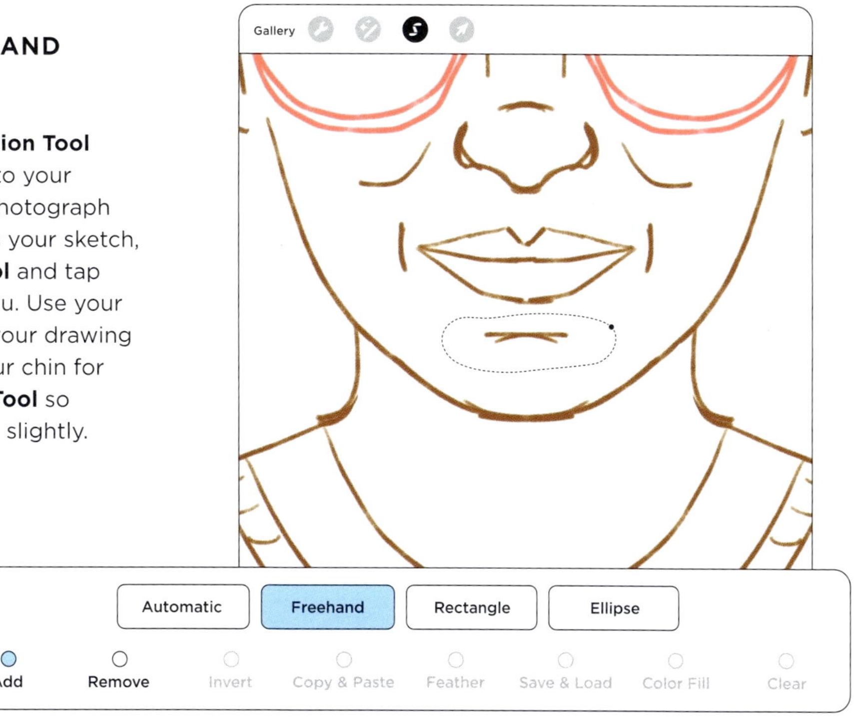

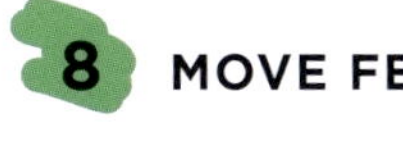

8 MOVE FEATURES AROUND

Turn off **Magnetics** and **Snapping** in the **Snapping Settings** if they are currently on, then move your "chin line" up and down to get it into the desired place. Repeat this process with any features you want to change to improve your portrait. Perhaps you'd like to raise one eyebrow, or make your nose a little lower? Subtle tweaks like this can change the personality of your drawing quite a bit.

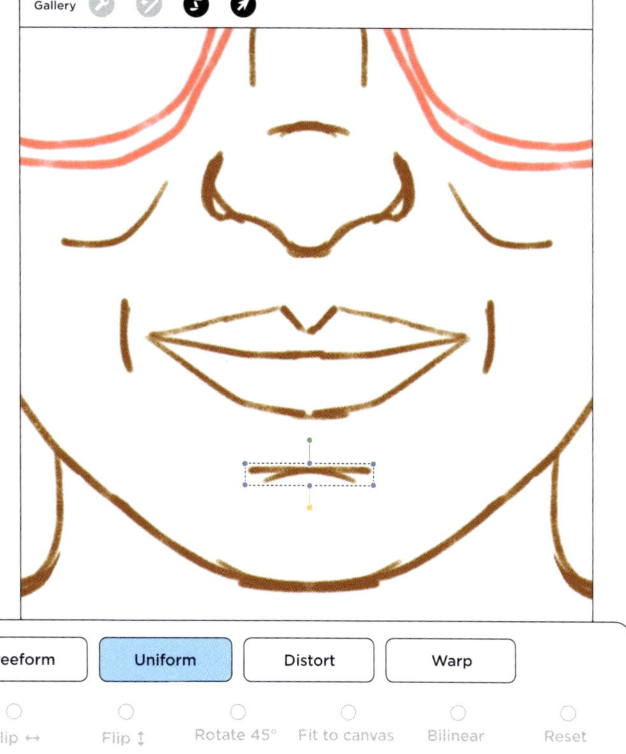

9 ADD SOME COLOR

Use the Fluid Ink brush to block in the main shapes of your avatar, making sure to put each new color on its own layer. This makes it easy to "try things on," like different colored glasses or accessories, or to leave things off all together.

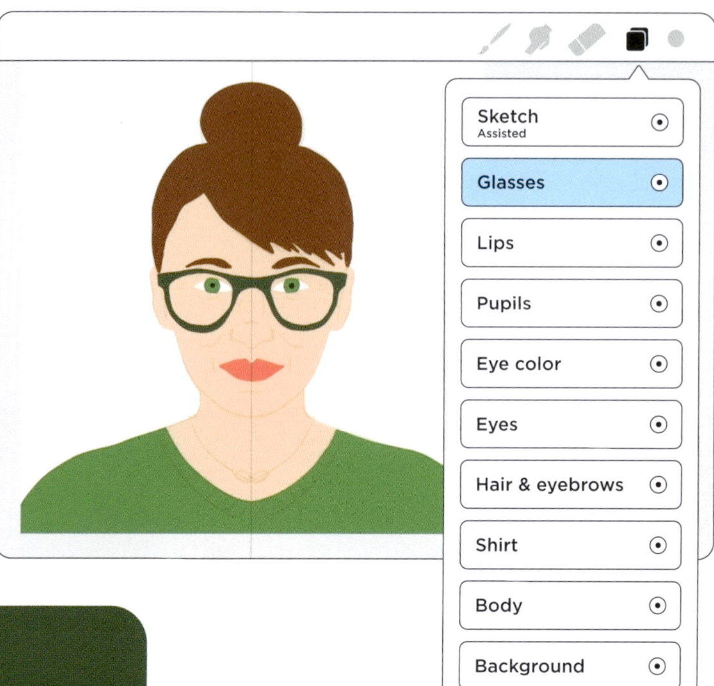

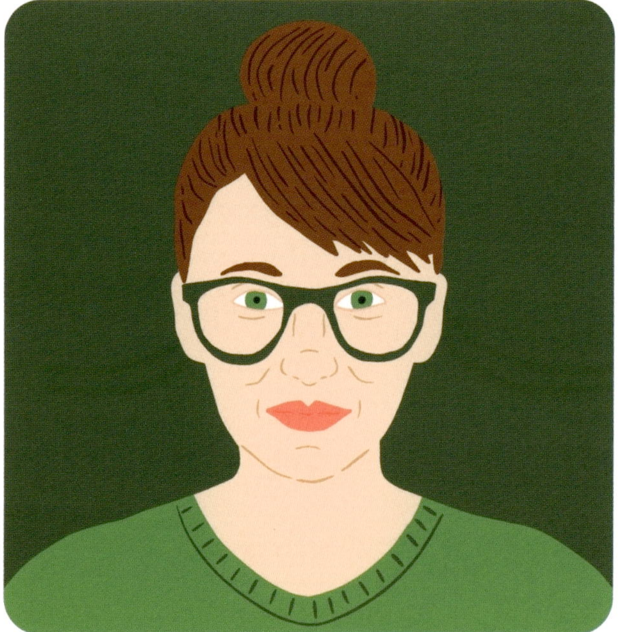

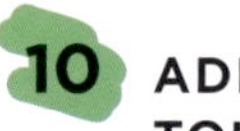

ADD THE FINISHING TOUCHES

Finally, use the same brush to add subtle details like the ribbing on the sweater or some subtle lines to show that you're smiling. Give your drawing a background color and you're done!

Keep It Going

Give yourself more personality-evoking elements like earrings, a necklace, or even a patterned wallpaper that shows your personal style. But how, you ask, do you even create a pattern? We'll be doing a tile pattern in the next project (see page 112), so read on to learn how and then come back to add it to your avatar project later.

The End Result

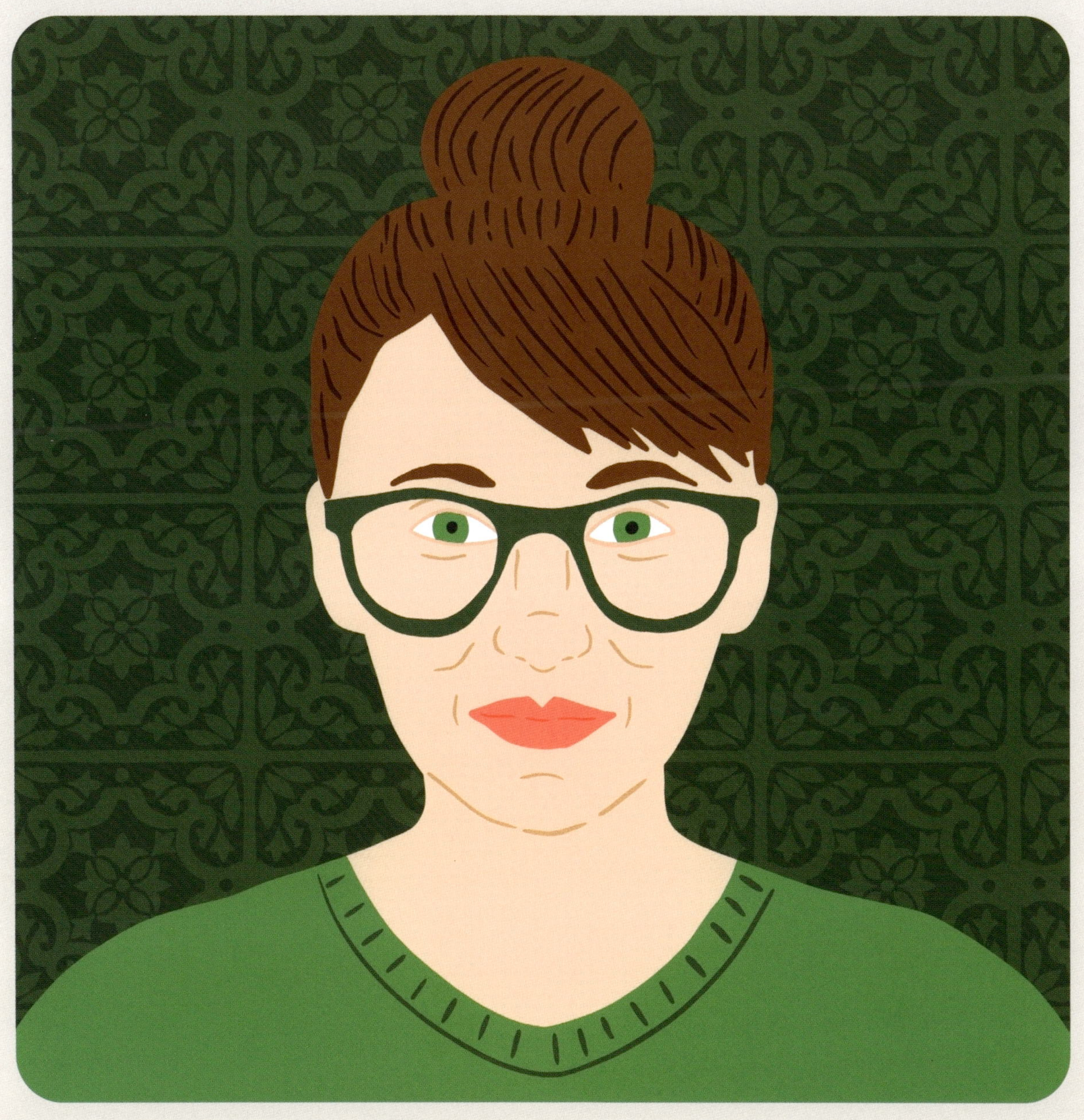

16

STEP OUT A *Flatlay*

Create an eye-catching composition by building up an illustration of patterned tiles on a floor. You'll also learn about Procreate Clipping Masks. This feature allows you to add details to various layers without worrying about Selecting, Alpha Locking, or editing your original layers.

What We're Learning:
Using **Clipping Masks**

Brushes:

Sketching Pencil

Rough Inking

Palette:
Muted Retro

Tomato Red #ff3100

Red Wine #981200

Cornflower Blue #597ce9

Blue Jay Blue #283c77

Glacier Blue #e0e4ea

Mountain Mist Blue #8799ad

Buttermilk Yellow #efb233

Oak Brown #916800

Dark Pastel Purple #917dbd

Plum Purple #493a62

Avocado Green #b1a450

Pickled Bean Green #595221

Flamingo Pink #f8abab

Valentine Red #e9605c

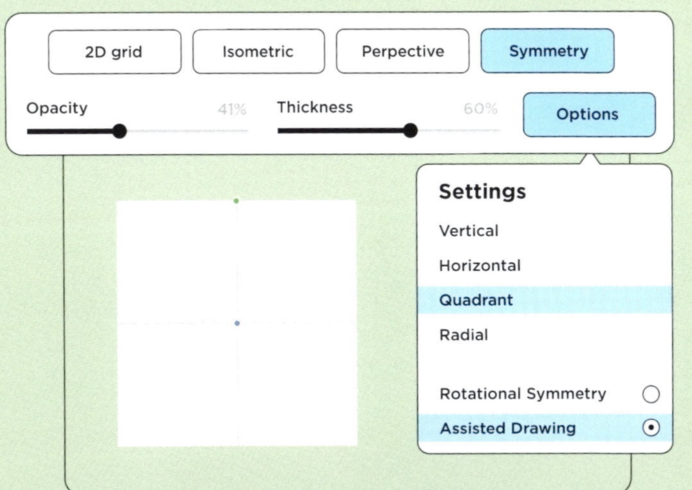

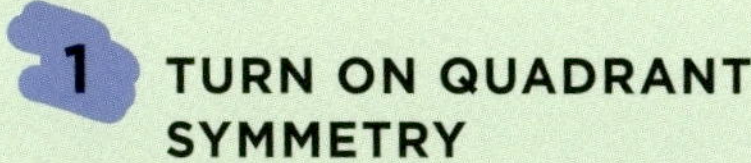

1 TURN ON QUADRANT SYMMETRY

First, find some inspiration for your tiles. You might search for something like "Morocco + tile" or "Spain + tile". Once you have some reference images, open a new canvas and turn on **Quadrant Symmetry** by going to **Actions**, **Canvas**, turn on the **Drawing Guide**, and then tap **Edit Drawing Guide**. On the bottom menu, turn on **Symmetry** and under **Options** choose **Quadrant**. Tap **Done** to save the symmetry setting.

2 DRAW YOUR TILE

Test your symmetry by drawing in the corner of the canvas. You should see the shape repeat on all four corners. Assuming that is working, draw your tile using your tile images as inspiration. The amount of space you leave on the borders of your canvas will determine the "grout" thickness, so keep that in mind as you draw your tile to edges. Your tile can be as simple or complex as you like, but you will be downsizing it significantly, so there is no need to draw in details that won't be visible at a small scale.

3 ADD A BASE COLOR

Now start inking the tile, beginning with the base color of the shape that will soon be covered in the pattern.

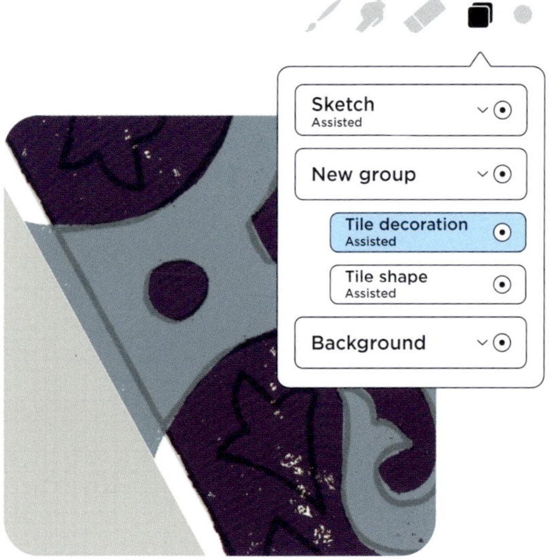

4 INKING THE TILE DESIGN

To demonstrate the **Clipping Mask** function, let's start with the elements of the tile design that go off the edge of the tile. First, ink the pattern elements that should go right to the edge of the tile. You'll notice that your inking will go right off the tile onto the white background of your canvas unless you do something to prevent it from doing so.

5 TURN ON THE CLIPPING MASK

To "clip" the pattern to the tile and prevent the new colors from going off the edge of the tile shape, turn the decoration layer into a **Clipping Mask**. To do this, tap on the Tile decoration layer and tap **Clipping Mask** on the flyout menu. The color will be clipped to whatever layer is beneath the **Clipping Mask** layer, which in this case is the tile shape.

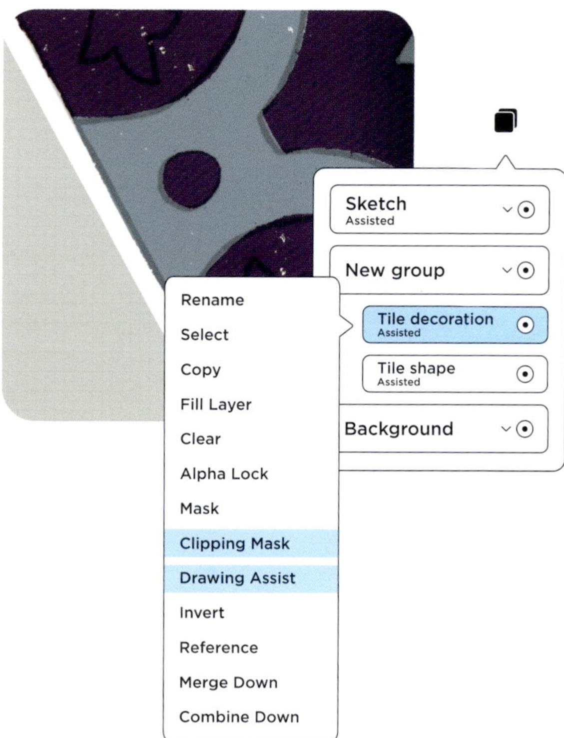

6 FINISH INKING THE TILE DESIGN

Repeat the inking process on all of your pattern shapes, using **Clipping Mask** layers for any elements that extend past the border of the tile. Then group the layers.

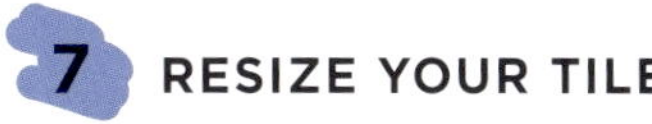

7 RESIZE YOUR TILE

Duplicate the group and resize your duplicate to the size that you would like it to be when you repeat it. Make sure to work with the duplicate so that if you change your mind about the sizing later, you can easily change it by redoing your tile. At this point, just make your tile about one fifth the size of your canvas.

Freeform | Uniform | Distort | Warp

8 DUPLICATE YOUR TILE

Make your original tile invisible (save it in case you want it later). Duplicate your smaller tile group and place the duplicate beside the first one, leaving some space for the "grout" between the tiles. Repeat this process, laying tiles down all over your canvas. If you want your tiles to be spaced by a specific amount, or if you want them to fit within a grid, you can turn on the **Drawing Guide** in the **Canvas Menu** and adjust the grid size to whatever size you'd like.

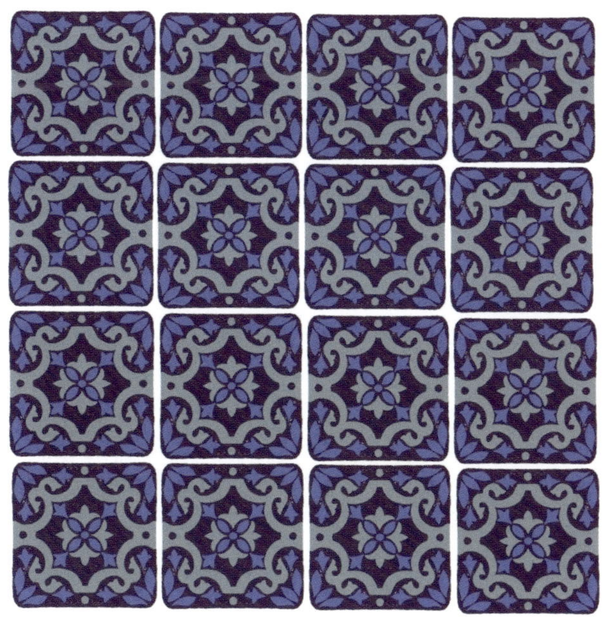

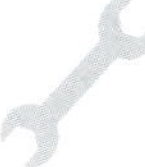

You will be racking up a sizeable layer count at this point. If you want to reduce your layer count and avoid lag in the Procreate app, you can merge some layers together. First, though, duplicate your original document to avoid losing all these layers. When you merge layers, you lose the ability to edit them separately.

9 ROTATE THE TILES

At this point, if you'd like to create a more interesting composition, you can rotate the tiles. To do this, tap the **Move Tool** and then use the **Rotate Handle** on the top of the selected groups to rotate everything. If any areas are missing tile pieces, you can continue duplicating one of the groups and putting them in place until all the spots are filled.

Freeform | Uniform | Distort | Warp

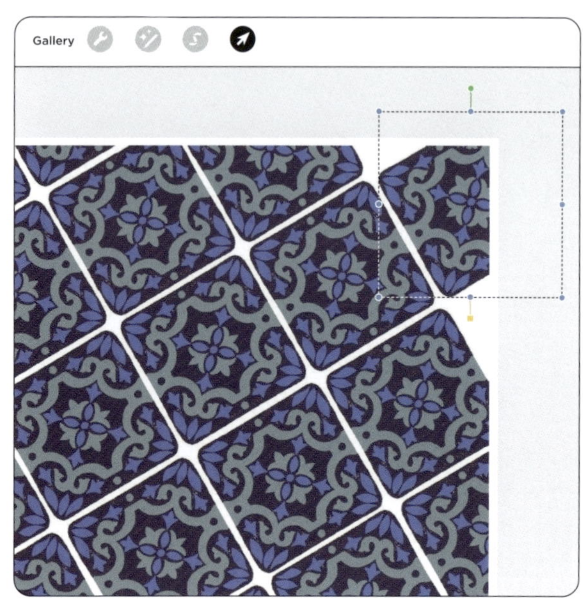

10 ADD SOME FEATURES

There is so much more you could add to this composition to give it life. Why not sketch in some feet using the same process we used in the Avatar project, or add in a plant seen from above. This could turn into a whole series about tiles from around the world or your feet in different places you visit. You might even add an open suitcase, map, or anything else to evoke the "traveling" theme in your composition.

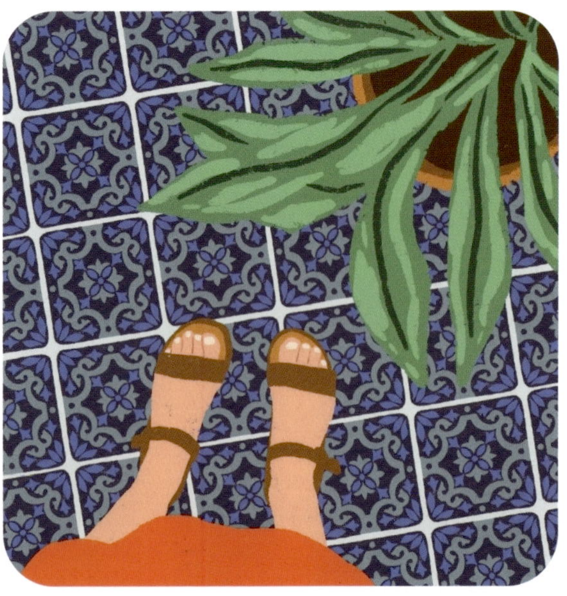

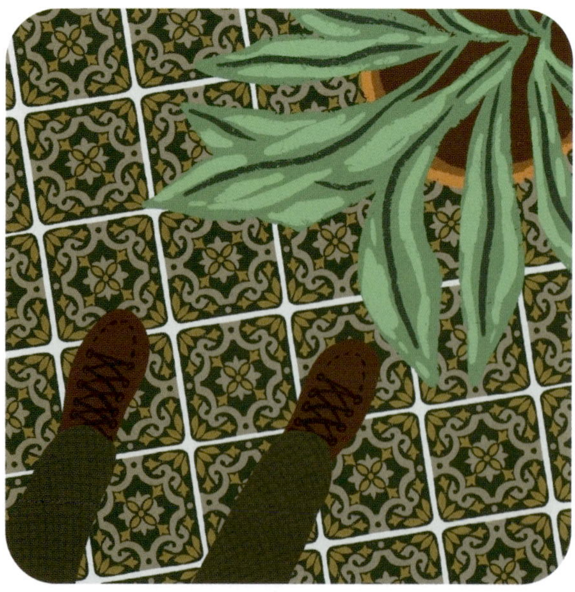

The End Result

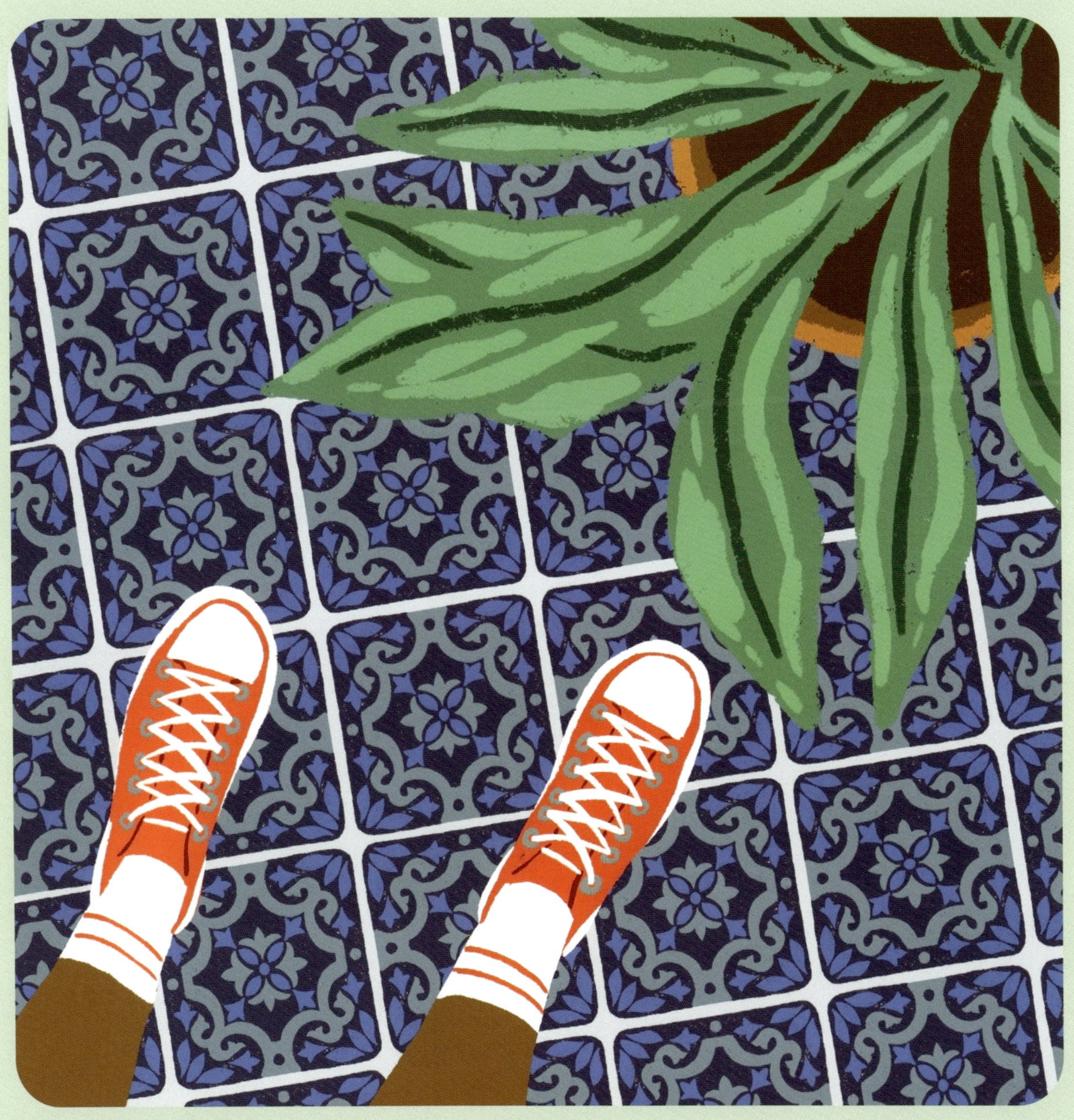

17

CREATE Jungle Textures

Discover how to make your own texture brushes. You've already used texture brushes in previous projects, like the Screen Print brushes and the Watercolor Paper brush, now it's time to make your own, 100% unique brush.

What We're Learning:
Creating texture brushes

Brushes:

Sketching Pencil

Fluid Ink

Cheetah Spots

Palette:
Funky Modern

- Reddish Orange #ff4b18
- Red Fox #d34925
- Rose Bud #ffb09b
- Dark Peach #d1725f
- Mango Orange #df8000
- Ginger Brown #9f5d00
- Pink Pearl #ff9ce2
- Neon Fuschia #ff54c2
- Lake Mist Blue #d7dce7
- Steel Blue #7297c9
- Aqua Forest Green #6b9b78
- Pine Green #3a5a44
- Pale Violet #eda7fc
- Amethyst Purple #ac4cc1

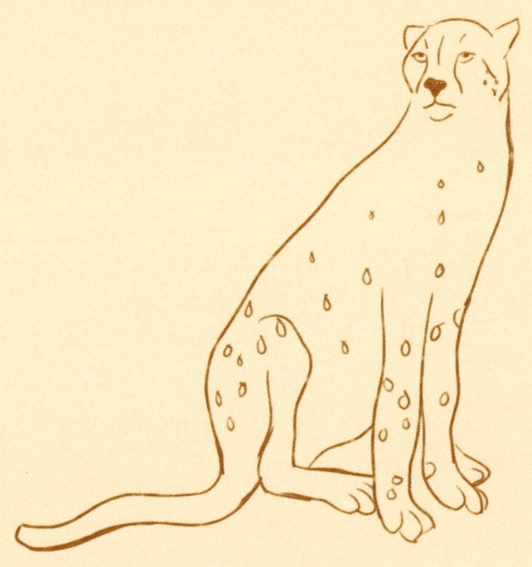

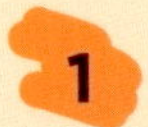

1 CHOOSE YOUR ANIMAL

The Cheetah Spots brush in the **Brush Sampler** is used as an example in this project, and you are free to use that, or you could choose your own animal to make the project more challenging—an animal with spots or stripes is ideal. You could trace an existing photograph of an animal, then change parts of it so that you aren't copying the reference image exactly, or you can draw your animal from scratch by combining poses from your reference images—the latter method is demonstrated below.

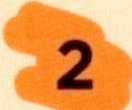

2 DRAWING FROM SCRATCH

To draw an animal from scratch, first draw a line from nose to tail. This is called the "action line" and it helps produce a natural pose. Block out the shape of the animal using geometric shapes, then draw a contour line along the edges of your sketch to work out the details. Drawing animals is a skill that takes practice, so don't be disheartened if your first animal is a little wonky. If that is the case, feel free to go back to the tracing step.

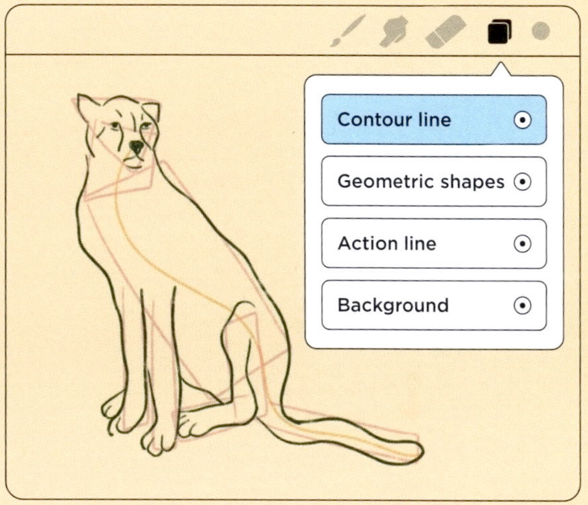

3 START INKING

Ink your animal artwork and add some defining lines on the areas that need some more detail to show where the body parts of the animal lie.

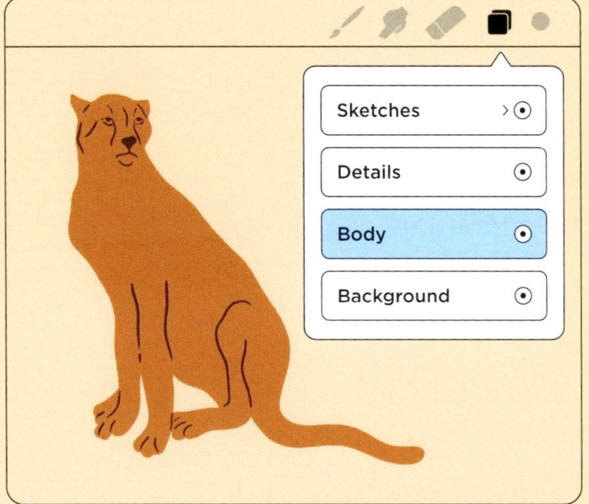

4 TEXTURE BRUSHES

The next step is to create a texture brush, also known as an “allover” brush, because it is made of an image that can be swiped all over the canvas with no seams. To see what this means, make all your other layers invisible, select the Cheetah Spots brush, then swipe it all over the canvas on a new layer. You can fill the entire space with cheetah spots because this brush has no beginning or end to its shape.

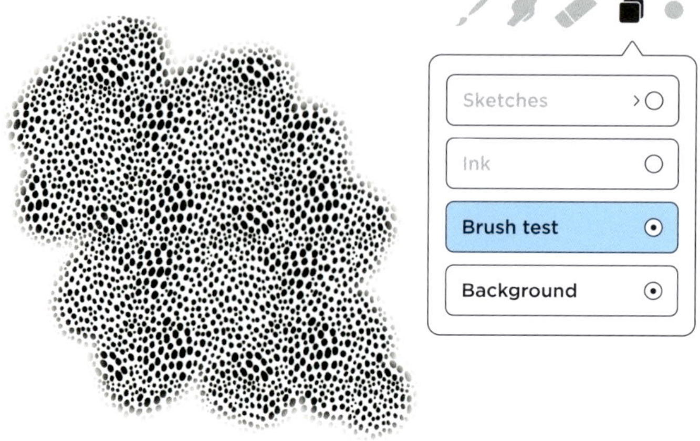

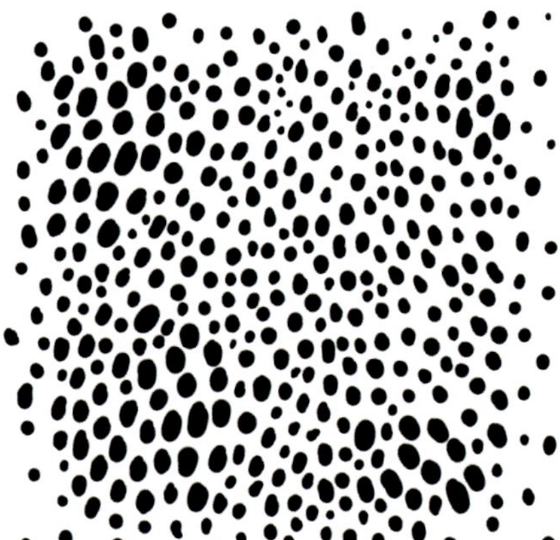

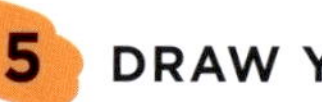

5 DRAW YOUR TEXTURE

Create a new layer and start inking some spots or stripes based on whatever animal you are drawing. You can change the scale of your brush later, so the scale of the texture isn't important. It's more important that your texture looks like the animal and fits together nicely, just as you'd see on the animal's fur. As with all brushes you create, use pure black for this step.

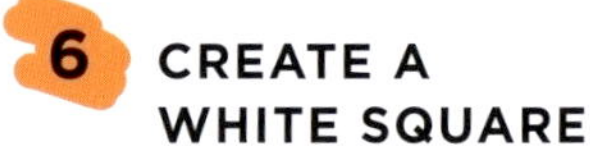

6 CREATE A WHITE SQUARE

To turn this shape into a seamless pattern, you first need to merge it with a white square. To do this, create a new layer and put it under your spots/stripes layer, then double tap in the white area of the **Color Disc** to get a pure white, tap on the new layer, and tap **Fill Layer**. You should now have a pure white square that you can merge with your black spots/stripes.

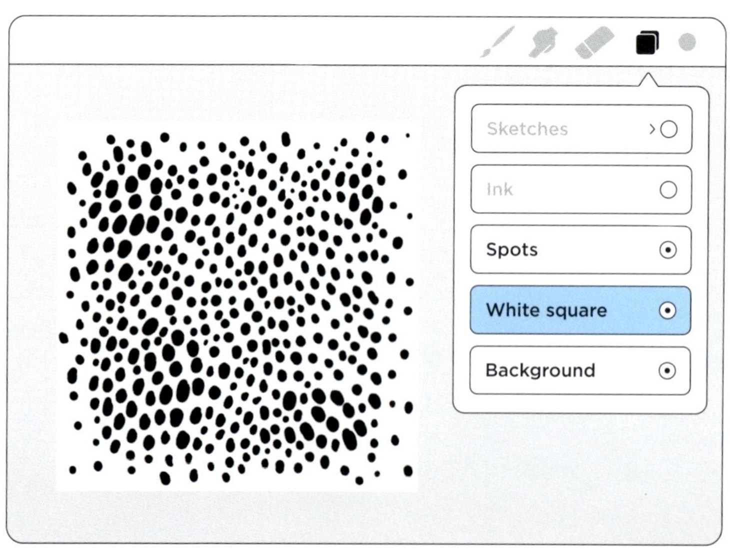

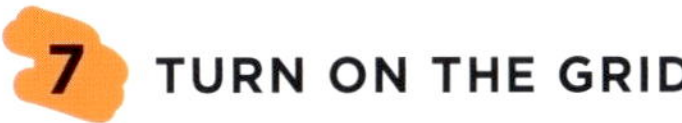

7 TURN ON THE GRID

Duplicate the merged layer three times so that you have four in total, then turn on the **Grid** by tapping on **Canvas**, turning on the **Drawing Guide**, and tapping **Edit Drawing Guide**. Increase the **Grid Size** to **Max** so that you just have a crosshair guide on your canvas. You can make your grid easier to see by adjusting the **Opacity**, **Thickness**, and **Color** before tapping **Done** to set the guide in place.

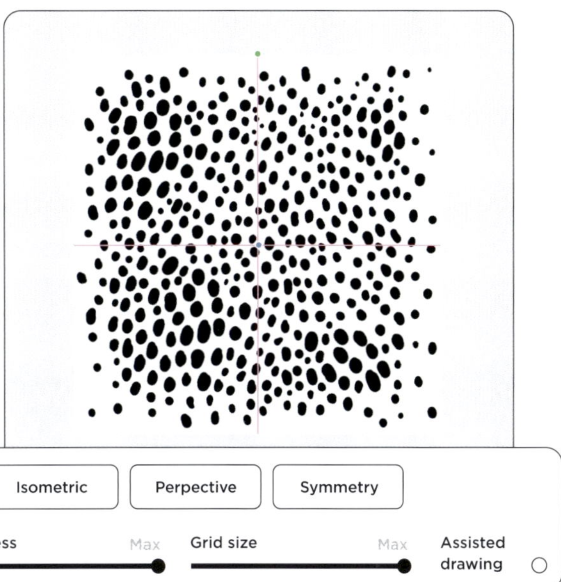

8 MOVE THE SQUARES TO THE CANVAS CORNERS

Move the squares to the corners of the canvas by tapping the **Move Tool**, turning on **Snapping** and **Magnetics** in the **Move Tool** settings, and dragging the shapes to the corners. Make sure you see an orange guide snap in a plus sign over your canvas to indicate that you are putting the square in the exact center of your canvas. Being just a pixel out can give your brush a slight gap in the artwork, so take the time to do this accurately.

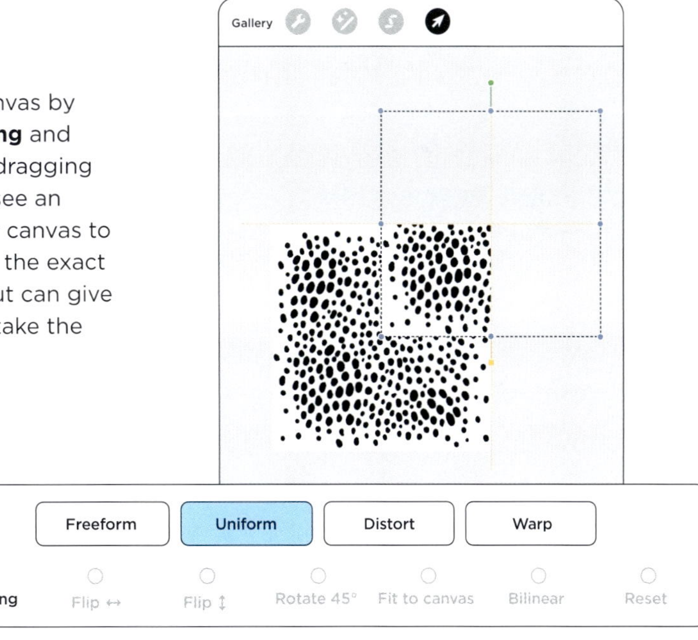

Tip Creating seamless blocks like this may seem complex at first, but they are more simple than they seem. Take a look at this simple seamless block. The stars need to line up at the top and bottom, and on the left and right, so one star has to overlap the edge so that it matches up on the other side. This is exactly what you are doing with your spots/stripes brush image, just with a lot more shapes!

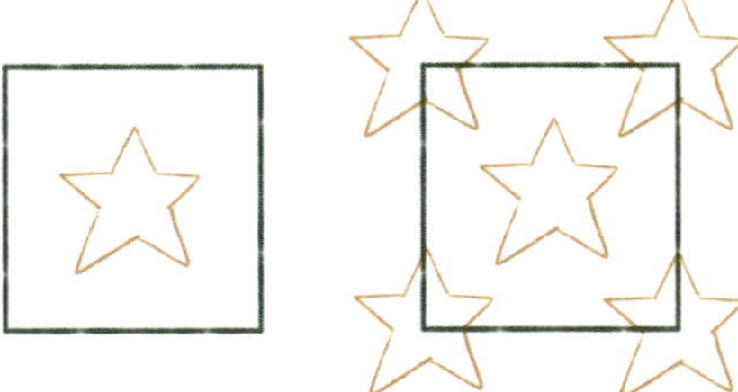

9 CREATE YOUR BRUSH

Create a new layer above the four positioned blocks and fill the space completely with more of your texture, taking care not to touch the canvas edges. You can save the image as a **JPEG** by going to **Actions**, **Share**, **JPEG**, then insert the image as the **Grain** on a duplicated version of the Cheetah Spots Brush—just as you did when you made your stamp for the Star Print project. The only difference is that when you make a texture brush, you insert the artwork into the **Grain Section**, rather than the **Shape Section**, of the brush settings.

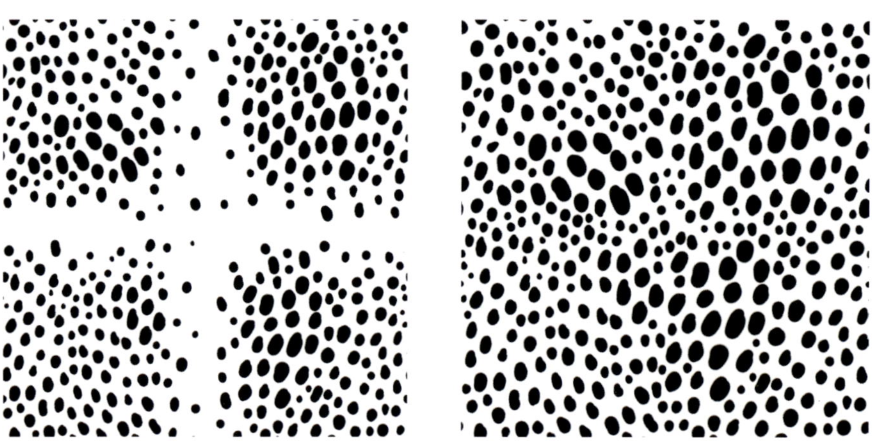

10 USE YOUR NEW BRUSH!

Test your brush by swiping it over your animal, then make sure that layer is just above your animal and turn it into a **Clipping Mask** layer so it clips to your animal. You may need to erase a few spots if they overlap with some of your detail lines, but otherwise all you need now is a background color. Why not fill the background with some plants that are native to the habitat where your animal lives? Draw them loosely on the canvas, then added some filler dots and lines.

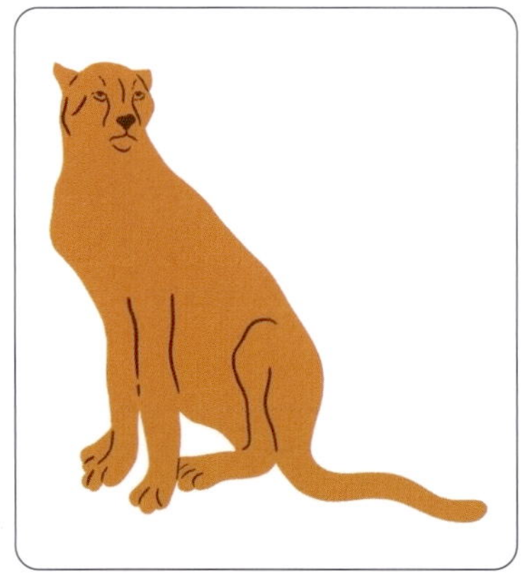

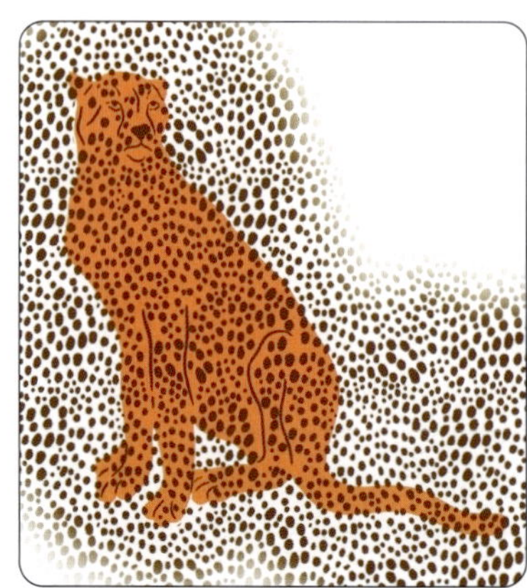

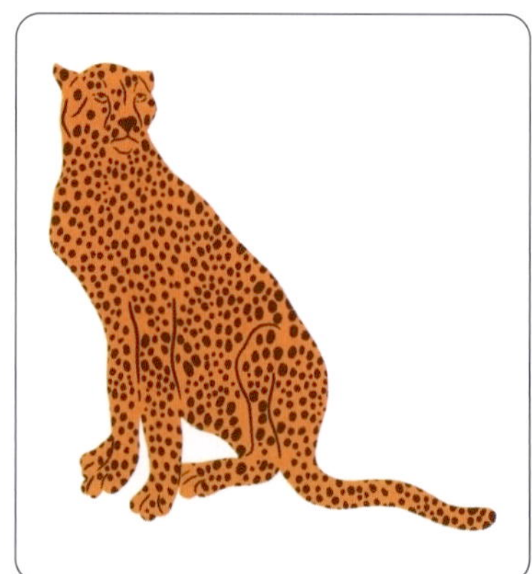

The End Result

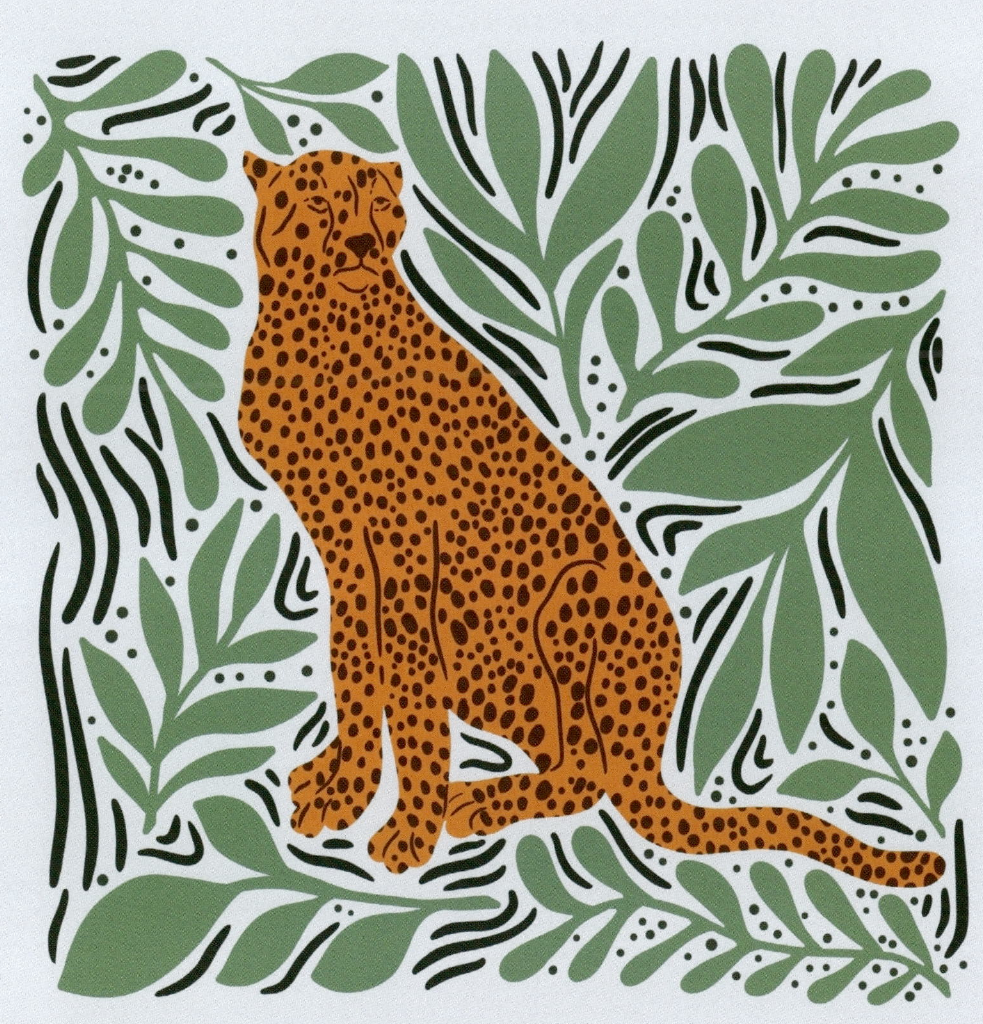

18

Get Rolling WITH LAYERS

Create a hobby-inspired composition featuring a lot of different individual parts. We'll practice managing large numbers of layers while avoiding lag or the app shutting down unexpectedly. There are layer limits in Procreate, so we need techniques to manage layer numbers successfully.

What We're Learning:
Managing a large layer count

Brushes:

Sketching Pencil

Dark Gouache Glaze

Palette:
Midnight Desert

- Hot Sun Yellow #ffc500
- Earthy Desert Yellow #ab7e00
- Buff Pink #ffc1ce
- Prom Dress Pink #b0707e
- Orange Sherbert #ff7c50
- Rusty Orange #ab3d17
- Electric Pink #ff3fc4
- Raspberry Pink #be0d7d
- Hazy Sky Blue #97aedc
- Deep Waters Blue #415888
- Ginkgo Leaf Green #69766b
- Aloe Plant Green #2d4934
- Lavender Purple #c1abf3
- Dark Iris Purple #210439

1 CHOOSE YOUR SUBJECT

Decide on a hobby to depict and find reference images for five to 10 objects related to the hobby. In this example, the hobby is roller-skating so the images relate to the gear you use when roller-skating. Once you've gathered images, create a rough and refined sketches for each object. Create each of these on a new layer and draw one object at a time. Draw more objects than you think you'll need; that way you can keep the ones that work best and delete the rest or save them for another project.

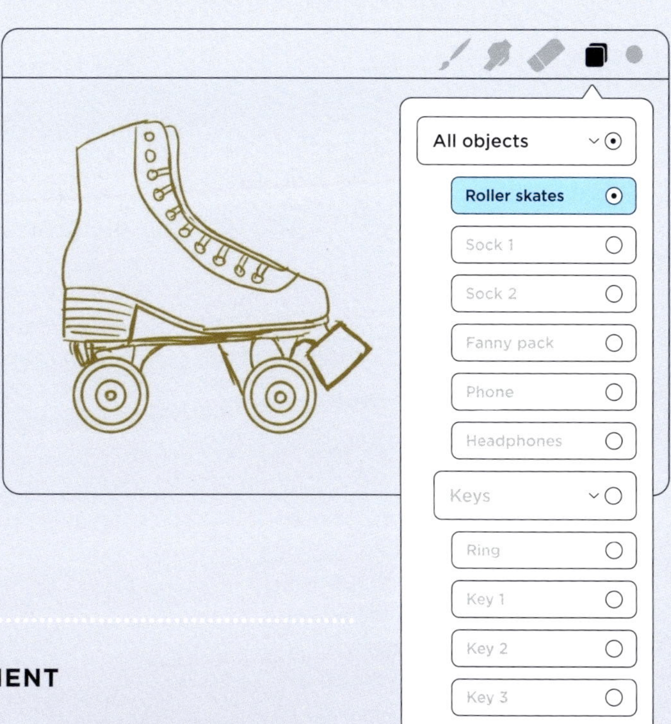

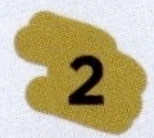

2 PLAN YOUR COLOR ARRANGEMENT

Because this composition has a limited color palette, it's a good idea to start thinking about how you will break up the color on the objects as you draw them. You can sketch areas in different colors to help with the process of visually breaking up the object. For example, on the fanny pack, the zipper and outer pocket will be separated from the strap and buckle using just a few simple colors.

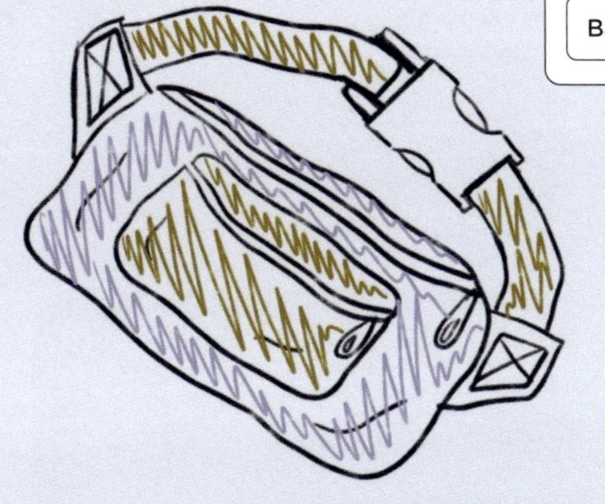

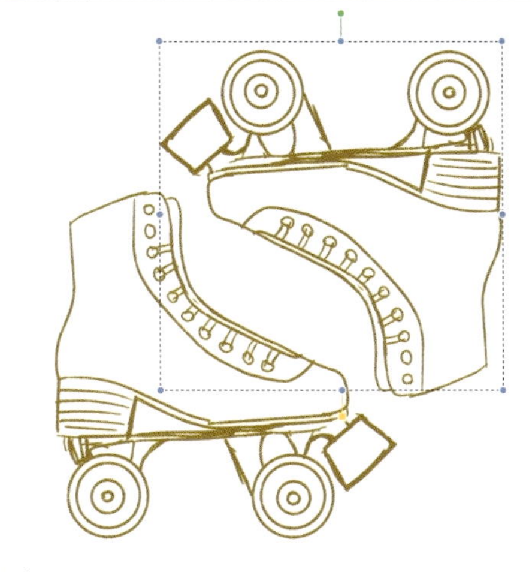

3 FLIP AND DUPLICATE

For some objects (like the roller skates) it isn't necessary to draw the object twice. Instead, you can draw the object just once, then **Duplicate** and **Flip** it to quickly produce both a left and right skate.

Freeform | Uniform | Distort | Warp

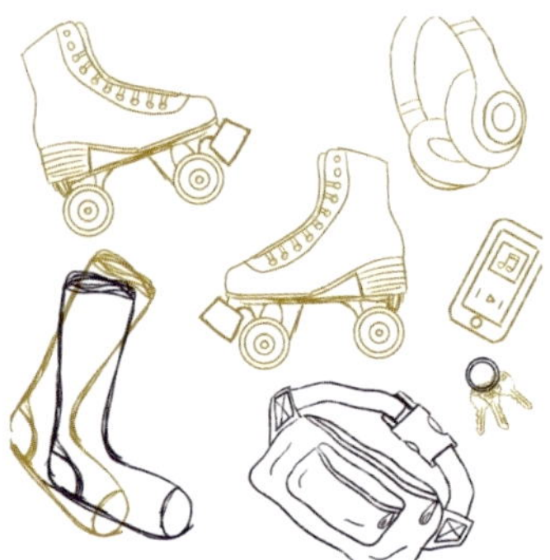

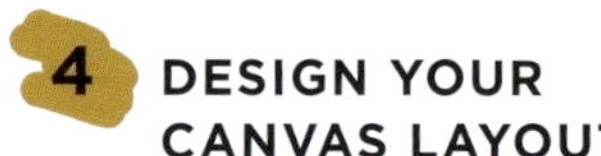

4 DESIGN YOUR CANVAS LAYOUT

Now reduce the size of the sketches so that you can comfortably fit all the objects on your canvas and scatter them around in whatever fashion you like. You could design a more organized layout (think gardening tools lined up in a row) or a loose and wild layout (think painting supplies scattered over a desk). Now, ink the objects one at a time, keeping each color on its own layer

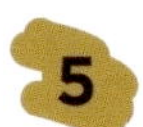

5 START TO ORGANIZE YOUR GROUPS

At this point, you have a decision to make: do you want to group your items by object or color? You could have a group for socks and one for earphones, or you could group all the same colors together—there is no "right way" to do this. For now, let's group by object; this will help you retain the ability to change every color and layer individually. The object groups are in the main group of Paint, which separates the sketches from the inking groups. If you put a group in the wrong place, you can drag it back to where you need it and keep going.

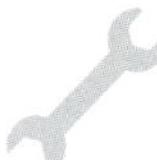

If you have an older or smaller iPad, you might start running into layer limits with a drawing like this. Check your layer limit by going to Actions, Canvas, Canvas Information, Layers. This will tell you how many layers you can have, how many you have used, and how many are still available.

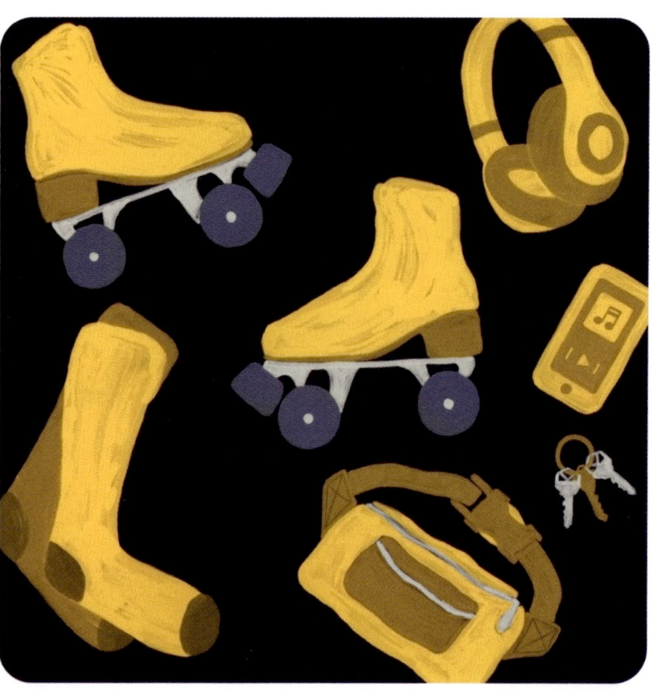

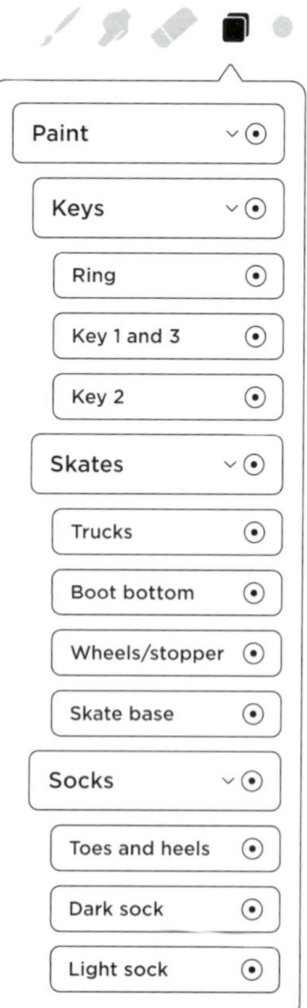

NAME YOUR LAYERS

At this point, take some time to name your layers, or at the very least, name your groups. While this can be boring, it's always a good idea (especially with tiny objects like the keys or the buttons on the phone) to be able to easily see from the **Layers Panel** what each element is. When you get into making color versions of the objects later on, you'll thank yourself for naming the layers on your original!

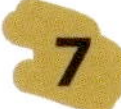

ADD DETAIL AND MOVEMENT

As you are inking, consider adding in a few extra elements to give the composition some movement. Here, the skate laces flow around the ground in a loose way, rather than being tied up in a bow. Little touches like this can help lead the viewer's eye around the canvas, which helps them take a longer look at your work. Sometimes, that is the difference between buying some artwork from an artist or passing it over.

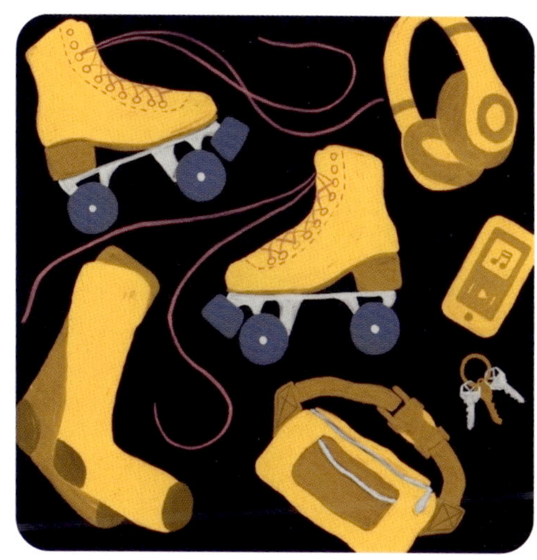

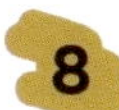

TRY DIFFERENT COLORWAYS

Once you feel confident about your layers and detail work, create some different color versions. To do that, head back to the **Gallery**, tap **Select**, then tap **Duplicate** a few times. Try a different color version for each canvas. When you work with duplicated canvases in this way, you can ignore the fear of "messing up" because you can just duplicate and ignore that doubting voice in your head telling you you're getting it wrong.

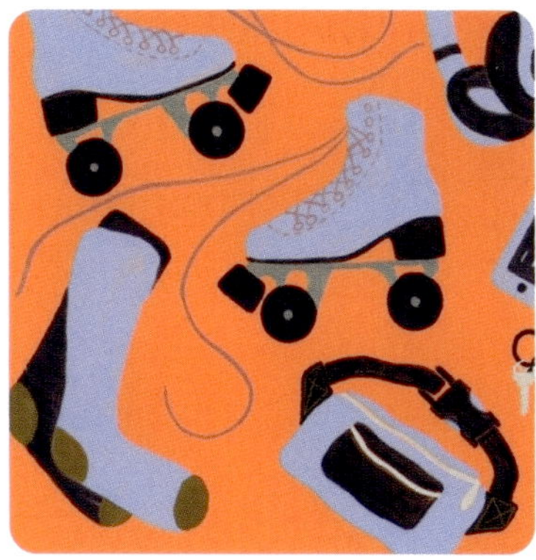

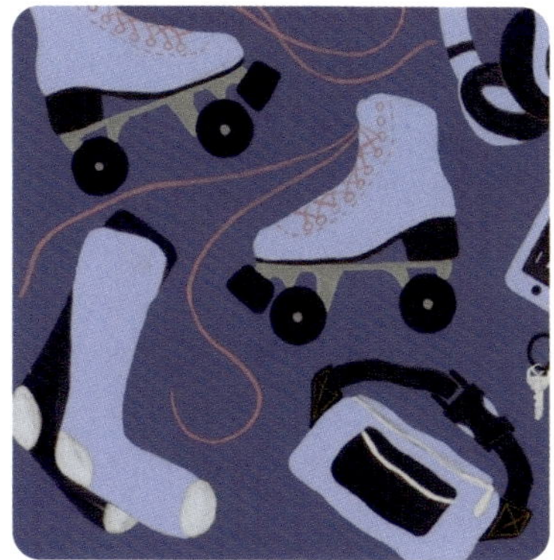

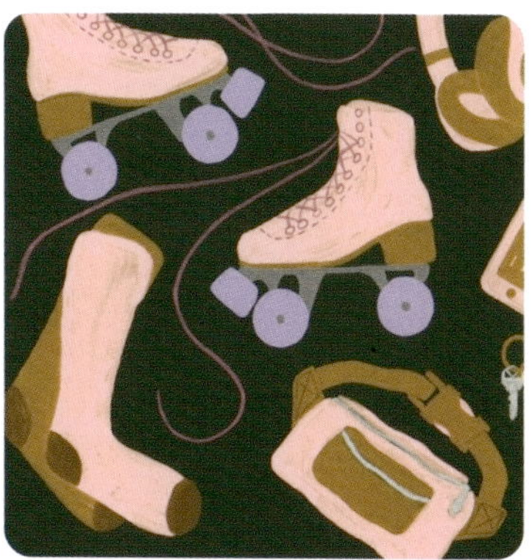

9 PREVIEW YOUR WORK

Now you can preview your color versions. Go back to the **Gallery**, tap **Select**, then tap on all the color versions you have created. Now tap **Preview** to be shown your artwork in large scale with no distracting icons or other gallery images in the background. You can swipe from left to right to preview your work, and ponder the pros and cons of each color version.

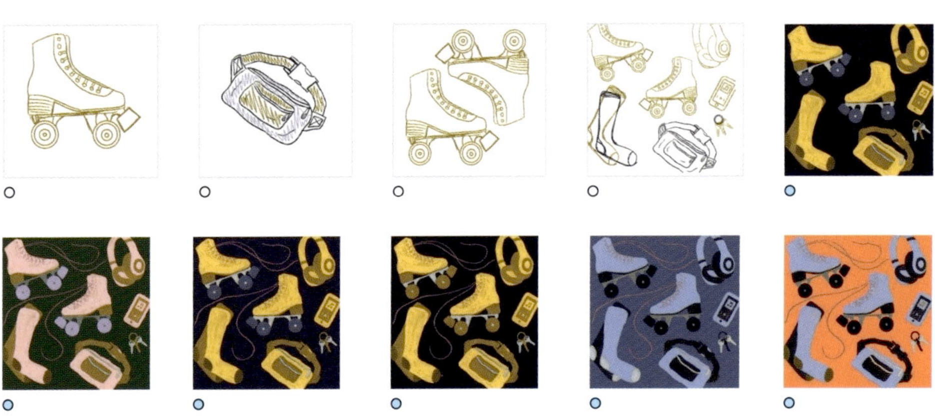

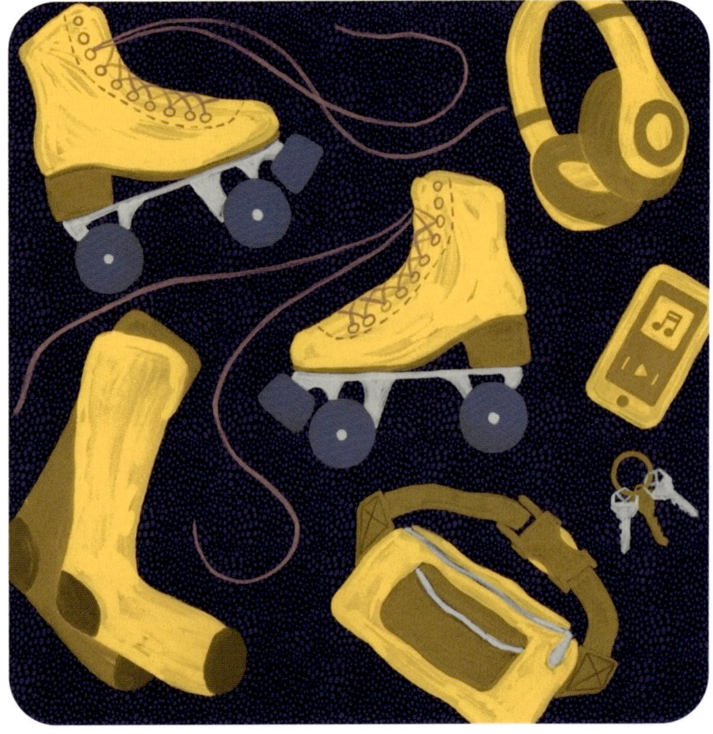

10 ADD A BACKGROUND TEXTURE

Now that you have an interesting composition with some objects on it, why not try adding a background surface that is related to your hobby. For example, for an art supplies theme you could add some wood grain to depict an artist's table, for a cooking theme you could depict a granite countertop. The Cheetah Spots brush has been used here, with the scale reduced so the spots read as pebbles instead of animal spots.

The End Result

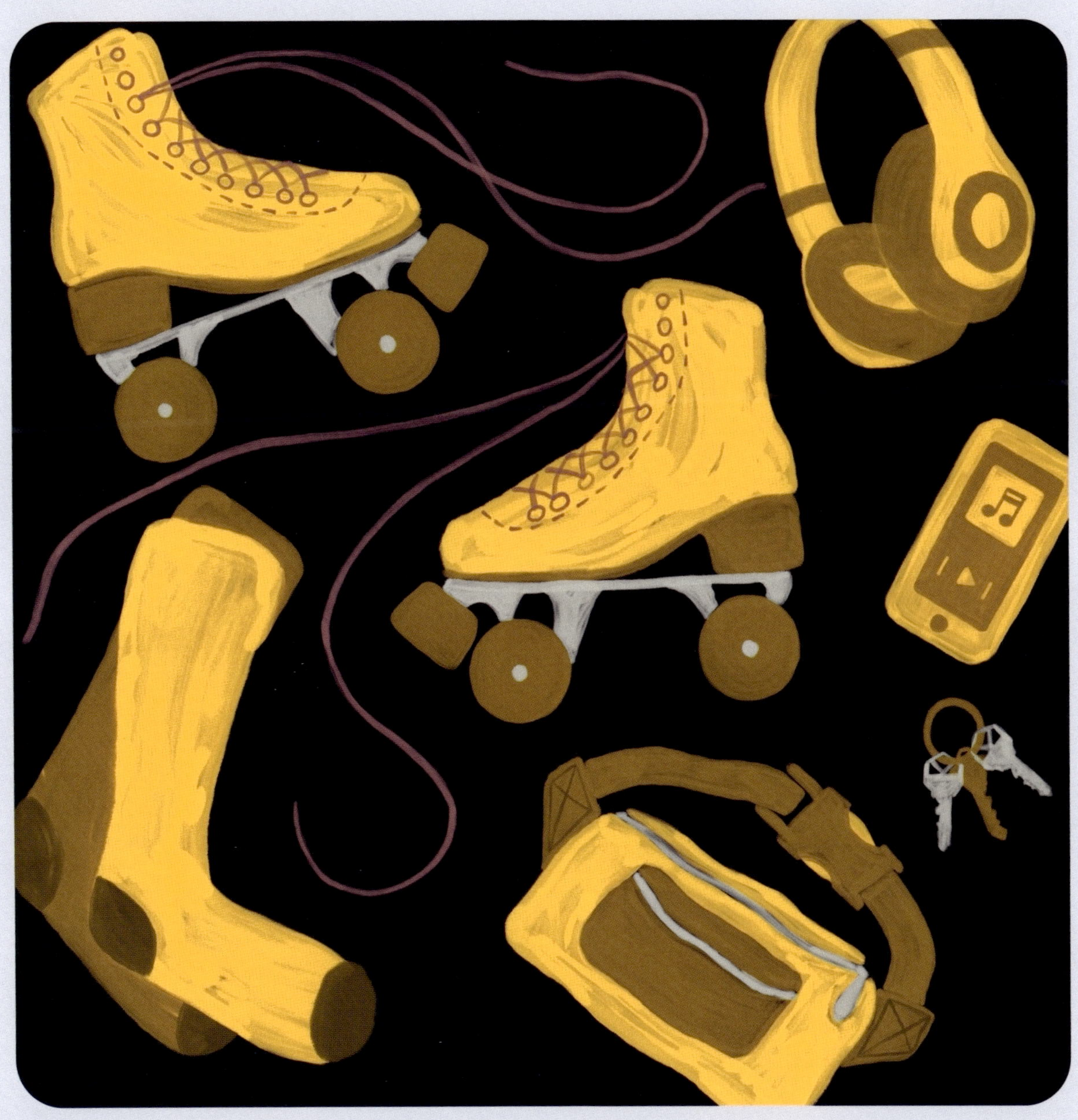

19

CREATE A Botanical Repeat

In this project, you will draw a repeat block with a botanical theme, so that you will learn how to hand draw seamless repeat patterns to create a fluid and interesting composition.

What We're Learning:
Drawing a repeat block

Brushes:

Sketching Pencil

Fluid Ink

Palette:
Muted Retro

Tomato Red #ff3100

Red Wine #981200

Cornflower Blue #597ce9

Blue Jay Blue #283c77

Glacier Blue #e0e4ea

Mountain Mist Blue #8799ad

Buttermilk Yellow #efb233

Oak Brown #916800

Dark Pastel Purple #917dbd

Plum Purple #493a62

Avocado Green #b1a450

Pickled Bean Green #595221

Flamingo Pink #f8abab

Valentine Red #e9605c

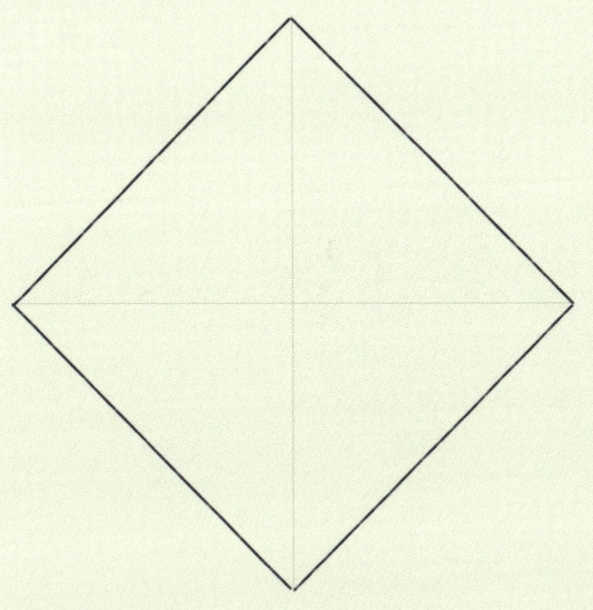

1 DRAW A DIAMOND SHAPE

First, find some reference images of plants you would like to draw. They could be florals, fruit, or leaves and berries. Choose a few and combine features of each in your rough sketch. Once you have your images, draw a diamond shape on the canvas by turning on the **Drawing Guide** to **Max** scale to get a plus symbol on your canvas, then draw lines between each of the points of the plus sign to produce a diamond.

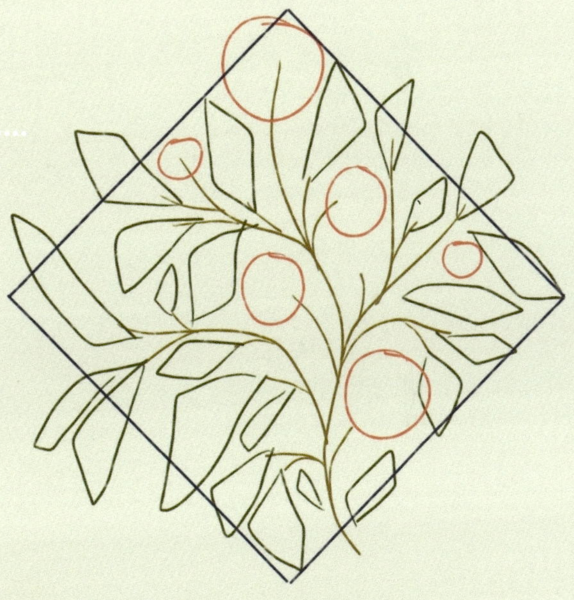

2 DRAW THE ROUGH SKETCH

Create the rough sketch for the first part of your pattern, starting out with simple lines and circles to show where the vines and flowers will be. At this early stage, using simple geometric shapes to block out areas is a great way to build a varied and interesting composition.

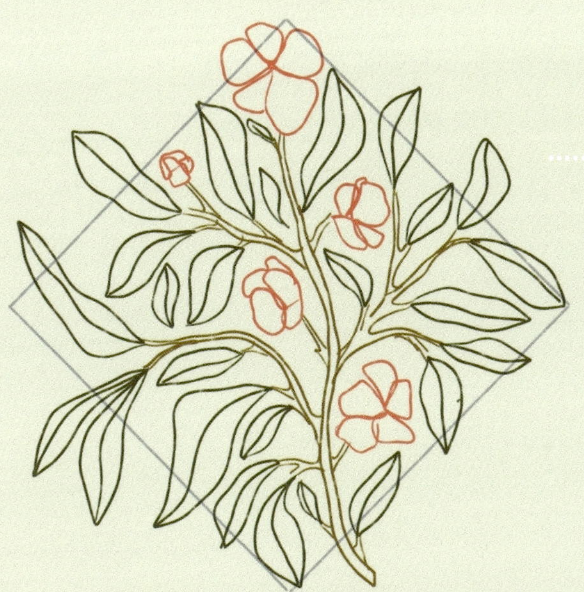

3 REFINE YOUR SKETCH

Next, create a more detailed sketch of your shapes focusing on details like the wavy edges of the leaves and the details on the flowers.

4 THE "DIAMOND 1" GROUP

Group all the sketch layers into one group and title it "Diamond 1". This will help you to remain organized as you build the other part of your repeat. Duplicate the Diamond 1 Group and name it "Diamond 2," so that you can differentiate it from your original. Now we are going to start building the repeat block.

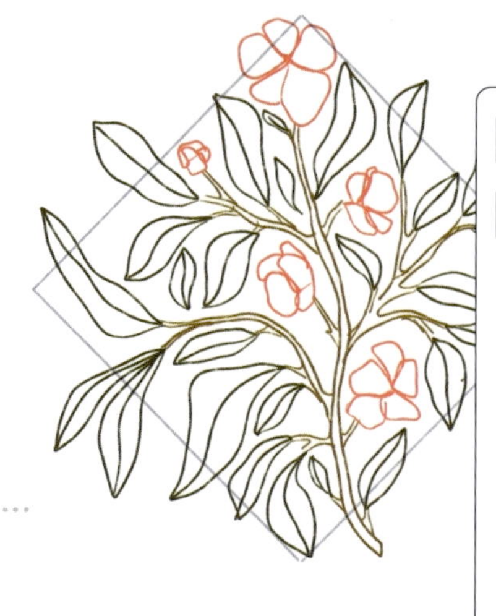

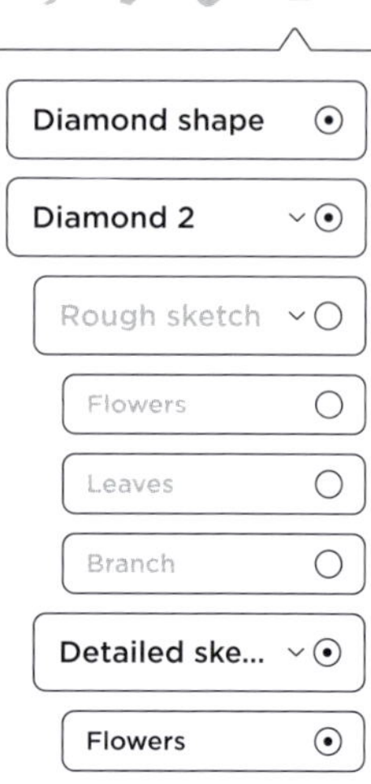

5 MOVE THE BLOCKS TO THE CANVAS CORNERS

Merge all the sketch layers in the Diamond 2 Group, create a white layer under the sketch layer and merge the two layers together, then duplicate and move the blocks to the corners of the canvas. Use the **Move Tool** to accurately place the four squares in the canvas corners, so that you end up with an open area in the center. For more information on this process, see the Jungle Textures project on page 118.

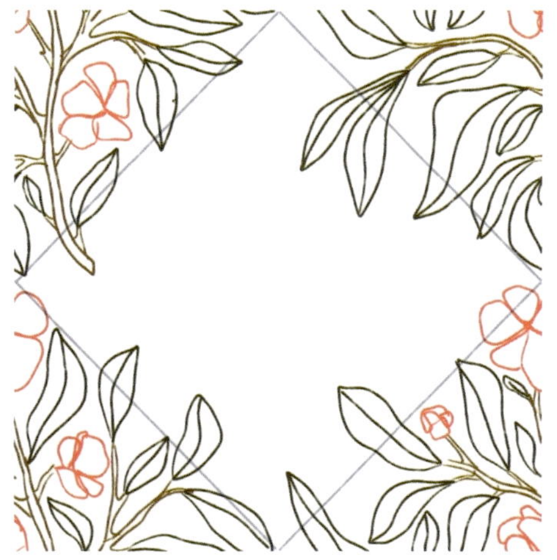

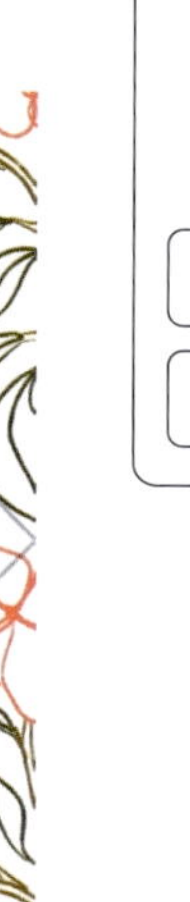

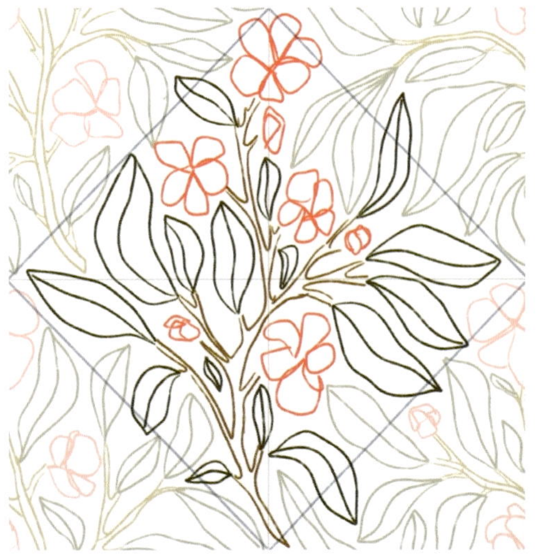

6 FILL THE GAPS IN THE PATTERN

You should now have a new empty diamond shape in the center of the canvas, because the four triangles that made up the first diamond have been placed so that they create a new diamond shape. Now draw flowers and leaves in the empty space in a way that makes them fit like puzzle pieces into the existing shapes. You can now also merge all your "white fill" layers together to save some space in your **Layers Panel**.

7 TEST YOUR REPEAT BLOCK

Now try your repeat block to see how it looks. Make your diamond layout visible, make all your detailed sketch layers 100% opacity, then save the image as a **JPEG** file. Insert the **JPEG** and resize the image using the **Move Tool** (make sure that the block snaps to the grid), then duplicate that block three times and put the blocks in place. If you see any areas in your repeat that need improvement, mark them with Red Pencil brush, then head back to your sketching layers and improve those spaces.

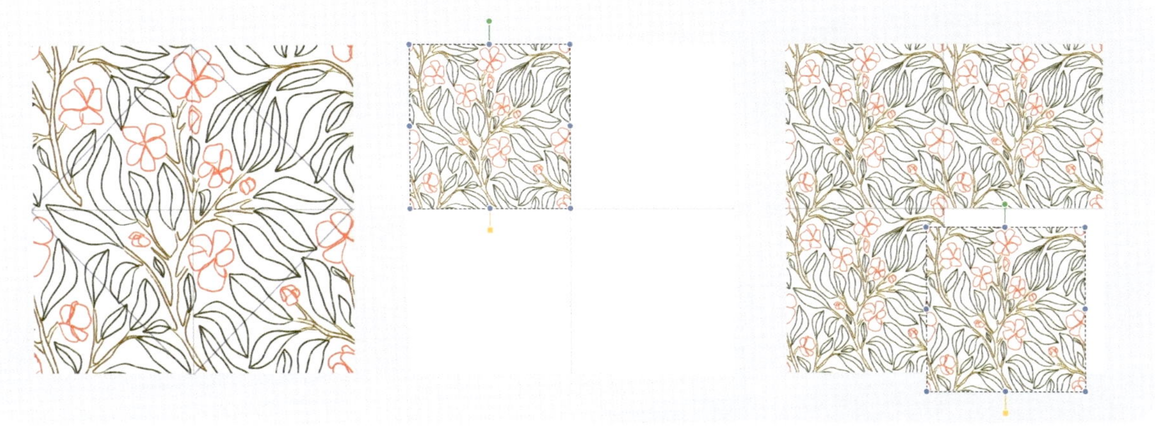

8 ADD COLOR AND DUPLICATE THE GROUP

Go back to the original Diamond 1 layer and add an inking group to that group, including a filled background layer at the bottom of the group. Ink the group, then duplicate that group three times and move the duplicated groups to the corners of the canvas, just as you did with your sketch in step 5. It's best practice to always make a fifth duplicate that you make invisible and call your "original" inked diamond just in case something goes wrong in the repeat making process.

Tip **If you have trouble getting your repeat squares perfectly into the corners of your canvas, remember that you can zoom in to the pixel level to check your placement. Line up the Move Tool dots and dotted lines of the grid on your canvas to get a perfect fit.**

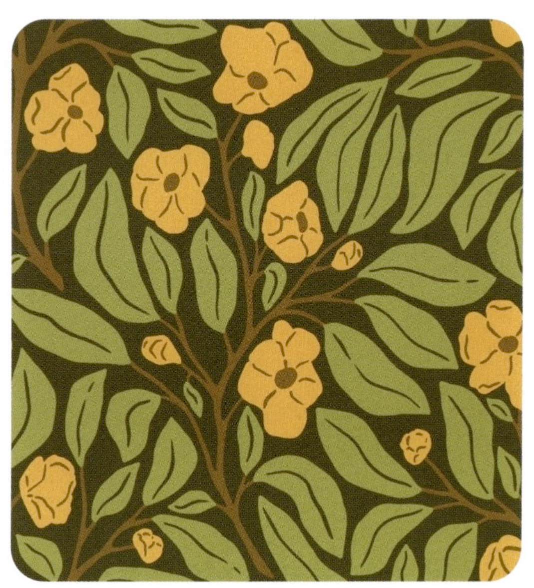

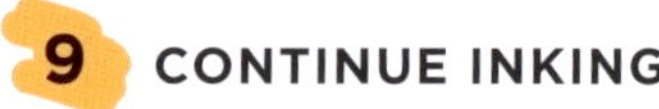

9 CONTINUE INKING

Now you can ink your second diamond and see how your repeat starts to come together as you ink each leaf and flower.

10 TRY OUT DIFFERENT COLORS

Take some time to play with color choices and subtle adjustments to each of your shapes until you are happy with the overall layout. Then you can repeat your pattern just as you did in step 7 to check if it works as a repeated tile.

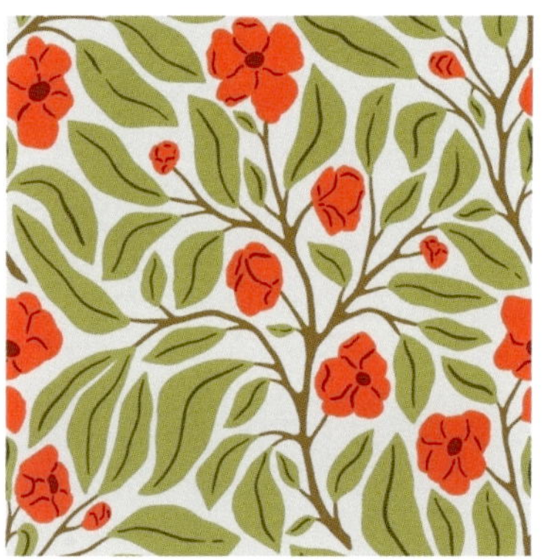

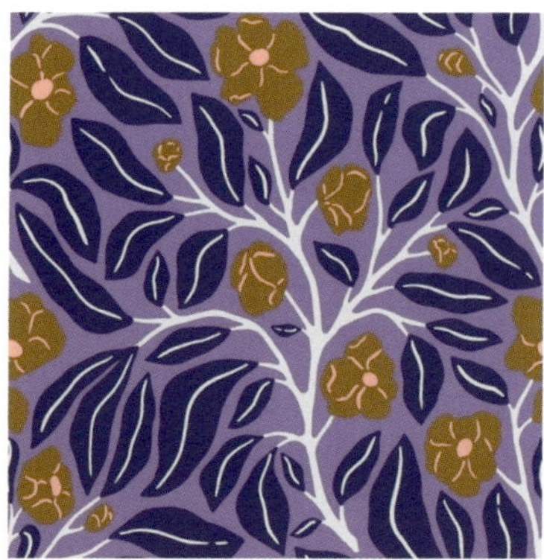

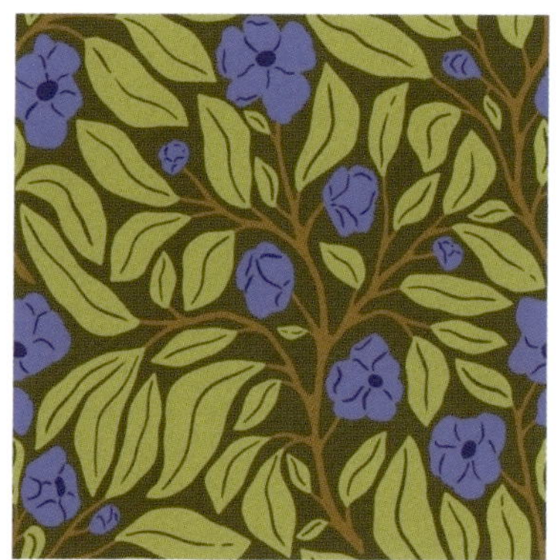

Keep It Going

Artists often feel tempted to give up on a drawing halfway through creating it because it seems like it's going to be a failure, but remember that the last step of adding fillers like dots or leaves is sometimes the final touch that can take a drawing from boring and flat, to interesting and varied.

The End Result

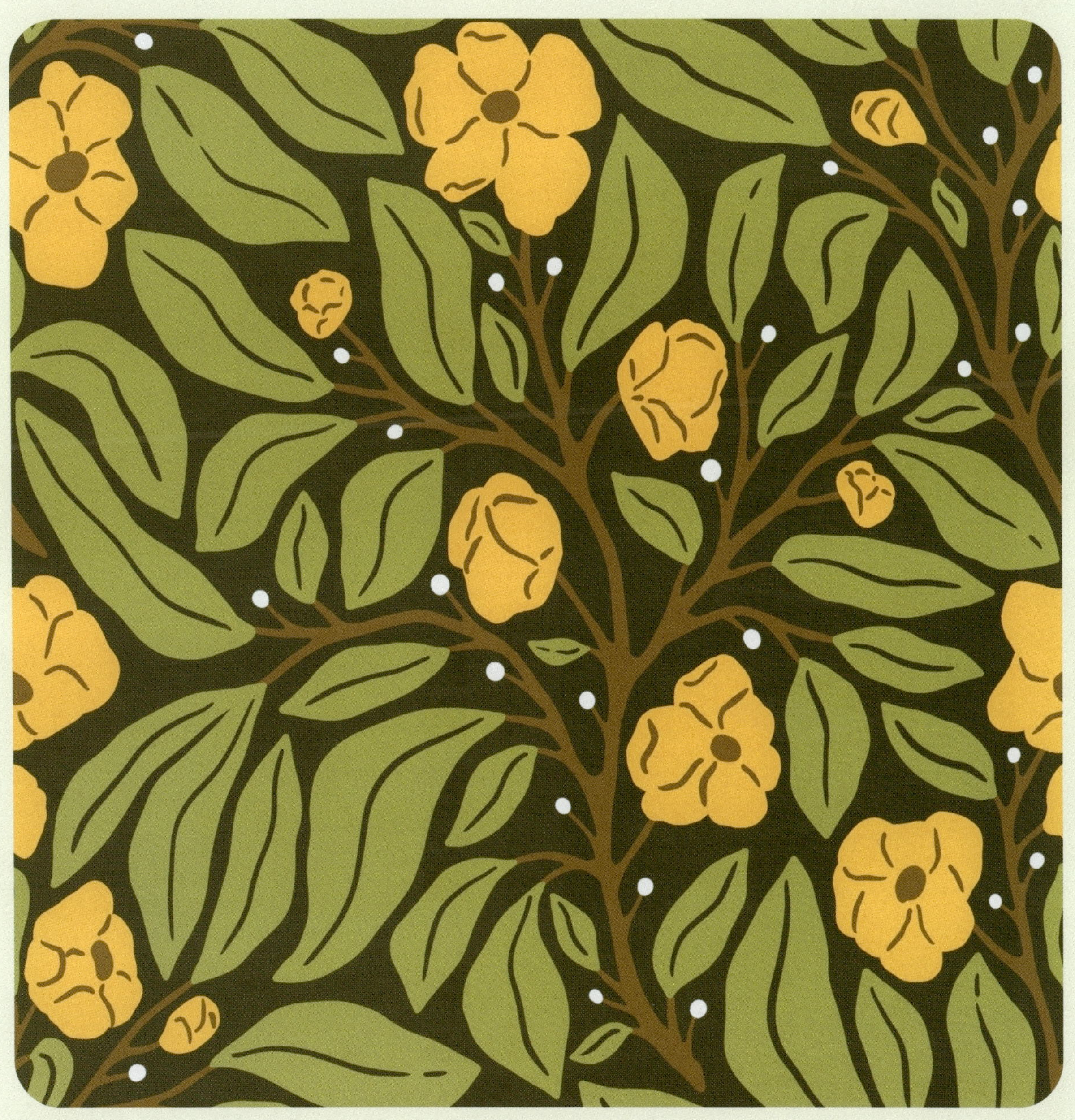

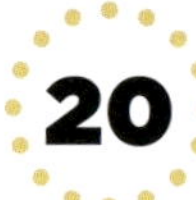

MAKE A Flame Flicker

In this project, we'll experiment with Animation. Adding a simple animation to projects can help increase viewer engagement with your work online and it's also a fun way to give your artwork some life and movement.

What We're Learning:
Using **Animation Tools**

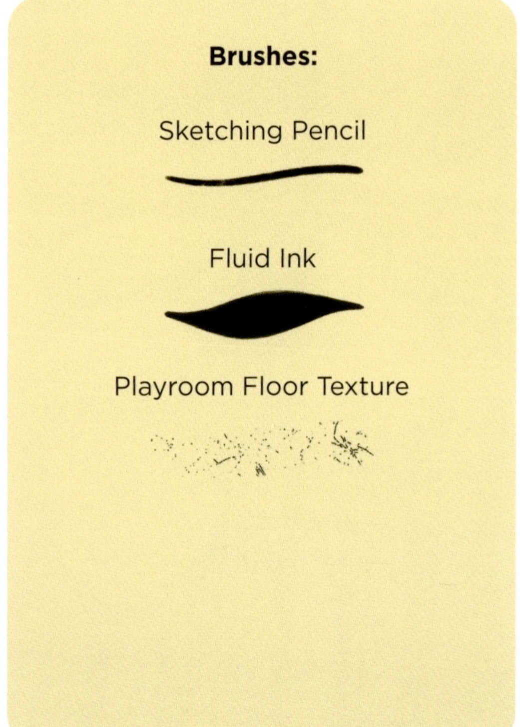

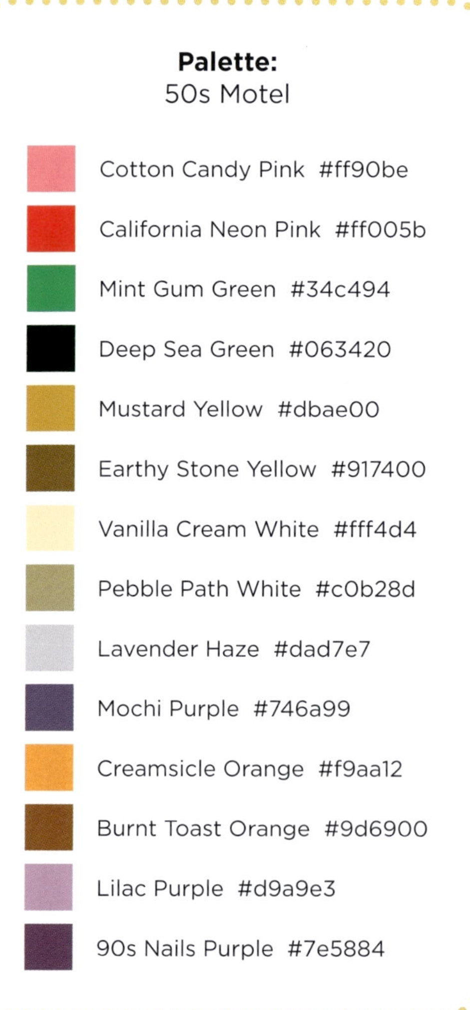

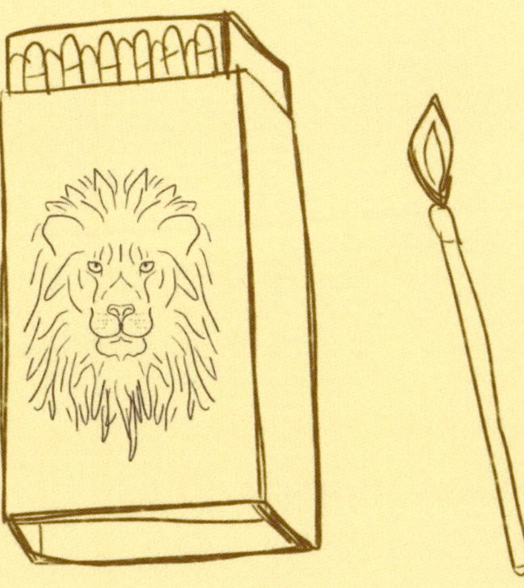

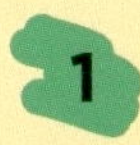

FIND SOME REFERENCE IMAGES AND START SKETCHING

Search online for reference images of vintage matchboxes and a fierce-looking animal that you would like to feature on the packaging—instead of an animal, you could use lettering, a symbol, or just patterned decoration. Searching for vintage matchboxes online should give you some great ideas for your matchbox illustration, but if not, follow this example and use a lion as your subject. Create a rough sketch of your matchbox, match, and decoration element.

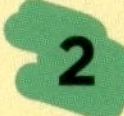

REFINE YOUR SKETCH

Create a detailed sketch of your matchbox, using **Quickline** to get the edges straight, and duplicating one original shape for repeated items like the heads of the matches.

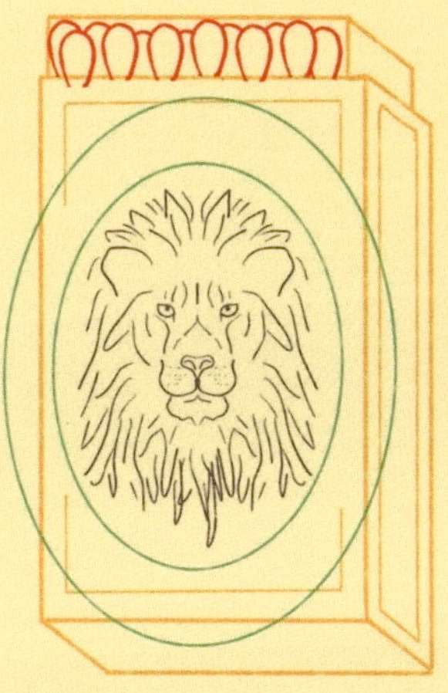

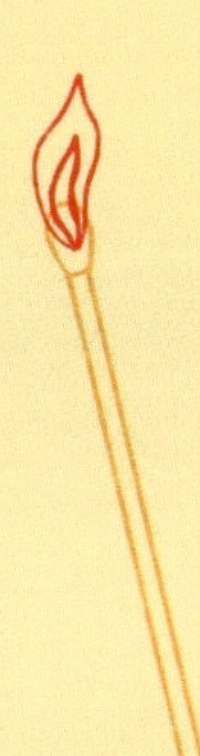

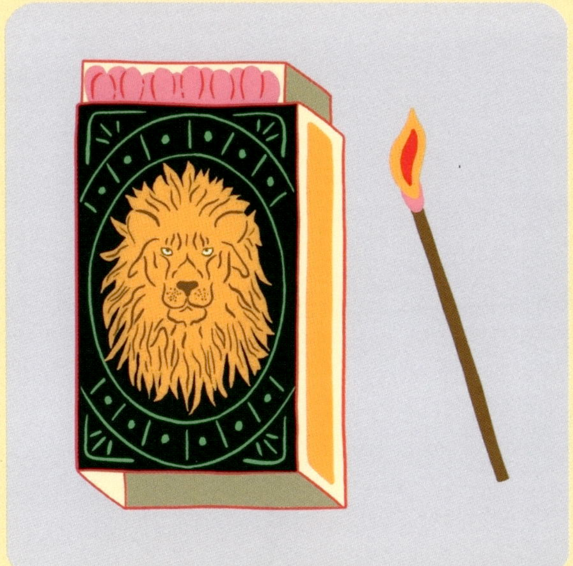

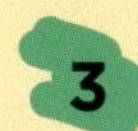

ADD COLOR

Ink your illustration using any of the styles that have been demonstrated in this book. By now you probably have an idea of what brushes you like, what colors you are drawn to, and how you like to lay out your **Layers Panel**.

4 ADD TEXTURE

One extra finishing touch you could try is adding a texture—such as the Pencil Taps or Playroom Floor Texture—on top of the whole illustration, then set it to a **Blend Mode** that produces the effect you like. In this example, the Playroom Floor Texture is used, set to the Color Dodge **Blend Mode**.

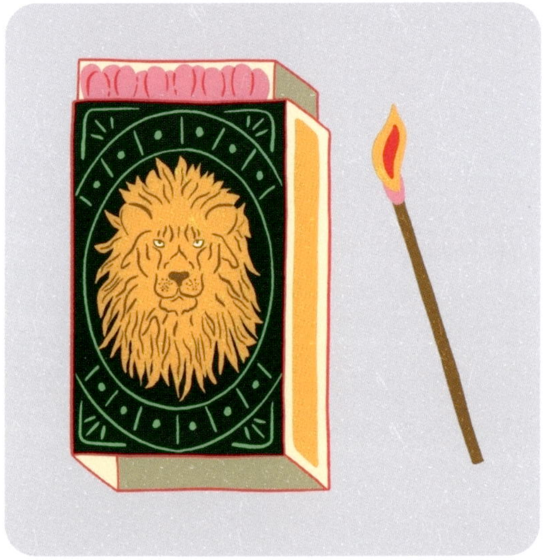

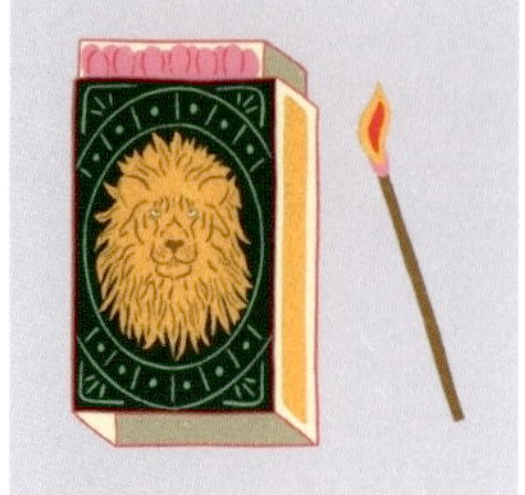

Lion

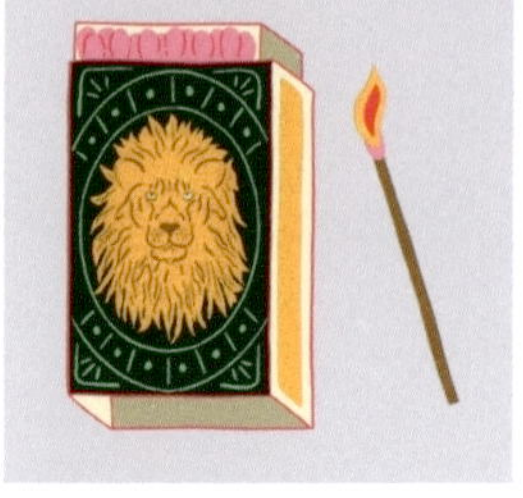

Matchbox animation

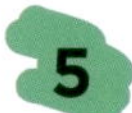

5 DUPLICATE YOUR ORIGINAL

Once you are happy with the illustration, it's time to add some animation! It's important to begin by making a duplicate of your original illustration—you don't want to lose all of your original layers, and the animation process requires you to merge some layers, so go to the **Gallery**, tap **Select**, and then tap **Duplicate**. Tap on the name of the document and name it "Matchbox animation" to differentiate it from the original.

6 ORGANIZE THE LAYERS PANEL

Open the duplicated document and tidy up your **Layers Panel** by deleting the sketch groups and merging shapes together into two groups: what will be animated and what will not be animated. In this case, the only thing that will move is the flame, so you can merge all the layers that aren't part of the flame. You will be left with three layers: a texture, a flame, and everything else.

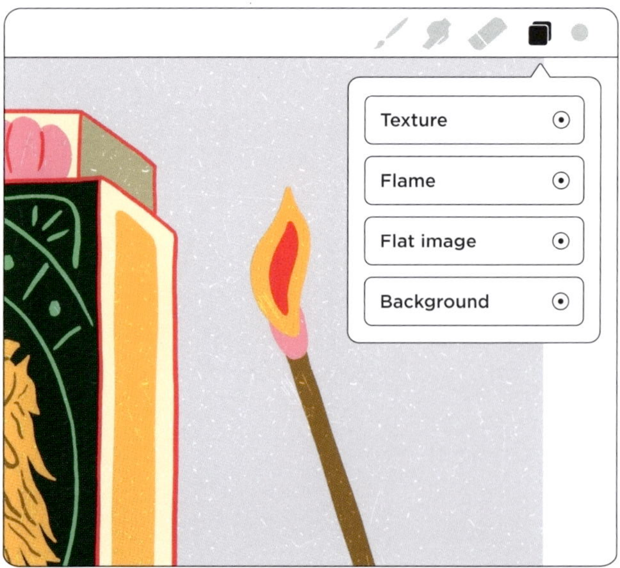

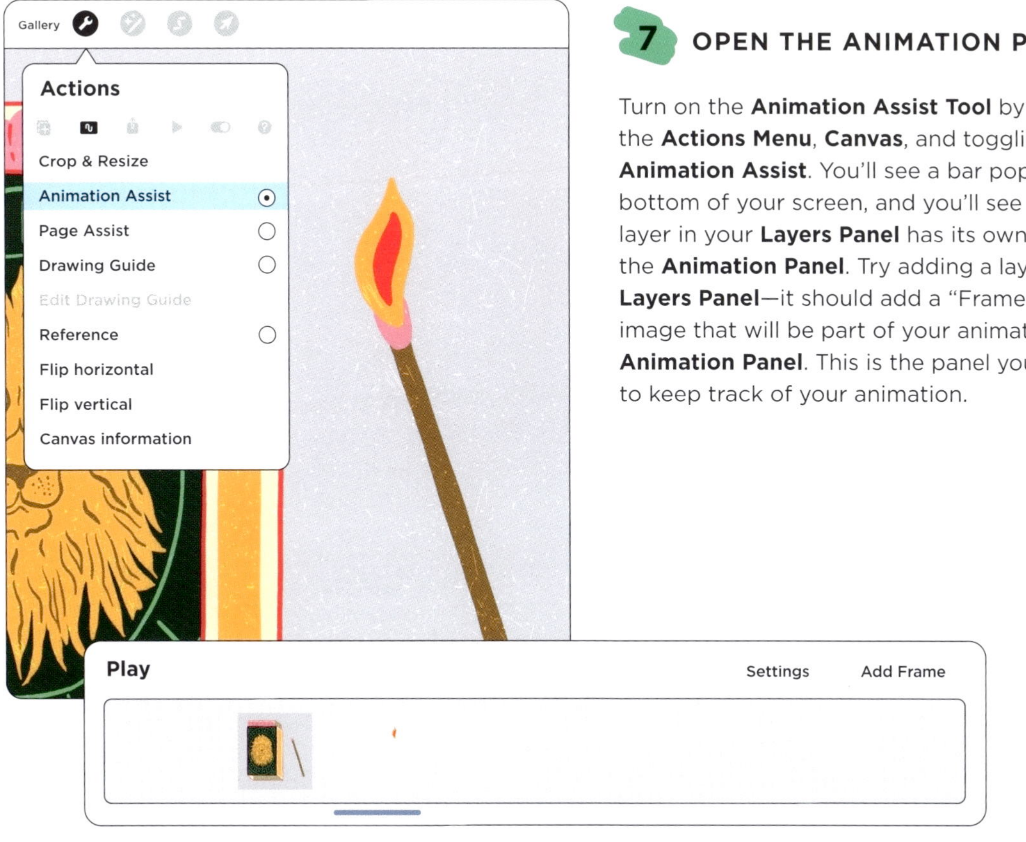

7 OPEN THE ANIMATION PANEL

Turn on the **Animation Assist Tool** by tapping the **Actions Menu**, **Canvas**, and toggling on **Animation Assist**. You'll see a bar pop up at the bottom of your screen, and you'll see that each layer in your **Layers Panel** has its own square in the **Animation Panel**. Try adding a layer to your **Layers Panel**—it should add a "Frame" (an image that will be part of your animation) to the **Animation Panel**. This is the panel you will use to keep track of your animation.

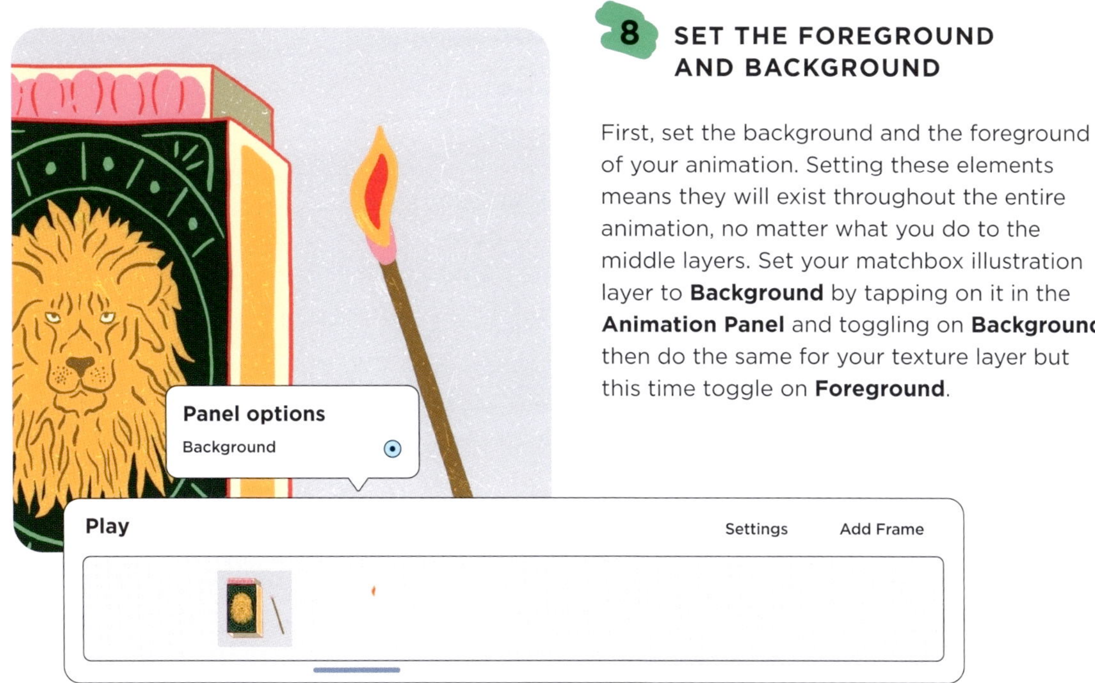

8 SET THE FOREGROUND AND BACKGROUND

First, set the background and the foreground of your animation. Setting these elements means they will exist throughout the entire animation, no matter what you do to the middle layers. Set your matchbox illustration layer to **Background** by tapping on it in the **Animation Panel** and toggling on **Background**, then do the same for your texture layer but this time toggle on **Foreground**.

9 DRAW YOUR ANIMATION FRAMES

Now start redrawing the flame repeatedly on different layers, just above one another, to create the frames of your animation. You will need to create at least five or six layers of flame with slightly different positioning in order to produce an interesting animation.

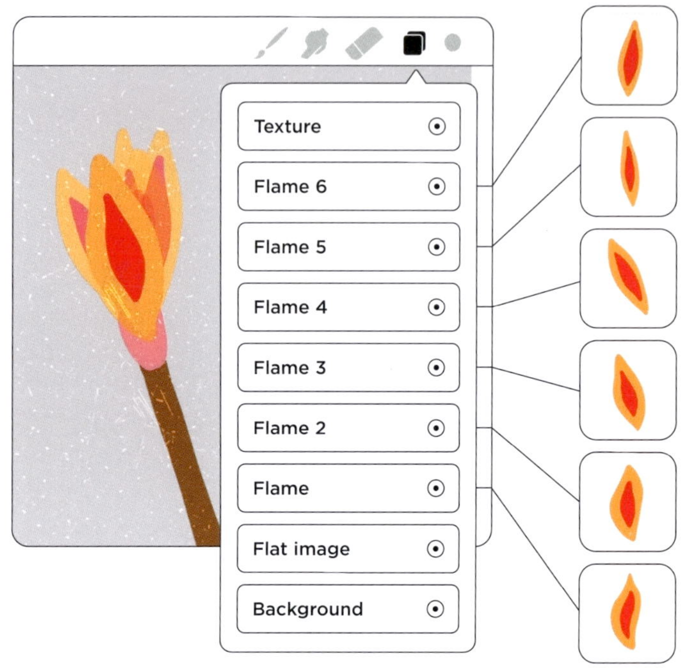

10 ANIMATE YOUR FLAME

After you've drawn a few layers, tap **Play** on the **Animation Panel**, then tap **Settings** to change the speed and type of animation. Try setting **Ping-Pong** at a speed of 8 frames per second for a start, then play around with the settings to see how each one results in a different effect for your animation. Continue making more flames if you want to develop your animation further.

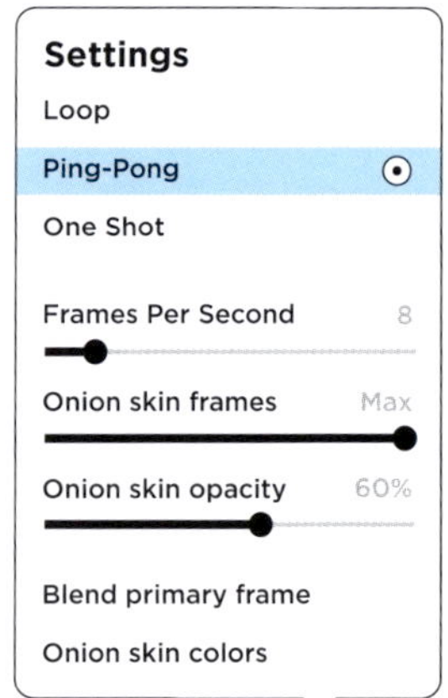

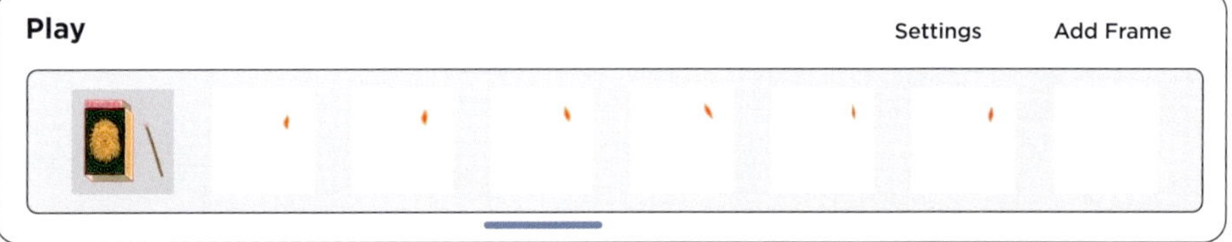

Keep It Going

Now that you know how to animate, why not add some more animation to this composition? You could make your lion's eyes blink or make the mane blow in the wind. Every little bit of movement you add to the composition gives it life.

The End Result

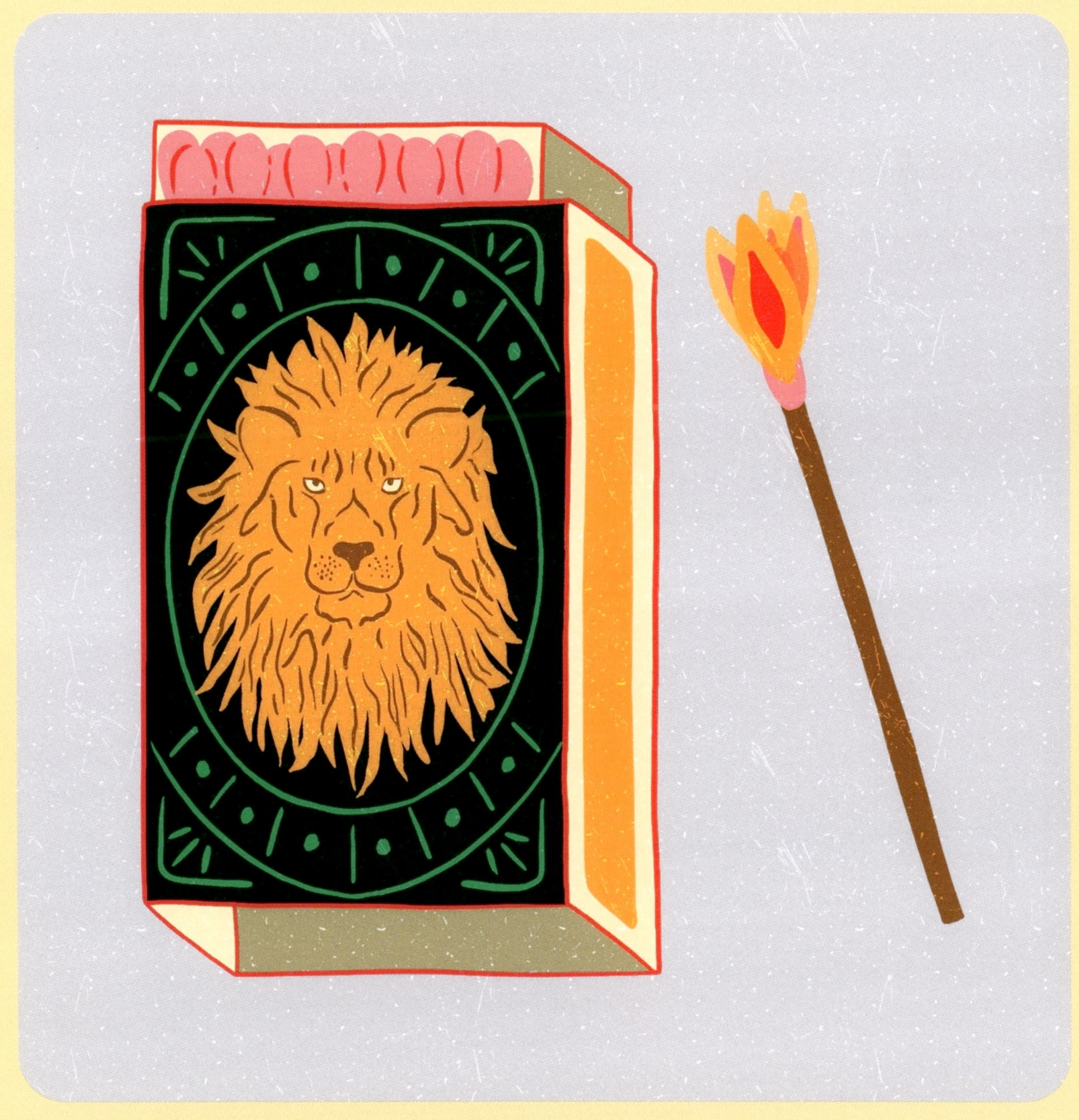

What Comes Next?

Now that you know how to create artwork in Procreate, it's time to start sharing your work with the world. You'll find some tips below on exactly how to do this and on how to keep developing your art skills.

WAYS TO SHARE YOUR ARTWORK

You can share your art on social media, a website, print-on-demand websites—where you sell your artwork to consumers—or even print your art out to hang on your wall or give as gifts.

SHARE YOUR MESSES

Finished artwork is not the only thing that you can share! Creatives and non-creatives alike love seeing an artist's process, so share your sketches, inked drawings, and color versions to get people interested in your work.

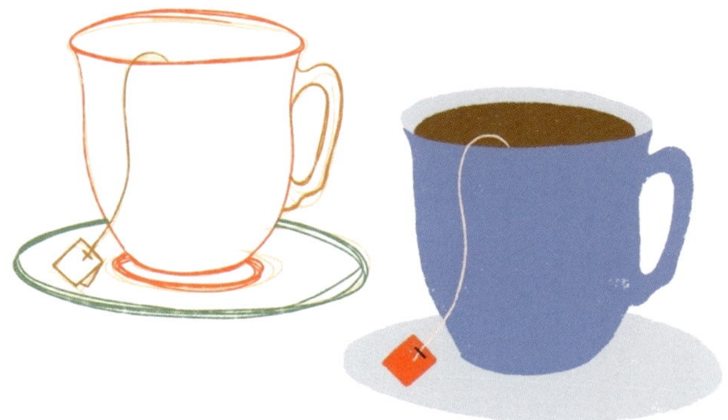

TAG YOUR FRIENDS

When you share your artwork online, tag or share it with friends and family. Starting by sharing with the circle of people who are already around you is the best way to start getting your work found online. If you post your work on Instagram, tag me @lizkohlerbrown, so that I can see it and cheer you on!

KEEP LEARNING AND GROWING

In this book, we have only touched the tip of the iceberg when it comes to the possibilities within Procreate. As you create more artwork and develop your style, you will get a sense for what you are drawn to, and can take that opportunity to start doing deep dives into subjects you love. Go with your gut and take months to explore a single style to build up your gallery of work to share with the world and uncover your personal style.

PROGRESS IS SLOW AND STEADY

Remember that every artist started at the beginning, just like you. The more you focus on one or two things, and hone your skills in those areas, the faster you will reach your desired goals. You may also find it encouraging to keep a log of your progress, perhaps saving a drawing each month and looking back over your progress periodically.

BACKING UP YOUR WORK

Once you start building up a sizeable gallery of artwork, you should consider backing up your work to a cloud storage service like iCloud, Dropbox, or Drive.

To do this, tap **Select** in the **Gallery**, tap on a **Stack**, then tap **Share** and choose Procreate as the file type to save your original Procreate files, just in case something happens like a stolen iPad, fire, or flood!

Index

ACKNOWLEDGMENTS

To the editors and publisher whose expertise and guidance have been invaluable in bringing this project to fruition, I offer my deepest thanks. To Lindsay Kaubi and Dee Costello, I am truly grateful for your tireless ability to edit kindly and patiently what came out of my sometimes-chaotic creative brain. To Lindsey Johns, the designer who took my hundreds of messy canvases and turned them into a gorgeously organized layout for this book, thank you for helping me look so neat and tidy and for making my ideas come to life.

A special note of appreciation goes to my husband, whose support has allowed me to pursue my creative career since we met in college in 2007. His willingness to live an unusual life with me (including selling all our possessions and moving to Thailand, living in the woods in an off-grid cabin, and taking the leap into building our own location-independent businesses) has made my creative career possible. Not to mention that he regularly wrangles our unusually energetic children with love and care while I occasionally sneak away to draw. Thank you for being my best friend, and the biggest supporter of my creative business from day one.

To the members of The Studio, whose creativity and enthusiasm have fueled my own artistic journey, I owe a debt of gratitude. Your years of unwavering support and encouragement have been a constant source of inspiration, driving me to explore new seemingly out-of-reach projects and push the boundaries of my craft. Thank you for being a part of this incredible creative community and for inspiring me to keep creating each and every day.

With heartfelt appreciation,

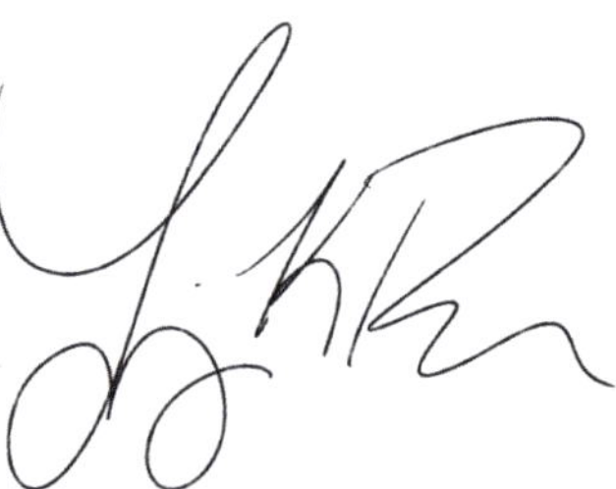

Liz Kohler Brown

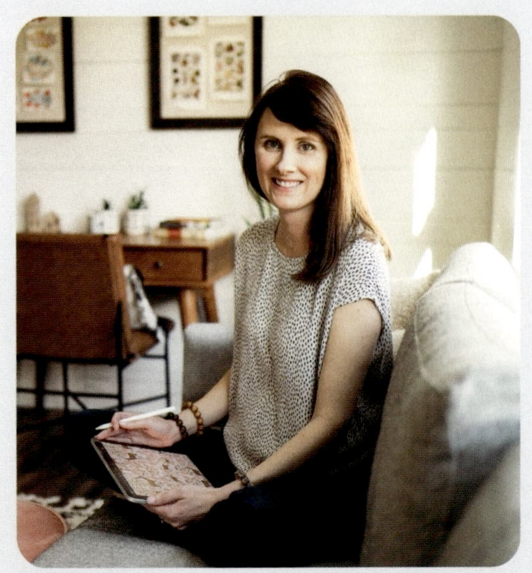

ABOUT THE AUTHOR

Liz Kohler Brown is a designer and letterer based in North Carolina who loves using vintage inspiration to create bold artwork for fabric and stationery. Her work is vibrant, playful, and full of surprising combinations. Liz's patterns and illustrations have been sold all over the world through online and in-person stores including Target, Hawthorne Supply Co., and Inkwell Greeting Cards. In her membership program, The Studio, artists can stay up to date on art and design trends, learn how to create income from their creative work, and develop a personal style that attracts clients and companies.

www.lizkohlerbrown.com